James Murdoch

A History of Constitutional Reform in Great Britain and Ireland

With a full account of the three great measures of 1832, 1867, and 1884

James Murdoch

A History of Constitutional Reform in Great Britain and Ireland
With a full account of the three great measures of 1832, 1867, and 1884

ISBN/EAN: 9783337295387

Printed in Europe, USA, Canada, Australia, Japan

Cover: Foto ©ninafisch / pixelio.de

More available books at **www.hansebooks.com**

A HISTORY

OF

ONSTITUTIONAL REFORM

IN

GREAT BRITAIN AND IRELAND;

WITH

A FULL ACCOUNT OF THE THREE GREAT MEASURES OF
1832, 1867, AND 1884.

BY

JAMES MURDOCH,

Member of the Faculty of Procurators in Glasgow; author of "Manual of the
Law of Insolvency and Bankruptcy;" &c.

BLACKIE & SON:
GLASGOW, EDINBURGH, AND LONDON.
1885.

PREFACE.

Now that the Reform Act of 1884—one of the charters of British freedom, has been secured, it may not be unfitting to inquire what it means, what it is worth, who have fought for it, and how it has been won. It is not much more than half a century since this great empire was really governed by a few thousands—by a mere oligarchy —and now we find that the political power of the country has been transferred to five millions of our fellow-countrymen, being perhaps three-fourths of the manhood of the nation. It is the object of these pages to present a short review of the successive reforms by which this emancipation was effected.

The history of human government exhibits an organic growth or development—it has a beginning, middle, and end. It begins with despotism, runs a course of constitutionalism, and ends with self-government. It is the constitutional phase of the political government of the country that has been selected for treatment here; that portion of its history during which we see the process going on whereby despotism was put under harness, and political power secured by the people at large. In the course of our review we endeavour to estimate at their true value the comparative benefits that have accrued from the acquisition of Magna Charta, the Revolution Settlement of 1688, and the Reform Bills of 1832, 1867, and 1884—those five great charters by which political power was successively conferred upon the barons, the land-owners, the middle classes, the artisans in the towns, and finally the agricultural labourers in the counties. All this involves a period of perhaps six hundred years.

There is no contentious matter introduced, no doubtful history referred to, no bias consciously permitted. In what narrative there is, the author proceeds on the broad lines of well-known history, and with an effort to point out the different stages of the evolving process that has been going on, and also with a strong disposition to acknowledge that each successive phase was unavoidable in the growth of the nation, and was therefore good in its season. Every public document bearing on the subject of reform has been made use of, every great leader in the cause has been acknowledged, and every speech of consequence, whether in Parliament or out of it, and whether from the promoters or the opponents of reform, has been carefully abridged and reproduced from the *Annual Register*, from *Hansard*, and other authentic sources.

CONTENTS.

		Page
I. THEORY OF POLITICAL GOVERNMENT, - - - -		9
II. CONTESTS FOR SUPREMACY BY THE THREE ESTATES, -		12
III. THEIR *Status quo* IN 1688, - - - - - -		21
IV. POSITION OF THE COUNTRY AT THAT TIME, - - -		24
V. PERIODS OF REFORM, - - - - - - - -		25
(1) First Reform, - - - - - - - - -		25
Constitution of 1688, - - - - - -		25
Working of Constitution, - - - - - -		25
Laws passed under it, - - - - - -		27
Government Tyrannical, - - - - - -		30
Discontent, - - - - - - - -		31
Opposition to Reform, - - - - - -		32
State of the Representation, - - - - -		33
Mr. Pitt's Motions of 1781 and 1782, - - -		35
Mr. Pitt's Resolutions of 1782, - - - - -		35
Mr. Pitt's Bill of 1785, - - - - - -		36
Mr. Flood's Bill, 1790, - - - - - -		40
Mr. Grey's (Earl Grey) Motion, 1792, - - -		48
Agitation in Scotland, 1793, - - - - -		50
Sir F. Burdett's Motion, 1819, - - - - -		55
Lord John Russell's Motion, 1819, - - - -		59
Mr. Lambton's (Earl Durham) Bill, 1821, - - -		61
Lord John Russell's Motion, 1821, - - - -		61
Lord Archibald Hamilton's Motion, 1821, - - -		63
Lord John Russell's Motion, 1822, - - -		64
Lord John Russell's Motion, 1826, - - - -		79
Marquis of Blandford's Motion, 1830, - - -		81
Daniel O'Connell's Bill, 1830, - - - - -		82
First Reform Bill of 1831, - - - - -		83
Second Reform Bill of 1831, - - - - -		113
Third Reform Bill of 1831, - - - - -		139
Extent of the Reform of 1832, - - - - -		162

CONTENTS.

	Page
(2) Second Reform,	163
Constitution of 1832,	163
Results of the Act of 1832,	163
Its Defects,	163
State of the Franchise,	164
Mr. Hume's Motion, 1848,	165
Mr. Locke King's Motion, 1851,	169
Mr. Hume's Bill of 1852,	170
Lord John Russell's Bill of 1854,	170
Sundry Motions on Reform in 1858,	175
Mr. Disraeli's Bill of 1859,	175
Lord Palmerston's Bill of 1860,	187
Sundry Motions on Reform in 1864,	199
Mr. Baines' Bill of 1865,	200
Mr. Gladstone's Bill of 1866,	201
Mr. Disraeli's Resolutions of 1867,	232
Mr. Disraeli's Bill of 1867,	242
Extent of the Reform of 1867,	262
(3) Third Reform,	263
Constitution of 1867,	263
Results of the Act of 1867,	264
Its Defects,	264
State of the Electoral Roll,	265
Mr. Trevelyan's Motions for Reform,	267, 268, 269
Mr. Gladstone's First Franchise Bill, 1884,	270
Mr. Gladstone's Second Franchise Bill, 1884,	393
Mr. Gladstone's Redistribution Bill, 1884,	397
Extent of the Reform of 1884,	398
VI. REFORM—ITS RESULTS AND FURTHER OBJECTS,	399
INDEX,	402

A HISTORY

OF

CONSTITUTIONAL REFORM.

I. THEORY OF GOVERNMENT.

NATIONS originally in a savage state, until they rise to
the privilege of self-government, have a wondrously long
journey before them. They have to go through the successive stages of slavery and serfdom before they reach
that of freedom. This requires a very long time, a great
deal of effort, and involves many changes. Some nations
progress faster than others; some seem to be more highly
favoured; while some can adapt themselves more speedily
to what is before them.

Meanwhile they require a governor. They must
attend both to internal and external government. They
are quite disunited among themselves—the strong tyran- Despotism
nize over the weak—and there are common enemies to
provide against. They elect a governor, and give him
despotic powers. It has been so in all ages. They cannot read; they have no written constitution, no body of
laws. The rule therefore of the monarch is arbitrary.

By and by this rule is felt to be oppressive. The
monarch then associates the nobles into the government,
and there is gradually formed an aristocracy. He makes
a constitution with them; he grants them a charter of

their liberties, and the monarchy becomes limited. These nobles consist of those who are powerful enough, from the extent of their possessions, from their personal character, and from the influence they possess over those under them, to keep the monarch in check. They include at this stage all the freemen of the country, at least all those who are able to contribute to the defence of the country.

This contract between the monarch and the nobles is the rallying-point round which their contests may go on for centuries. There is no external authority that can keep the parties to their bargain. If the monarch is a capable man he may, and generally will find means to act as despotically as he can; while the nobles, if they are united as a body, will not only hold the monarch down to his charter, but reduce him to still further concessions as an opportunity occurs. At this stage there is very little attention paid to a contract. It is a question of *power*, unless indeed there be a church in the land, to which all parties may pay some little reverence.

The next stage is the rise of a larger body, of humbler men, into existence, men who have begun to possess wealth, and who are not serfs nor yet nobles. They are freemen. The king sees that they are able to bear some of the burdens of his government, and he orders them to be summoned to send deputies to a parliament in order that the people may be taxed. These deputies sit by themselves and form a Lower House, or House of Commons, while the nobility constitute the Upper House, or House of Lords. The power of each Estate is defined as well perhaps as it can be. Nevertheless frequent encroachments take place, frequent disputes arise, concessions are made, and victories won in the strife. As a rule the Estate has the greatest power whose policy is mostly in accord with the opinion of the people.

Another power now makes its appearance on the scene. It is the country itself. It is not content with giving a passive support to any one of the Estates. It is going to take an active part in the business of government. It is not content with seeing those three Estates spending their time in strife, spending the people's blood in wars, spending their money upon themselves. The country sees that it has no control over any one of the Estates. It has no control even over its own deputies. These deputies, although intended to represent the country, and who do really bind the country, are nominated by the crown and the nobility; they only attend when summoned; they are only summoned when the monarch pleases. The country therefore remonstrates against all this; it agitates, it threatens. Reform is granted; the system becomes representative so far as the House of Commons is concerned, and the people have control of their deputies.

Self-government.

The process goes on. The hereditary principle is taken out of the aristocracy, and the second chamber becomes elective and representative. It is also taken out of the monarchy, and it also becomes elective and representative. The government is now republican. The people have a system of self-government—each of the three governing powers exercising its own functions; the deputies representing the interests of the nation, the second doing deliberative work, and the monarch or president exercising the function of the executive. The whole departments of the government are filled by the fittest.

Such are the processes of evolution in a state that is progressive. It begins with a monarch who is a despot. The nobility join him in the government and it becomes a limited monarchy. The structure broadens downwards, and the deputies of the people are admitted to a share of political power. These three Estates combined—the Crown, the Lords, the Commons, rule the people with no responsibility. By and by the people arise and assume the ultimate position—they are masters—and those who once were masters are now the people's servants. Thus does Democracy supersede Aristocracy, and also the Monarchy, and converts the tyrants of these earlier systems into the officials of a Republic. Such is the result of political evolution.

II. CONTESTS FOR SUPREMACY BY THE THREE ESTATES.

The evolution of the governing powers of England took place in the most ordinary way. The system had the usual despotic beginning. Under the Britons, the Romans, the Saxons, the Danes, and at first under the Normans, the rule in all the departments of life was arbitrary. There was no fixed constitution, no written laws. The history of that long period is really a narrative of attempts to limit the power of the monarch, and it will be seen as we go on that these were not absolutely successful till the settlement of 1688. During this lapse of time many compacts were made and broken between the king and his subjects, many insurrections and wars followed, several monarchs lost their lives, more than one revolution happened as well as a change of dynasty, and it required them all to bring about a fixed constitution, a suitable body of laws, and what was of more importance, a disposition and an interest on the part of the various estates of the realm as well as of the nation generally, to adhere to them. This only happened with the ascension of the Prince of Orange and his wife, and when it is said that all this occurred in the most ordinary way, what is meant is, that what happened in this country has happened in all countries that have *grown* out of the past. It was political conflict from first to last.

Let us begin with the Conqueror. It was seen by William that for the stability of his government, and in order to retain the allegiance of his barons, it was necessary to create a constitution. He therefore established the feudal system. He retained a large portion of the Feudal lands of the dispossessed Saxons to himself, and he system. awarded the remainder to his barons on the condition of obtaining certain military services from them. The larger barons did the same to the lesser barons, and they in their turn to vassals lower still, all on similar conditions. The lowest classes were not included in this system. They were mere serfs. William and his son Rufus worked this system in a very arbitrary way. The system was in fact kingly despotism, limited only by the strength of the nobility. "The prince finding that greater opposition was often made to him when he enforced the laws than when he violated them, was apt to render his own will and pleasure the sole rule of government, and on every emergency to consider the power of the persons whom he might offend rather than the rights of those whom he might injure."[1] During the reigns of Henry I., Stephen, Henry II., and Richard I., the government was administered in the way we have described. At times there were difficulties in the king's way, and occasionally there were dangers, and Henry I. actually executed a

[1] Hume's *History of England*, chap. vi.

charter in order to gain the affections of his subjects, and
deposited copies of it in the various abbeys of the country. But he never observed it, nor did any of his immediate successors, and it had not the effect of preventing
them from levying taxes whenever they saw that the imposition would be submitted to. It was in the reign of
John that the mischief came to a head, and when the
royal prerogative began to be systematically assailed by
the barons—John had been acting foolishly, not only to
the pope but to his nobility, and they each in their turn
had to humble him—the barons exacted from him the
Magna Charta, which was a formal constitution, and by
it gained many important concessions. Among others, the
king renounced the right of levying taxes from the nobles
beyond their charters, also from burghs and cities without
the consent of the Great Council or Parliament, which
consisted of earls, great barons, and prelates. This may
be said to be the formal establishment of the House of
Lords. His successor, Henry III., went further than
John. He renewed the charter with additional concessions in it. He afterwards confirmed it, and was not permitted to violate its main provisions during the whole of
his reign. The king's prerogative during this reign was
greatly reduced, the barons usurped the right of government to a large extent, and it was now that the Commons
came first upon the scene. But it was altogether different
with Edward I., who was the ablest, the most warlike,
and the most ambitious of all these early princes. He
required money for crusade purposes and raised it without hesitation, trampling charters of all kinds in the
dust. The contentions with his barons were serious
throughout this reign, but at last a compromise was made,
the right of levying taxes of his own prerogative was

abandoned, and the Great Charter was again established. By this time the confirmations from different sovereigns were above thirty in number. In the next reign, that of Edward II., the prerogative was at the lowest point, in consequence of the personal incapacity of the monarch; but Edward III. was a sovereign of a different stamp. He reigned on the most arbitrary principles, he fought France and Scotland single-handed, he kept down the nobility with a high hand. He openly avowed that he would not levy money unless it was necessary, he systematically broke the Great Charter and ratified it over and over again. He was a monarch of great capacity, and his reign was both brilliant and successful. This arbitrary system ran continuously down through the reigns of the remaining Plantagenets, through the houses of Lancaster and York, and through the dynasties of the Tudors and Stuarts. The royal prerogative would rise and fall according to the capacity of the monarch, sometimes according to the necessities of his reign, and sometimes according to the divisions among his subjects. The authority of the monarch was lowest, and that of the aristocracy highest, on the whole, prior to the reign of Henry VII. After his ascension, and throughout the reigns of the succeeding Tudors, the royal prerogative was at its height. A proclamation was equal to a law. Perhaps Henry VIII. and Elizabeth were the most arbitrary monarchs that ever reigned in this country. The Stuarts tried to maintain it, and their dynasty perished in the attempt.

The nobles were organized as an Estate of the realm in the reign of John. No doubt they would constitute a consulting council some time before, but it was by the Great Charter that they were assigned certain political functions

Confirmations of Magna Charta

with regard to the country generally. They had to consent to their order being taxed when the taxation was
beyond the limits of their charters; they had to advise
the king, and without them it was incompetent to levy
money on the cities and burghs. The barons at this
time were very powerful, and there can be little doubt
that a sense of insecurity had the effect of keeping them
united as a body, and perhaps political ambition contributed to give force to the union for some centuries to
come. Whether they really ever aimed at the creation
of a system of aristocratic government is perhaps a little
Usurpations doubtful, but it is pretty obvious from what took place
of the
barons. that their aim was to aggrandize their order to such an
extent, and so shape their proceedings that the monarch
would be a mere puppet in their hands. It is also obvious
that but for the rise of Edward I., Edward III., and
Henry VII., three of the most capable of the early
monarchs, they would perhaps have been successful. In
the reign of John we are told, on the authority of Hume,[1]
that " the barons obliged the king to agree that London
should remain in their hands, and the Tower be consigned
to the custody of the Primate till the 15th of August
ensuing, or till the execution of the several articles of the
Great Charter. The better to ensure the same end, he
allowed them to choose five-and-twenty members from
their own body as conservators of the public liberties; and
no bounds were set to the authority of these men, either
in extent or duration. If any complaint were made of a
violation of the Charter, whether attempted by the king,
justiciaries, sheriffs, or foresters, any four of these barons
might admonish the king to redress the grievance; if
satisfaction were not obtained, they could assemble the

[1] Chap. xi.

whole council of twenty-five, who, in conjunction with the Great Council, were empowered to compel him to observe the Charter, and in case of resistance might levy war against him, attack his castles, and employ every kind of violence, except against his royal person and that of his queen and children. All men throughout the kingdom were bound, under the penalty of confiscation, to swear obedience to the twenty-five barons; and the freeholders of each county were to choose twelve knights who were to make report of such evil customs as required redress conformably to the tenor of the Great Charter." In the reign of Henry III. a similar step was taken by the Parliament of Oxford. The barons brought with them to that Parliament all their military vassals, and compelled the king to submit to their terms. Twelve barons were selected from among the king's ministers, twelve more were chosen by Parliament; to these twenty-four unlimited authority was given to reform the state; and the king himself took an oath that he would maintain whatever ordinances they should think proper to enact for that purpose. "But the subsequent proceedings of the twenty-four barons were sufficient to open the eyes of the nation, and to prove their intention of reducing for ever both the king and the people, under the arbitrary power of a very narrow aristocracy, which must at last have terminated either in anarchy or in a violent usurpation and tyranny." So in a similar way Edward II. was obliged to sign a commission empowering the prelates and barons to elect twelve persons to assume the royal functions, and consenting that their ordinances should thenceforth and for ever have the force of laws.[1] There was another attempt of that kind made in the reign of

Parliament at Oxford.

[1] Hume, chap. xiv.

B

Richard II. "Gloucester and his associates observed their stipulation with the king, and attacked no more of his ministers; but they immediately attacked himself and his royal dignity, and framed a commission after the model of those which had been attempted almost in every reign since that of Richard I., and which had always been attended with extreme confusion. By this commission, which was ratified by Parliament, a council of fourteen persons was appointed, all of Gloucester's faction, except Nevil, Archbishop of York; the sovereign power was transferred to these men for a twelvemonth; the king, who had now reached the twenty-first year of his age, was in reality dethroned; the aristocracy was rendered supreme, and though the term of the commission was limited, it was easy to foresee that the intentions of the party were to render it perpetual, and that power would with great difficulty be wrested from those grasping hands to which it was once committed."[1] The efforts of the nobles continued persistently from the time of John till that of Henry VII., nearly three centuries, but this last-named monarch was too powerful for them. Besides, the nobles themselves and the times were changed. Entails were broken, and a new race of nobles had taken the place of the old. The old race were greatly cut up by the wars of the Roses. Religious differences had crept in among them. They were not allowed to keep armed retainers as of old. Be the causes what they may, the aristocracy of England never afterwards occupied the same position as they did. They never troubled the monarch to the same extent; they may be said to have become from that date superseded in the possession of most of their political functions by a most formidable rival—the rising House of Commons.

[1] Hume, chap. xvii.

In 1258, at a Parliament held at Oxford by Henry III.
and the barons, an order was given that four knights
should be chosen for each county, that they should make
inquiry into the grievances of which their neighbourhood
had reason to complain, and they should attend the ensuing Parliament in order to *give information* to that
assembly of the state of their particular counties.[1] This
was the forerunner of the House of Commons. It seems
to have answered the purpose, for we find in the same
reign, but seven years later, a return was ordered to be
made not only of knights from each shire but of deputies
from the boroughs. This has been considered to be the
beginning of the House of Commons. At the same time
it is to be noted that the Parliament which gave those
orders was a little irregular in its character, and may be
said to have been entirely an usurpation of authority by
the barons. The summons given by Edward I. was quite
regular. In 1295 he issued writs to the sheriffs, enjoin-
ing them to send to Parliament, along with two knights
of the shire, two deputies from each borough within
their county, and these provided with sufficient power to
consent in the name of their community to what the
king and his council should require of them. They composed not, properly speaking, any essential part of the
Parliament; they sat apart both from the barons and the
knights, who disdained to mix with such "mean person-
ages." After they had given their consent to the taxes
required of them, their business being then finished, they
separated, even though the Parliament continued to sit
and canvass the national business.[2] It does not appear
exactly when the House of Commons began to discuss
national affairs and take a part in legislation as well as

Origin of the House of Commons.

---

[1] Hume, chap. xii.   [2] Ibid. chap. xiiI.

in the execution of the laws. They first began to discuss grievances, and endeavoured to make the granting of supplies dependent upon redress. It would appear that it was perhaps in the reign of Henry VI. when the House of Commons first began to take the position of a deliberative assembly, and it had to pass through a fiery ordeal before it was finally permitted to do so. The House could not meet unless it were summoned, it fell to be dismissed at the king's pleasure, the members had no freedom of speech, they were subject to arrest at the king's order, and for a long period of time they were not allowed to discuss national affairs at all. In 1552 Edward VI. ordered circular letters to be sent to all the sheriffs to enjoin the freeholders to choose men of knowledge and experience for their representatives, that the assembly may be composed of those best fitted to give *advice* and *good counsel*. This was very amiable in the young prince, but his strong-minded sister did not see the matter in that light. Elizabeth allowed them very limited power. She would not permit the question of her successor to be discussed by the Commons, nor her royal right of purveyance to be questioned. She expressly prohibited them from interfering with affairs of state and religion; she told the speaker she was highly offended at their presumption, and directed one of the offenders to be imprisoned in Tilbury Castle. When the speaker at the opening of Parliament petitioned for liberty of speech, freedom from arrest, and access to her person, he was distinctly informed that those could only be granted under great limitations—so much so as to amount to a refusal. In the reign of James I. the Commons became bolder—they resolved to have the royal prerogative curtailed. The king threw some of the members into prison.

They offered counsel on matters of state, but the king
objected. They insisted upon freedom of speech, and the
leading members were thrown into the Tower. Charles
I. was even more tyrannical than his father. When the
House of Commons refused supplies he also threw some
of the members into prison. He then proceeded to levy
money without them. The House objected, and was
dissolved. The king resolved to dispense with a Parliament altogether, which he did for a period of twelve
years, until he summoned the Long Parliament, which
immediately proceeded to the assumption of sovereign
power. Charles II. and James II. both governed on the Rise of the
same despotic principles, and in 1688, when James abdi- Commons.
cated, the great contest of the three estates—latterly of
the King and Commons for political supremacy in the
country—came to a close. The House of Commons had
won the victory.

III. THE STATUS QUO IN 1688.

By the settlement that took place on the ascension of
William and Mary the results of the great conflict that
had then been going on for six hundred years were defin-
itely ascertained. The throne was fixed to be open to Revolution
Protestants only, and an annual sum was awarded to the settlement.
king to meet the expenses of the civil list, while all the
remaining revenue was left in the hands of the Commons
to support the army and navy and defray the cost of
government. The old constitutional form of government
was maintained, of King, Lords, and Commons, the king
acting as the executive through his ministers and according to statutes agreed on (Wm. and M. c. vi., 1688),

each estate of the realm being necessary to the transaction of legislative business, and each being entitled to an equal vote. The laws, such as were not questioned by any of the parties, and such as had been observed during recent times, were to be upheld, but as many of the prerogatives as well as laws had been the subject of question and of strife, it became necessary to frame a special settlement with reference to them. A statute was therefore passed for that purpose, which enacted—

laws in

1. That the pretended power of suspending of laws or of the execution of laws by regal authority, without consent of Parliament, is illegal.

2. That the pretended power of dispensing with laws or the execution of laws by regal authority, as it hath been assumed and exercised of late, is illegal.

3. That the commission for erecting the late court commissioners for ecclesiastical causes, and all other commissions and courts of like nature, are illegal and pernicious.

4. That levying money for or to the use of the crown by pretence or prerogative without grant of Parliament for longer time, or in other manner than the same is or shall be granted, is illegal.

5. That it is the right of the subjects to petition the king, and all commitments and prosecutions for such petitioning are illegal.

6. That the raising or keeping a standing army within the kingdom in time of peace, unless it be with consent of Parliament, is against law.

7. That the subjects which are Protestants may have arms for their defence suitable to their conditions and as allowed by law.

8. That election of members of Parliament ought to be free.

9. That the freedom of speech and debates on proceedings in Parliament ought not to be impeached or questioned in any court or place out of Parliament.

10. That excessive bail ought not to be required, nor excessive fines imposed, nor cruel and unusual punishment inflicted.

11. That jurors ought to be duly empannelled and returned, and jurors which pass upon men in trials for high treason ought to be freeholders.

12. That all grants and promises of fines and forfeitures of particular persons before conviction are illegal and void.

13. And that for redress of all grievances and for the amending, strengthening, and preserving of the laws, Parliament ought to be held frequently.

There were certain things that were not defined by this constitution, such as the position of the king's cabinet of ministers, nor expressed, such as the privilege of the House of Commons with regard to money bills. However, it clearly meant that all political authority was vested in the three estates, and that in legislation they were equal. But their relations to one another were very peculiar, and such as could only be provisional. It was government in a circle—each estate controlled the other, and the three estates governed the country. For instance, the king controlled the Peers by the power of creation; the peers virtually nominated the House of Commons; the Commons kept the king in order by holding the public purse. This triangular control, like a triangular duel, in which each combatant fired into his neighbour, was a rough way of regulating the action of the different estates. Such clumsy machinery could never have worked at all satisfactorily but for the rise of another power, whose business it was to place these estates in a proper position towards one another and in a state of subordination to itself.

Be that as it may, it is worthy of remark, as showing the progress of the Anglo-Saxon race, that this settlement has never been questioned. Many constitutions had been made before. They were not observed, nor meant to be observed. On the contrary, private vows were sometimes registered that they would not be kept, and reasons assigned why they should not. Then there was the court

of Rome to appeal to. The pope would absolve the
monarch from keeping his contract, and in a moral sense
this was one of the most pernicious practices of the pon-
tiffs of those days. But since 1688 let us be thankful for
the moral development of the race, and say that in high
places an obligation was expected to be kept and not to
be evaded, and that a public oath was sacred.

IV. POSITION OF THE COUNTRY IN 1688.

We have been discussing the position of the three
estates to one another and towards the country—not the
position of the country towards *them*. The country had
no constitutional control over the monarch nor over the
House of Lords. It had not even a control over the
House of Commons, although it was a house supposed to
be representative of the nation. It was nominated, or at
least a large majority of its members were nominated by
the nobility. This was done quite openly, and the practice continued down to 1832. The country had no control either over its meeting or its parting. The king
could summon it when he pleased, or dismiss it when he
pleased. No pressure of public business, no public want,
no emergency could give the people any voice in the
business. Even when the House of Commons met, the
public had no control over the members. They could
not recall them; they cannot do it even yet. They had
to wait for three years, and then for seven years, before
they could even change the member—that is, in the few
cases in which the constituencies, such as they were, had
the power to do so. Then for many long years the

country had no opportunity of knowing what their representatives were doing. The debates and votes of the
House of Commons were not allowed to be published.
It was not till 1770 that publication of the proceedings
of Parliament was allowed. Meanwhile the members of
the House of Commons, partly from the blandishments
of royalty, partly from the bribes of ministers, and partly
from their anomalous and irresponsible position, were a
separate caste, and no true representatives of the people
at all.

V. PERIODS OF REFORM.

FIRST REFORM.

Before entering upon the subject of reform it will be Constitu-
necessary to advert to the working of the new constitu- tion of 1688
tion and also to the state of the representation. It may
be acknowledged at the outset that the system of government inaugurated at 1688 was a step in advance upon
what preceded it. It was a *regular* constitution. It consisted of the three estates of the realm, and each of them
had defined powers, and they had all to be consulted in
the government. There was surely not much beyond
that! This system of an equipoise in the three governing
authorities that had been at war for ages was, like the
balance of power in Europe, supposed to be perfection.
There were no questions *inter se*. If ever there was a
happy family party, this was surely it!

But *quoad* the nation, we are obliged to acknowledge Working of
that this threefold rule was severe, selfish, systematically it.
suppressive. In fact, the treatment of the people by the

three Estates for the period from 1688 to 1832 was perhaps worse than that under the most despotic of the monarchs, for it was tyranny under the sanction of law, and was upheld by a mixture of superior knowledge and military power. Look at the statute-book and see the long array of revenue laws and game-laws. Look at the laws for the protection of property—protection against trespass—protection against creditors, whether of the landlord or the tenant. Look at the long series of corn-laws—laws putting down combinations of workmen to protect themselves against the rapacity of their masters—criminal laws against workmen to compel them to fulfil their engagements—laws to compel men to work at such wages as a magistrate chose to fix. Look at the laws prohibiting public meetings and the discussion of grievances—at the variety and extent of indirect taxation, that made living to the poor man almost impossible—at the frightful punishments for the smallest offences. Then look at the great extravagance at headquarters—the enormous hereditary pensions that were granted—the corrupt system of dealing with the parliamentary representatives of the people. Then the final picture to look at was a nation great and wealthy and luxurious, and another nation poverty-stricken, ignorant, and debased, both living side by side in the same island, the one the governors, the others the governed.

In case it may be supposed that there is exaggeration in this indictment against the three estates under the new constitution, it may be interesting, and perhaps profitable, to look into the statute-book, and see how these early legislators spent their time after their inauguration into office.

We shall take their proceedings in chronological order,

and present the following to our readers as specimens of CONSTITU-
TION OF 1688.
their legislative work, viz. :—

1690 Act passed to give landlord power of sale over tenant's Laws passed
effects, and extending right of seizure over corn, loose, or in under it.
the straw, or in a granary, &c., 2 Wm. and Mary, session i. c. 5.

1691 Act for the discovery and punishment of deer-stealers, 3 Wm.
and M. c. 10.

1692 Act giving power to search for game, &c., 4 and 5 Wm. III.
c. 23.

1706 Act for preservation of game, and fine or imprisonment
imposed on an innkeeper or chapman found in possession of
game, 5 Anne, c. 14.

1709 Act giving a preference to landlords for one year's rent over
ordinary creditors, 8 Anne, c. 14.

1710 Act prescribing that a knight of the shire must have £600
a year, and a borough member £300 a year, of income from
land, 9 Anne, c. 5.

1710 Act against night poaching, 9 Anne, c. 25.

1711 Act restoring church patronage in Scotland, 10 Anne, c. 12.

1715 Act extending present and future Parliaments to 7 years,
1 Geo. I. c. 38.

1715 Act for the protection of trees, 1 Geo. I. c. 48.

1716 Act preventing landlords giving power to farmers to kill
game, 3 Geo. I. c. 11.

1718 Act for further punishment of deer-stealers, 5 Geo. I. c. 15.

1718 Act imposing 7 years' transportation on anyone entering a
park and killing a deer, 5 Geo. I. c. 28.

1719 Act to encourage the planting of trees, 6 Geo. I. c. 16.

1720 Act to prevent journeymen tailors in London from combining to raise wages or lessen hours of work—their hours
being from 6 A.M. to 8 P.M. with an hour for dinner, 7 Geo. I.
c. 13.

1721 Act for recovery of penalties under game-laws, 8 Geo. I. c. 19.

1725 Act to prevent weavers from combining to raise wages,
12 Geo. I. c. 34.

1729 Act to amend corn-laws, 2 Geo. II. c. 18.

1731 Act for ejection of tenants, 4 Geo. II. c. 38.

1731 Act to prevent frauds against the corn-laws, 5 Geo. II. 12.

Co.<small>NSTITU-</small>
TION OF 1688.

1732 Act fixing £100 per annum from land as the qualification of a justice of the peace, 5 Geo. II. c. 18.

1738 Act giving landlords power to recover their tenants' goods removed from premises, 2 Geo. II. c. 19.

1738 Act freeing peers from imprisonment even for a crown debt, 2 Geo. II. c. 24.

Laws passed under it.

1740 Act imposing hard labour in house of correction to a journeyman who neglects performance of engagement in making up gloves, boots, &c., 13 Geo. II. c. 8.

1741 Act making the stealing or killing of cattle felony without benefit of clergy, 14 Geo. II. c. 6.

1745 Act for the more effectual prevention of those of mean estate from becoming justices of the peace, 28 Geo. II. c. 20.

1747 Act providing hard labour in house of correction for artificers, labourers, &c., for misconduct, 20 Geo. II. c. 19.

1747 Act also provides for discharge to servant, if master guilty of misusage, cruelty, or want of necessary provisions, 20 Geo. II. c. 19.

1749 Act extending 13 Geo. II. c. 8 to workers in woollen and linen goods, whereby anyone not fulfilling engagement to be sent to house of correction, 22 Geo. II. 27.

1751 Game Act for Scotland, 24 Geo. II. c. 34.

1755 Act amending game-laws, 28 Geo. II. c. 12.

1757 Act extending 20 Geo. II. c. 19 to agricultural labourers, 31 Géo. II. c. 11.

1760 Act prescribing time for killing game in Scotland, 1 Geo. III. c. 21.

1762 Act for England, 2 Geo. III. c. 19.

1765 Act imposing transportation on anyone who destroys or takes conies in the night time, 5 Geo. III. c. 15.

1766 Act imposing 3 months in the house of correction on apprentices, handicraftsmen, or labourers, for not fulfilling contract, 6 Geo. III. c. 25.

1766 Act imposing 7 years' transportation for destruction of trees or shrubs in night time, 6 Geo. III. c. 36.

1770 Act imposing not more than 6 months, and not less than 3 months, for killing game in night time, 10 Geo. III. c. 19.

1773 Corn-law—if wheat at or about 48s., duty 6d., 13 Geo. III. c. 43.

1773 Act fixing time for killing game in Scotland, 13 Geo. III. CONSTITU-
c. 54.   TION OF 1688.

1773 Act amending English game-law, 13 Geo. IIL c. 55.

1773 Act providing that the wages of journeymen weavers of
silk in London and Middlesex be periodically fixed by lord-
mayor or justice of peace—that masters paying more or less
shall forfeit £50—that men asking or taking more or less Laws passed
forfeit 40s., 13 Geo. III. c. 68.   under it.

1773 Act to amend law as to night poaching, 13 Geo. III. c. 80.

1776 Act consolidating laws against deer-stealing, 13 Geo. IIL
c. 30.

1777 Act ordering journeymen in hat trade, on appealing to
quarter session anent raising wages or lessening hours of work,
to find sureties to abide judgment, 17 Geo. III. c. 55.

1780 Act prohibiting anyone from having a county vote, unless
assessed for land tax, for 6 months, 20 Geo. III. c. 17.

1782 Act imposing a fine of £500 and imprisonment for 12 months
on anyone contracting with or encouraging a workman in
calicoes or linens to leave country, 22 Geo. III. c. 60.

1785 Act extending this to workers in iron or steel, 25 Geo. III.
c. 67.

1791 Act imposing heavy corn duties if wheat 44s., duty 5s.,
31 Geo. III. c. 30.

1796 Act prohibiting assemblies of 50 persons to petition Parliament or discuss grievances, unless 7 householders give notice
to authorities and the meeting was advertised—and at such
meeting nothing to be done to stir up hatred or contempt of
the government or constitution on pain of death, without tho
benefit of clergy, 36 Geo. III. c. 8.

1796 Places for lectures on grievances to be licensed—*ibid.*

1796 Act prohibiting the shooting of partridges in England till
September 14, 36 Geo. III. c. 39.

1796 Do. for Scotland, 36 Geo. III. c. 54.

1796 Act against combinations of workmen in paper-works for
raising wages or lessening hours, 36 Geo. III. c. 3.

1799 Act fixing shooting of partridges to begin on September 1,
39 Geo. III. c. 34.

1799 Act to suppress societies formed for overturning government, 39 Geo. III. c. 79.

CONSTITU-
TION OF 1688. 1799 Act consolidating laws against journeymen of all kinds, combining to raise wages or lessen hours or quantity of work, and
imposing 3 months' imprisonment or 2 months of the house
of correction, 39 Geo. III. c. 81.

1800 Act imposing 40s. or 6 months' imprisonment on a collier
who refused to fulfil engagement, 39 and 40 Geo. III. c. 77.

Laws passed
under it. 1802 Act imposing 7 years' transportation for hunting, snaring,
or injuring deer within an inclosure, and penalty of £50 if
uninclosed, 42 Geo. III. c. 107.

1803 Act extending to Ireland the combination act as to wages,
&c., 43 Geo. III. c. 86.

1804 Act imposing very heavy corn duties—duty on wheat 24s. 3d.,
44 Geo. III. c. 109.

1807 Act extending to Ireland the laws for having wages of
artificers, labourers, and servants fixed by a justice of the
peace, 47 Geo. III. c. 43, session 1.

1810 Act limiting imprisonment of a woman having a bastard
child chargeable to parish to 1 year to house of correction
with hard labour, and not less than 6 weeks, 50 Geo. III. c. 51.

Legislation of the above character began now to cease,
as it was apparent that the country would not submit
further. It had indeed gone very far—so far as to make
the life of the working-men of the country one of legal-
ized oppression. The specimens given are not all, nor
nearly all, for it was in the administration of the laws
where the despotism was chiefly felt. This was done in
a pitiless manner. It was not uncommon to have a sentence of death pronounced for an offence which is now
Government
tyrannical. petty larceny. The punishments especially for offences
against property were fearful, and the state of the prisons
was enough to make one shudder. The number of taxes
too, and their vexatious character, bore with great severity on the mass of the people. Indeed it would seem to
have been the delight of Parliament after Parliament from
1688 down to 1810, to do little else than sit, and raise

and spend money, carry on war, and execute their cruel Constitu-
tion of 1688. laws with all possible severity. ?

All this time there was no check on these estates of the realm. On a review of the legislation over the period from 1688 to 1810 it would appear that there was a system of property being created, and a monopoly of government being practised, which gave tremendous power and tremendous wealth to a class—that class was the aristocracy, the old nobility, and those that elbowed themselves up to position. Of course there were other No check on two estates to be consulted and carried along with them. estates. There was the monarch. He had to be largely subsidized; and when it came to the time of the prince-regent it was not easy subsidizing *him.* Then the Commons— at least a majority, and certainly the most prominent of them—had to be bribed. The corruption that was systematically carried on was on a large scale; it was not hidden, but openly paraded and freely avowed, and it was times without number charged against the ministry, in the House of Commons, without contradiction and without complaint. Indeed Sir Robert Walpole is reported to have said that every man in political life had his price. The subsidizing of the monarch and the corruption of the Commons was the *quid pro quo* paid by the aristocracy for the constitutional privilege of plundering the nation.

It is not to be supposed that discontent existed all Discontent. through the period we have named. For the first century after 1688 there was not much discontent in the country. The system had not had time to tell. The country besides was in the midst of war through almost the whole of that period. There was the French war, under the management of King William and the Duke of Marlborough; there were the wars afterwards with

Constitu-
tion of 1688. France in India and America. Then there was the
American War of Independence, and afterwards followed
all the wars arising out of the French Revolution. These
kept the nation preoccupied and in a state of excitement.
In fact, it was not till towards the end of the eighteenth
century that the pressure of things was felt, and that
discontent first took shape. No doubt the French Revolution added intensity to the feeling. The people then
began to realize their position, and a cry for reform
began to be heard. The cry was to break in upon this
circle—this "ring"—this equipoise—and to give the country a command of the House of Commons. No doubt
many of the fiery spirits would have gone further, and
were disposed to demand a republic, in imitation of their
neighbours in France. The most moderate, and, indeed,
all the respectable and even the independent classes were
inclined to postpone the whole subject. They were
alarmed at the progress of the revolution, and saw that
things had gone too far.

All through this long period of about a century and
a half there was a stern front held towards Reform. It
was not to be supposed that there was anything to
reform. The "glorious revolution" had completed all
reform. Indeed, at first the stream was running in quite
an opposite direction; for there was in 1710 an act passed
whereby a knight of the shire must have £600 a year
and a borough member £300 a year of income from land;
and then in 1716 the act was passed for extending the
duration of Parliament from three to seven years, which
Opposition
to Reform. was a most obnoxious measure to a true reformer of that
period; and lastly, there was in 1771 a powerful effort
made to prevent the publication of the debates of the
House of Commons, so that the people whose house it

was were not only to have no command over it, but were
not to be permitted the satisfaction of knowing what their representatives were about. This, after several prosecutions against the printers of the debates, was abandoned. Thereafter the attempt was made to tax the American colonies, and this gave rise to the War of Independence. It was the conduct of this war that first called the attention of the country to the state of the House of Commons. It came to be felt that the country could not be properly represented in the House of Commons, else the great blunder of that war could hardly have been committed. This was what led to the beginning of the great reform movement; but before entering upon that subject it will be as well to see what was the state of the House of Commons.

The representation of the country in the House of
Commons, prior to the first Reform Act, was quite a farce. In early times the seats had to be distributed at the will of the sovereign. He enfranchised and disfranchised places at his pleasure; but this prerogative had been suspended since the time of Charles II., so that the inequalities and defects had attained the most monstrous proportions by the middle of last century. Bribery was openly practised; seats were as openly bought and sold. In many boroughs the constituencies were very small, with possibly not more than eight or ten voters in each. In larger boroughs the member was elected by the town-council, and it, in its turn, was self-elected. In the general case the members were nominated by some influential peer, or by a wealthy landowner, or by the crown, and returned as a matter of course. It was well known that out of a house of 658, being 513 for England and Wales, 45

members was 487—there being 371 for England and Wales, 45 for Scotland, and 71 for Ireland. Those for England and Wales were nominated by 87 peers, 9 commoners, and 16 by the crown. The Scotch nominee members
were returned by 21 peers and 14 commoners, and the Irish by 36 peers and 19 commoners. In all there were only 202 individuals who had the nomination of those 487 members, which constituted a very large majority of the house.[1] These were well-known facts.[2] It was well known that the Duke of Norfolk returned 11 members, Lord Lonsdale 9, and Lord Darlington 7. It was also a well-known thing that seats could be got by purchase in the open market. It was also well known that the representation in Scotland was quite as bad. In no county were there more than 240 voters, in one there were only 9. In 1831 the whole constituency of Scotland did not exceed 4000, the counties having 2500 and the burghs 1440, while the population of the country amounted to over two millions. The cities of Glasgow and Edinburgh had each a constituency of 33.

So much for the constituencies. The right of voting was very anomalous. It might be the paying of parish
rates, the membership of a corporation, the being a householder, or by virtue of some extraordinary custom of the burgh; but generally it arose from the ownership of a 40s. freehold, or in Scotland of a superiority to that amount.

From these various causes the House of Commons, in the words of a constitutional authority, was at the same time dependent and corrupt. The crown and the dominant political families readily commanded a majority of that

---

[1] Oldfield's *Representative History*, vol. vi. pp. 285 and 300.
[2] Sir Erskine May's *Constitutional History*, vol. i. p. 306.

assembly. A large proportion of the borough members Mr. Pitt's Resolutions. were the nominees of peers and great landowners, or were mainly returned through the political interest of those magnates. Many were the nominees of the crown, or owed their seats to government influence. Rich ad- House of Commons non-repre- sentative. venturers having purchased their seats of the proprietors, or acquired them by bribery, supported the ministry of the day for the sake of honours, patronage, or court favour. The country members were generally identified with the territorial aristocracy. The adherence of a further class was secured—places and pensions—by shares in loans, lotteries, and contracts, and even by pecuniary bribes (May, i. p. 277).

It was the great Pitt who first attempted legislation Mr. Pitt's motion, 1781. on the subject of House of Commons reform. In 1781 he endeavoured to have a measure introduced, but failed. On May 7, 1782, he brought the subject of reform in the constitution of Parliament again before the house. The insuperable difficulties that had occurred in bringing the friends of such reform to agree on any specific pro- position, induced him on that occasion to vary the mode of procedure, and to move "that a committee be appointed Motion in 1782. to inquire into the state of the representation in Parlia- ment, and to report to the house their sentiments there- on." The debate was long and ably supported by the Debate. mover, as well as by Mr. Sawbridge, Mr. Fox, and others, on the side of reform; by Mr. Powys, Mr. T. Pitt, and the Lord Advocate of Scotland against it. On a division the motion was rejected by 161 to 141.

On May 7, 1782, Mr. Pitt made another motion re- Mr. Pitt's Resolutions. 1782. specting the reform of parliamentary representation, and as the mode of proceeding by a committee proposed on the previous occasion had formed one of the principal

Mr. Pitt's objections against the reform itself, he thought it more
Resolu- advisable to bring forward some specific propositions.
tions, 1782. These were:—

1. "That it was the opinion of the House that measures were highly necessary to be taken for the future
prevention of bribery and expense at elections.

2. "That for the future, when the majority of voters
for any burgh shall be convicted of gross and notorious
corruption before a select committee of that House,
appointed to try the merits of any election, such burgh
should be disfranchised, and the minority of voters not
so convicted should be entitled to vote for the county in
which such burgh should be situated.

3. "That an addition of knights of the shire and of
representatives of the metropolis should be added to the
state of the representation."

He left the number for future discussion, but said he
should propose one hundred.

The debate continued till near two o'clock without any
novelty of reasoning or diversity of argument. The
number of petitioners this year had decreased. Only
fourteen counties appeared, and most of the petitions had
a very inconsiderable number of names subscribed. The
whole amount was said not to reach 20,000. Amongst
the converts to the question appeared Mr. Thomas Pitt,
and the Lord-Advocate for Scotland, Mr. Dundas. The
former of those gentlemen made the House an offer of
Resolutions the voluntary surrender of his burgh of Old Sarum. The
rejected. House divided on the order of the day—ayes, 293; noes,
149. The motion was lost.

Mr. Pitt's The last attempt at reform by Pitt was made on April
Bill, 1785. 18, 1785. The weight and influence of the government had hitherto been exerted more or less against any

measure of reform; but Mr. Pitt, who was now premier, MR PITT's
having pledged himself both as a "man and a minister" BILL, 1785.
to make every personal effort to attain it, the opportunity
that then offered itself was looked upon as the most favourable *it could ever experience.* There can be no doubt that
George III. was opposed to it, but when Pitt laid his
plan before him, the conscientious old monarch gave
him full permission to proceed, at same time signifying his
disapproval but informing him that he would not com-
municate his opinion on the subject to anyone but himself.

Notwithstanding the coldness of the king on the sub- Mr. Pitt's
ject, Pitt brought his proposal forward with great energy speech.
in the House of Commons: "That leave be given to
bring in a Bill to amend the representation of the people
of England in Parliament." The plan which he proposed
was to transfer the right of choosing representatives from
thirty-six of such boroughs as had already fallen or were
falling into decay, to the counties, and to such chief
towns and cities as were then unrepresented; that a fund
should be provided for the purpose of giving the owners
and holders of such boroughs disfranchised an appreciated
compensation for their property; that the taking this
compensation should be a voluntary act of the proprietors,
and if not then taken should be placed out at compound
interest until it became an irresistible bait to such proprietors; and that the right of voting for knights of the
shire to copyholders as well as freeholders should be
extended. Such was an outline of the measure, and it
sounds strange at this period of time to hear of a man of
Pitt's intelligence talking of the right of nomination as
being a *right of property,* and it is still more strange to
see how careful he is in providing compensation for the

MR. PITT's
BILL, 1785.

invasion of the right, and delicately trying to tempt the landowners to accept the money. In the course of his speech Pitt remarked: "The number of gentlemen who are hostile to reform are a phalanx which ought to give alarm to any individual upon rising to suggest such a measure. Those who, with a sort of superstitious awe, reverence the constitution so much as to be fearful of touching even its defects, have always reprobated every attempt to purify the representation. They acknowledge its inequality and corruption, but in their enthusiasm for the grand fabric they would not suffer a reformer with unhallowed hands to repair the injuries which it has suffered from time. Others who, perceiving the deficiencies that have arisen from circumstances, are solicitous for their amendment, yet resist the attempt under the

His speech.

argument that when once we have presumed to touch the constitution in one point, the awe which had heretofore kept us back from the daring enterprise of innovations might abate, and there was no foreseeing to what alarming length we might progressively go under the mask of reformation."[1] The chief arguments, however, in favour of reform were derived from the defective and partial representation of the kingdom at large. It was urged that an active reforming and regulating principle which kept pace with the alterations in the state was requisite to preserve the constitution in its full force and vigour; that as any part of the constitution decayed, it had ever been the wisdom of the legislature to renovate and restore it by such means as were most likely to answer the end proposed, and that hence had arisen the frequent alterations that had taken place with respect to the rule of representation both before

[1] The particulars of debates cited in these pages are taken from the Annual Register and from Hansard.

and at the Revolution. On the other hand, it was objected to the motion that it was not called for by the people, and particularly not by the unrepresented large towns and cities, which it was stated had a right to claim the benefit which would result from such a measure; that if a bill of reform was once introduced men's minds were so unsettled and various on the subject that there was no knowing to what extent it might be carried; that what were called rotten and decayed boroughs were frequently represented by gentlemen who had the greatest stake in the country, and consequently were as much concerned in its welfare and in that of the constitution as any other species of representatives, in whatever manner they might be chosen, could be; and finally, that whilst no necessity was shown for such a reform, and whilst the rights and liberties of the people remained safe and secure under the present mode of representation, it was hazardous in the extreme to alter what was found by experience to be good. Mr. Fox particularly objected to the mode laid down of purchasing the boroughs, though he approved of the measure in other respects. Mr. Pitt did not think proper to make use of his ministerial influence on the occasion, and was doomed to suffer a defeat. The proposal was rejected by 248 against 174. It does not appear that Pitt was very sanguine of success, but there seems no reason for questioning his sincerity, as has been done. The French Revolution soon followed, and it was enough to change most men's minds. At all events it was enough to disturb the ordinary course of legislation, and it certainly had the effect of retarding reform for nearly half a century. It was a revolution which carried a terror for popular government all over Europe, and drove men into Toryism. It was enough to account for the attitude taken

Mr. Flood's
Bill, 1790. up by the great minister during the remainder of his career, that it was not opportune. It was held to be so by very many others, for we find that it was not taken up by any responsible statesman till 1819, when Lord John Russell appeared on the scene.

It does not follow, however, that nothing was done or attempted by irresponsible statesmen. On March 4, 1790, the question was raised in the House of Commons by Mr. Henry Flood, an Irish orator, who asked for leave to bring in a bill to amend the representation of the people in Parliament. The grounds on which Mr. Flood proceeded were those—That as by the general law of the constitution the majority is to decide for the whole, the representative must be chosen by a body of constituents whereby the elective franchise may extend to the majority Mr. Flood's
speech. of the people; for if the constituent body consisted of but one thousand for the whole nation, the representatives chosen by that thousand could not in any rational sense be the actual representatives of the people; that nothing less than a constituent body formed on a principle that extends to the majority can be constitutionally adequate to the return of an actual representative of the people; and that unless the people be actually represented, they are not constitutionally represented at all. He admitted that property to a certain degree is a necessary ingredient to the elective power, that is to say, that franchise ought not to go beyond property, but at the same time it ought to be as nearly commensurate to it as possible. Property, by the original principle of the constitution, was the source of all power both elective and legislative; the *liberi tenentes,* including at that time in effect the whole property in the country and extending to the mass of the people, were the elective body. The persons whom they

chose to represent them in Parliament sat in right of the Mr. Flood's property of those electors, and the barons sat in right of Bill, 1790. their own baronies, that is to say, of their own property. At that time the latter were not creatures of royal patent as now. But now that the Lords are creatures of royal patent merely, and that freehold property is but a part of the property of the nation, the national property is not as fully represented as it was originally, and as it ought to be still, by the constitution; that the constituent body is also defective in number as well as in point of property, the whole number of electors being infinitely short of what it should be; and what is worse, the majority of representatives who decide for the whole, chosen by a number of electors not exceeding 6000 or 8000, though these representatives are to act for 8,000,000 of people. That a new body of constituents is therefore wanting, His speech and in their appointment two things are to be considered—one, that they should be numerous enough, because numbers are necessary to the spirit of liberty; the other that they should have a competent degree of property, because that is considered to be the spirit of order. To supply this deficiency both in the representative and constituent body, Mr. Flood proposed that 100 members should be added, and that they should be elected by the resident householders in every county. _Resident_, first, because they must be best acquainted with local circumstances; and next, because they can attend at every place of election with the least inconvenience and expense to themselves or to the candidate. _Householders_, because being masters of families they may be sufficiently responsible to be entitled to the franchise. There is no country in the world, he said, in which the householders of it are considered as the rabble, no country can be said to be

Mr. Flood's
Bill, 1790. free where they are not allowed to be efficient citizens. They are exclusive of the rabble, the great mass of the people; they are the natural guardians of popular liberty in the first stages of it. Without them it cannot be retained. As long as they have this constitutional influence, and till they become generally corrupt, popular liberty cannot be taken away. In order to evince the necessity of the reform proposed, Mr. Flood used the following argument. The constitution, he said, consists of three orders—one monarchial, one aristocratic, and one popular; the balance consists in maintaining the equipoise between them. This balance was lost in the first part of the Norman era; it was recovered in some degree afterwards; it was impaired again in the period of the Tudors and Stuarts; at the Revolution it was sup-
His speech. posed to have been again recovered. Let us see whether it has not been impaired since. The Lords have been the most stationary, yet by a great increase of their numbers of late, the Upper House has obtained a great many patrimonial and private boroughs, thereby obtaining an influence over the House of Commons which does not constitutionally belong to them. But the great alteration has appeared on the part of the crown. On this point he quoted the authority of Mr. Justice Blackstone and Mr. Hume, and lastly the memorable resolutions of the House of Commons "that the influence of the crown had increased, was increasing, and ought to be diminished." Does any man, he said, doubt this authority? Were not they who voted it witnesses of the fact as well as judges of the proposition? But it does not rest on their authority. An act of the whole legislature has since confirmed their words; they have been made statute by the act of reform that passed afterwards. But what has happened

since? An East India Bill has passed and a declaratory law, and what is the consequence? No man who has any modesty, or who ever expected to be credited, will deny that by those laws more influence has been conveyed to the crown or the ministry than was subtracted by that act of reform. After answering the objections that might be made to his motion, as ill-timed, innovating on the constitution, and tending to excite discontents among the people, Mr. Flood concluded to the following effect. "Montesquieu has said that a free people will pay more taxes with greater alacrity than a people that are not free, and he adds the reason, because they have a compensation in the rights they enjoy. The people of England pay fifteen millions and a half annually to the revenue. This purchase they pay for the constitution. Shall they not have the benefit of it? Every individual pays fifty shillings a year. How many enjoyments must every inferior individual relinquish and how much labour must he undergo to enable him to make this contribution? No people ever deserved better of government than the people of'this country. At this moment they have not only submitted with alacrity to this enormous mass of taxation, but when the health or the rights of their sovereign were at stake, they gathered around the throne with unexampled zeal. Can such a people be denied their privileges? Can their privileges be a subject of indifference or remissness to this House? I cannot believe it, and therefore I move for leave to bring in a bill to amend the representation of the people in Parliament."

The motion was seconded by Mr. Grigby, and opposed by Mr. Wyndham, who observed that, in his opinion, before the House could receive the motion the right honour-

MR. FLOOD's BILL, 1790. able gentleman ought first to make out some specific grievance arising out of the present mode of representation, and then propose his remedy; and when the House was put in possession of both it would be for it to judge how far the first was ascertained and the second proportionate, and to decide whether the remedy ought to be adopted or not. Mr. Flood had said that the representation was inadequate without producing any fact in Mr. Wyndham's speech. proof of the allegation, except an arithmetical calculation, which only proved it to be, what needed no proof, unequal. The right honourable gentleman seemed to have confounded the end with the means. Experience had convinced them that the representation was not inadequate, but that the House of Commons, constituted as it was, answered all the beneficial purposes that could possibly be desired. This was a case in which we might lose everything and could gain nothing. The liberty of the country stood in need of no speculative security. It could not be better secured than it was. Mr. Flood having adduced the support given in Parliament to the American War contrary to the sense of the people as a proof of the necessity of a reform, Mr. Wyndham denied that the continuance of the American War had been owing to the inadequacy of representation. On the contrary, he said it was the war of the people, a better proof of which need not be desired than what had happened to the member for Bristol, a right honourable friend of his (Mr. Burke), who had been turned out for opposing its continuance. Towards the close of that war, which had been undertaken with no better reason, he was afraid, than the hope of saving themselves by taxing America, a clamour indeed was raised on account of the expense and ill success attending it, and the cry was for a reform of representation in Parliament as a remedy for the evils Mr. Flood's Bill 1790. which the people had at least a share in bringing upon themselves. He had hoped that the wild notions which were generated during that war had happily subsided never to rise again, and he was sorry to find that, like locusts, they had only lain torpid, and had been brought to life again by the heat and fermentation which prevailed in the affairs of the Continent. He was sorry to hear them again buzzing about, and thought it por- Mr. Wyndham's speech tended no good to the verdure and beauty of the British constitution. But if he had approved ever so much of the right honourable gentleman's proposition for a parliamentary reform, he should object to it on account of the time at which he had thought proper to introduce it. What! he said; would he advise them to repair their house in the hurricane season! Speculatists and visionaries enough were at work in a neighbouring country; there was project against project, and theory against theory. He entreated the House to wait a little for the event, and in the meantime to guard with all possible care against catching from them the infection.

Mr. Pitt followed Mr. Wyndham, and said that after Mr. Pitt's speech. the extraordinary display of ingenuity and wisdom which the House had just heard, little remained to be said upon the merits of the motion. What he should say, therefore, would relate to the question so far as he might be personally concerned in it. He had brought forward some years back a proposition of the same nature, to which the opposition had been successful, though the times and a variety of other circumstances were then more favourable than at present. The chief objection then was the danger of innovation, and it was a knowledge of the impression that argument had made which rendered him desirous

Mr. Flood's Bill, 1790. of waiting till some more favourable moment than the present should offer itself, when he most certainly should again submit his ideas upon the subject to the House. At present, unless the right honourable gentleman would consent to withdraw his motion he should move to adjourn. Mr. Pitt declared that if he were forced to come to a specific vote upon the right honourable gentleman's plan for amending the constitution, he should be against it; and even if it were his own proposition he should act in the same manner, feeling that the cause of reform might suffer disgrace and lose ground from being

Speech of Mr. Fox. brought forward at an improper moment. Mr. Fox argued in favour of the motion, but at the same time candidly said that he believed the opinion he supported was not that of the majority either within or without the doors of Parliament. He differed from Mr. Wyndham on the point of the American War, and was of opinion that had the House of Commons been differently constituted at that time it would have put an end to that war much earlier. Sure also he was that what had happened in 1784 would never in that case have taken place. He differed totally from Mr. Wyndham in the sentiments he had expressed relative to France. That gentleman had asked, Would any man repair his house in a hurricane? Mr. Fox said he would be glad to know what season was more proper to set about a repair in than when a hurricane was near, and might possibly burst forth. He concluded with declaring that he thought the reform proposed by Mr. Flood the best of all he had yet heard suggested.

Mr. Burke's speech. Mr. Burke combated the various arguments that had been urged in favour of the motion. He particularly contended that the people did not wish for any reform,

and that such attempts did not originate with or were Mr. Flood's Bill, 1790
countenanced by them. He contended that the American
War was a war of the people, and that it was put an end
to by the virtue of the House of Commons with scarce
any interference of the people, and almost with their
consent.

Mr. Powys, Mr. Wilberforce, and Mr. Secretary Granville spoke on the same side, and Mr. Courtney, Sir
Joseph Mawbey, Mr. Martin, Mr. Duncombe, and others
for the motion. At last Mr. Flood agreed that it should Bill with-drawn.
be withdrawn.

We now come to the years 1792, 1793, and 1794, which
proved fatal to the cause of reform for many years. It
was a most tempestuous period, and was indebted for that
to the prevalence of the French Revolution. During the
first of these years those who were favourable to reform
formed themselves into a society called "The Friends of Society of "Friends of the People."
the People," and the two principles which it advocated
were an equal extension of the suffrage and the shortening
of the duration of Parliaments. These were two objects
quite legitimate in their character, and there was nothing
to prevent many moderate men in Parliament and the
country from becoming members of the association.
Many accordingly joined it, of high position and great
influence, but multitudes of others likewise became
members whose aims went considerably beyond mere
reform. The writings of Paine began to attract attention,
and there could be no doubt of their revolutionary character. Other writings followed still more inflammatory
in their nature, and the mind of the nation speedily
underwent a change. The upper classes got alarmed
and drew back, the lower classes wanted to go forward.
It was inevitable that there would be a collision. In

Mr. Grey's
motion,
1792. consequence of a resolution of this society, Mr. Charles Grey gave notice on April 30, 1792, of a motion he intended to make at some period in the next session, and made a speech on the subject. Mr. Pitt said, if ever there was a time when the subject of a parliamentary reform ought not to be agitated, the present was that period. When he had himself proposed a parliamentary reform, the complexion of the times was different in every respect from what it then was. Real grievances were practically felt, and a direct contrariety existed between the opinions of Parliament and the opinions of the people. The country was in a state of actual distress, a national bankruptcy dreaded, and the public mind almost bordering on absolute despair. In this situation Mr. Pitt's
speech. something, he had conceived, ought to be attempted to counteract such alarming evils by restoring to the people that confidence in Parliament which they seemed to have lost. A parliamentary reform had appeared to him adequate to such an effect, a measure which at the time would have satisfied the nation, and was not likely to have gone beyond its declared object. Moderate measures were not likely to satisfy reformers; they wished not to preserve, but to subvert the constitution. At the close of the American War little could have been lost; but now little could be gained, and all could be lost. He complained that instead of coming forward at once with some specific proposition on the subject, Mr. Grey had given an indistinct notice which would naturally agitate the public mind for a considerable period, and set to work many dangerous and designing theorists. Of this latter description he conceived some of that society to be, with which he grieved to find a man of Mr. Grey's talents and character unhappily connected. The aim of such people

was nothing less than to destroy the British constitution, Mr. Grey's MOTION, 1792. and to erect on its ruins that mad system which had been misnamed "Liberty" in another country—a system at war with freedom and good order, to which despotism itself was preferable. Mr. Fox, in his reply, remarked that if the allies of opposition were infuriated republicans, those of the minister were the slaves of despotism, both equally hostile to national liberty, but the former in the least degree. He conceived that Mr. Pitt, when he alluded to the mad speculators out of doors, principally had in view a book entitled The Rights of Man, which mocked all ideas of reform in our government, and rather went to a total change of it. Mr. Burke observed that amid all our political regulations, no essential change had Debate. ever taken place in our parliamentary representation. We had seen a reformation, a revolution, an abdication of the throne, and a change in the line of succession, but never till lately had any attempt been made to remodel the constitution of the House of Commons. The prudence, therefore, and caution of our ancestors in this respect he deemed it wise to imitate. Notwithstanding the informality of the proceedings, the debate was carried to a considerable length, several members strongly expressing their disapprobation of the society in which the measure had originated. The subject then dropped.

Meantime the country was kept in a state of excite- Riots. ment and alarm—riots had been taking place, societies of all kinds had been formed; and these societies, both in the metropolis and throughout the principal towns, began to be unusually active. They employed pamphlets, handbills, public advertisements, essays, paragraphs, in short, all the arts of the press, to assail every class and description of men, with addresses to their passions, pre-

D

judices, and interests; and to keep them more surely to one point, a new institution was formed under the name of the "London Corresponding Society." The special grievances from which the country was to be delivered were stated to be "royal prerogatives, a servile peerage, rapacious and intolerant clergy, and a corrupt representation." The government now thought it necessary to issue a royal proclamation against seditious meetings and writings, and this was laid before the Houses of Parliament on the 25th of May, when an address of thanks and support to the king was moved, and was ultimately carried in both Houses. Meantime a number of prosecutions followed; among others, one against the author of *The Rights of Man*, in which a verdict of guilty was obtained. Paine, however, escaped.

In the following year (1793) Mr. Grey made a second effort at reform in the House of Commons, and which was attended with failure; but a scene of another kind was being enacted in the Court of Justiciary in Edinburgh. The agitation in Scotland had been carried on with great activity, for the forms of despotism there were fully as

rigid as they were in the south. Lord Cockburn tells us: "With the people put down, and the Whigs powerless government was the master of nearly every individual in Scotland, but especially in Edinburgh, which was the chief seat of its influence. The infidelity of the French gave it almost all the pious; their atrocities all the timid; rapidly increasing taxation and establishments, all the venal; the higher and middle ranks were at its command and the people at its feet. The pulpit, the bench, the bar, the colleges, the parliamentary electors, the press, the magistracies, the local institutions, were so completely at the service of the party in power that the idea of independence, besides being monstrous and absurd, was suppressed by a feeling of conscious ingratitude. And in addition to all the sources of government influence, Henry Dundas, an Edinburgh man, and well calculated by talent and manner to make despotism popular, was the absolute dictator of Scotland, and had the means of rewarding submission and of suppressing opposition beyond what were ever exercised in modern times by one person in any portion of the empire."[1] If that was anything like the condition of Scotland at the period we refer to, there is little wonder that much discontent should exist, and that it should take the guise of "reform." But reform meant a different thing then in public estimation from what it did in Pitt's time, and from what it did in 1819, when Lord John Russell began to deal with the subject. At the time we are writing of, reform was understood to mean revolution—it meant a reconstruction of the constitution in the light thrown upon it by the French revolution. At all events this was what many really meant, and what many feared it to mean. There had been issued a great many pamphlets to stir up the public mind, many meetings had been held, and in imitation of the French a convention had taken place in Edinburgh, to which delegates came from all parts of the country. Mr. Thomas Muir, younger, of Hunter's Hill, near Glasgow, had, along with several others of good position, taken an active part in the proceedings. He was a young man of great promise, a member of the Scottish bar. He was indicted for sedition, and brought before the High Court of Justiciary on August 30, 1793, by Mr. Henry Dundas, as public prosecutor. The leading judge was Lord Braxfield, a man at once both merci-

[1] *Memorials*, p. 87.

less and unscrupulous. He had the selection of the jury that was to try Muir. There was permitted no challenge of jurors, either because of their being servants of the crown, or because they had become members of opposing associations, or because they had expressed opinions adverse to Muir. It was of no use. The trial proceeded, and Lord Braxfield summed up: "Now, before this question can be answered, two things must be attended to that require no proof. First, that the British constitution is the best that ever was since the creation of the world, and it is not possible to make it better. For, is not every man secure? Does not every man reap the fruits of his own industry, and sit safely under his own fig-tree? The next circumstance is, that there was a spirit of sedition in this country last winter, which made every good man very uneasy; and I coincide in opinion with the master of the Grammar School of Glasgow, the propriety of whose sentiments, I must own, struck me very forcibly, when he said that he had told Mr. Muir that he thought proposing a reform was very ill timed. Yet Mr. Muir had at that time gone about telling the folk that a reform was absolutely necessary for preserving their liberty, which, if it had not been for him, they would never have known was in danger. I do not doubt that this will appear to you, gentlemen, as well as it does to me, to be sedition. Mr. Muir might have known that no attention could be paid to such a rabble as he harangued. What right had they to representation? He could have told them that the Parliament would never listen to their petition. How could they think of it? A government in every country should be just like a corporation; and in this country it is made up of the landed interest, which alone has a right to be represented. As for the rabble, who have nothing but SCOTLAND IN 1793. personal property, what hold has the nation of them? What security for the payment of their taxes? They may pack up all their property upon their backs and leave the country in the twinkling of an eye, but landed property cannot be removed." Muir was unanimously found guilty, and sentenced to fourteen years' transportation. Four others were tried for similar offences—Gerald, Skirving, Palmer, and Margarot—and each received Muir's trial. a sentence of fourteen years' transportation.[1] There can be no doubt that these men were really only guilty of advocating universal suffrage and short parliaments; but such was the temper of the times, and with a judge such as Lord Braxfield, who was a disgrace even to that age,[2] it was easy to foretell the result.

In the beginning of the following year (1794) there Mr. Adams' motion for was notice of the trials taken in Parliament. It was appeal re-known during the previous year by a decision of the jected. House of Lords that there could be no review of such cases, and accordingly, on 27th January, 1794, it was intimated to the House of Commons by Mr. Adams that he would move for leave to bring in a bill to grant such an appeal, and that an instruction be given to the committee on the bill to insert a clause that should be retrospective, so as to admit of covering the trials in question. This was refused, but he gave notice that he would bring the subject forward in another form, while in the meantime Mr. Sheridan presented a petition from Mr. Palmer himself. The subject was debated on 10th March, on the motion of Mr. Adam for a review of the trials; but this motion was rejected, as well as one of a similar kind in the House of Lords. The government having thus

[1] Report of Trial, 1794. [2] Lord Cockburn's *Memorials*, p. 115.

SCOTLAND IN 1793.

been successful with the trials in Scotland, resolved to pursue the same measures with the English societies as they had with the Scottish convention and its leaders.[1] With this view they arrested the principal members of the Corresponding Society and the Constitutional Society as guilty of treasonable practices, and committed them to the Tower. Their names were Hardie and Adams, the two secretaries, Horne Tooke, Jeremiah Joyce, and John Thelwall—and afterwards a number of others. The trials of Hardie, Tooke, and Thelwall came on toward the end of the year, but they were acquitted, and the prosecutions as a whole were abandoned.

Thus ends the exciting period from 1792 to 1794. The spectre of the Great Revolution had frightened reform out of the land. Those who had attempted to move had been silenced, and a long interval of apathy was now to set in. The government was stronger than ever. The Tories had the control of the whole institutions of the country; the Whigs had in a measure actually left the House of Commons, and let the great minister rule as he pleased. With the exception of a debate on the subject of reform raised by Mr. Grey in the parliament of 1797, and one by Sir Francis Burdett in that of 1809, which were both quite fruitless, we hear no more of the cause for a period of a quarter of a century.

Postponement of Reform.

By the year 1817 the outcome of the policy of the government since 1688 began to become very visible. What occurred in 1793 was simply the contagion of the French Revolution, and was merely a species of philosophical radicalism. What the government had now to face was a cry of distress. It was starvation resulting from low wages and high prices. It was want of employ-

Distress.

---

[1] *Annual Register*, 1794, p. 263.

ment. There was manifest a deep discontent through- Sir F. Bur-dett's mo-tion. out the nation at large—there was open sedition—there was training of men to arms for purposes of war. There were assemblages of men discussing politics in every corner of the land; there were large meetings held in the large towns; there were petitions in thousands sent on to Parliament. There were proclamations issued by the government. Secret committees sat. Over and over again the *Habeas Corpus* Act was suspended. Arrests were made, and the jails were filled. Many political trials took place, and a good many capital punishments inflicted. The military were unsparingly used, and at Manchester, on one occasion, several people were killed, while hundreds were wounded. This did not continue all the time from 1817 to 1832, but abated for a few years, and then broke out again as we approach the year 1831.

Meanwhile the movement for a thorough reform of the House recommenced on the old lines and with renewed energy. On July 1, 1819, the subject was brought before Sir F. Bur-dett's mo-tion. 1819. the House of Commons by Sir Francis Burdett in a speech of great ability. He said that he had never entertained the apprehensions by which many had been disturbed, in a good principle being pushed to its utmost extent. He could fear nothing from pursuing to its utmost extent the ancient and recognized common-law maxim—the corner-stone of the edifice of our liberties—"that the people of England have a property in their own goods, which is not to be taken from them without their own consent; in other words, that they are not constitution-ally liable to be taxed without their own consent, ex-pressed by a full, free, and fair representation in Parlia-ment." On this principle he stood as upon a rock, from

SIR F. BUR-
DETT'S MO-
TION, 1819.
which he thought it impossible to be moved. He had abstained from bringing forward this motion earlier in the session, lest he should be accused of thwarting or interfering in any manner with the attempts of the gentlemen composing what was called "the opposition" to remedy those evils of which they so loudly complained, and also because he wished both them and the public to be convinced by experience how vain and futile were any efforts and all expectations of any important redress of grievances from a new Parliament constituted like the old. Much had been said about the infusion of independence into the new Parliament; the elections were said to have proved that the present system of ministers could

His speech.
not be continued; that the ministers must relax in their career of corruption, and adopt a plan of retrenchment and economy, or resign to those who would. Hopes were excited, both within and without the House, which nothing but the conduct of the Parliament and the evidence of facts could have dispelled. Nothing short of this could have induced men to concur with himself in opinion that an effectual remedy, a material amelioration in the condition of the people, was only to be expected from a radical reform. Had he sooner stirred this question he should have been accused of throwing the apple of discord among the Whigs maliciously and advisedly, for the purpose of defeating all those rational and moderate plans of reform, as they were falsely called, of which that party were the advocates. But now that all attempts at remedying minor abuses had failed, and the utter hopelessness and folly of placing any reliance on what was called a new Parliament had been made apparent, knowing the anxiety of the public mind, seeing the dissatisfaction everywhere expressed, and the cause of all—

the want of a fair representation—he felt it his duty to
bring forward the subject. He entertained no expectation of its being followed by the immediate adoption of
any measure, but he did not doubt that the principle if
adopted would have a practical and beneficial effect in
tranquillizing the mind of the country; and he was anxious
that it should be tranquillized, that the people might give
no pretence to the noble lord at the head of the administration for again proposing to this borough-mongering
Parliament the suspension of the *Habeas Corpus* Act. The
motion he should make would lay gentlemen under no
obligation to support general suffrage or annual parlia-
·ments, or even state explicitly how far they would go;
all he requested of them was an engagement to satisfy
the public mind that early in the following session some
remedy might be expected for an evil of such magnitude
as the people not being represented in the Commons
House of Parliament; and he did trust that all those
gentlemen who had talked so much of grievances would
support a resolution for taking into consideration this
matter—grievances so far from being wild and visionary
that the people are moderate and wise, their aims are
noble, their first wish is to be free. And yet so modest
are they in their demands, wild and visionary as they
are called, that they demand only to be restored to that
portion of their rights which is necessary for the security
of their property and of their persons; the appointment
of those men who are to have the disposal of the hard-
earned fruits of their industry and labour, and in whom
they can confide for the honest application of them to the
purposes of the state; to have some share in the appointment of those who not only raise taxes from their labour,
but who also exercise the power of taking the people

SIR F. BUR-
DETT'S MO-
TION, 1819.

themselves—using their limbs and shedding their blood —whenever the cause of the country demands the sacrifice. Is it, then, asking too much for men who are liable to be torn from their families, and exposed to all risks and dangers, that they should have some share in the election of the representatives who have the power of saying when and how their services should be demanded? That they should, appears to me both reasonable and just. After a reference to the comparative state of freedom of the people of England and of France in the time of Lord-chancellor Fortescue contrasted with that of the present day, the honourable baronet proceeded to remark on the grievance evinced by the noble lord opposite (Castlereagh) of the general state of distress and embarrassment now subsisting amongst all conditions of persons. At the commencement of the present session, he said, the noble lord dreamed that the agriculture, manufactures, and commerce of the country were in the most satisfactory state, and had recovered from that temporary pressure which he admitted they had undergone in the transition from war to peace. "I cannot but suppose those to have been the real sentiments of the noble lord, because he puts this language into the speech from the throne, but I will say that if the noble lord believed this he was the only person in the country who did." Mr.

Mr. Lamb's
speech.

Lamb, in seconding the motion, remarked that he wished to see the borough system purged of its corruption, the elective franchise extended to populous places where it did not now exist, and triennial parliaments restored. He begged to add, that whatever reception the present proposition met with he must still consider the members of that House as the constitutional representatives of the people. The other members who took part in the debate were, with scarcely an exception, gentlemen who usually vote on the side of opposition, and who were nearly unanimous in expressing their wishes for a limited reform of the representation, particularly as a means to the attainment of a reduction in the present profuse and corrupt expenditure of public money in every department of the national establishments; but most of them declared their averseness to pushing reform to the length contemplated by the honourable baronet, and several were opposed to the motion on account of the time at which it was brought forward. The others declared their intention of voting in its favour. After a reply from the honourable baronet the House divided on passing to the order of the day—Ayes, 153; Noes, 58.

On 14th December, 1819, Lord John Russell rose to bring forward a motion, of which he had given notice, respecting parliamentary reform. His lordship began with stating the anxiety under which he presented a measure for which the present period might appear to some peculiarly ill adapted. He was not unaware that there were many persons in the House and in the country opposed to all theoretical advantages to be derived from a change in the constitution of Parliament. These were willing that the constitution, like the temples of the gods at Rome, should remain with all its dust and cobwebs about it, and thought it profane in any hand to remove the corruption by which it was defaced. Their opponents, on the other hand, the champions of radical reform, seemed desirous to raise their name by applying a firebrand to a sanctuary which had stood for ages. But without entering on a discussion of abstract principles, he wished to draw the attention of the House to the unrepresented towns, many of which

LORD JOHN
RUSSELL'S
MOTION,1819.

had risen into places of great commercial wealth and importance, while others had sunk into decay, and become unfit to enjoy the privilege of sending representatives. On reference to the history of Parliament, it would be found that the principle of change had been often acknowledged, and the suffrage withdrawn and conferred on various occasions. Of this the noble lord proceeded to adduce several examples, and after making various remarks on the practical evils resulting from the corruption of small boroughs—most of which were represented by gentlemen who sought a seat in the House from private and personal views, and who uniformly voted with the government, he passed on to the

His speech.

evils of non-representation to the populous towns to which he alluded, and the benefits to be anticipated from extending to them this privilege—a privilege which could only be extended to them on this principle of change, since neither the principles of the Revolution nor the Act of Union would permit the sovereign to issue his writ for adding to the number of members. After expressing at large both his veneration for the constitution, and his ideas on the reforms which it required, and could safely receive, his lordship, amid the cheers of both sides of the House, proposed several resolutions which went to establish the principle of change which he had laid down, and some rules respecting the voters of disfranchised places on whom corruption should not have been proved. On the suggestion of Lord Castlereagh, who acknowledged the moderation with which the proposal of the noble lord had been brought forward, and manifested a desire to concur in its objects to a certain degree, and to conciliate whatever differences of opinion might still subsist between himself and the noble mover, Lord John Russell withdrew his present motion. MR. LAMB-TON'S BILL, 1821.

There was no notice of reform taken in the session of 1820, but in 1821 there was a trial of strength between the reform party and the government; several petitions had been presented in its favour, and public meetings had taken place, at which language of extreme violence had been used. A reform dinner had been given in the London Tavern on May 4th, which was numerously attended by gentlemen of consideration and property. On the same night the subject was brought forward in the House of Commons, and though the attendance was exceedingly thin the debate occupied the House during two evenings. Mr. Lambton proposed a detailed and elaborate plan of reform, the principle features of which were—the limitation of the duration of Parliament to three years; the extension of the elective franchise to all persons possessing property, however small in value, which contributed to taxation; and the abolition of rotten boroughs. The discussion was long and languid, and terminated abruptly in the absence of the mover. Ayes 43, and Noes 55. Renewed agitation. Mr. Lambton's Bill.

Notwithstanding this frivolous result, Lord John Russell brought on the subject again on May 9, in a more general shape, which, without adopting any specific plan, merely asserted the necessity of reform, and pledged the House to the consideration of the measures by which it might be best effected. This he did by moving these four resolutions:— Lord J. Russell's motion, 1821.

" 1. That grievous complaints are made in the kingdom, and manifestly appear to be true, of undue elections of members to serve as burgesses in Parliament, by gross bribery and corruption, contrary to the laws and in violation of the freedom due to the electors of representatives for the Commons of England in Parliament, to the great scandal of the kingdom, dishonourable and may be destructive to the condition of Parliament.

" 2. That in order to strengthen and maintain the necessary connection between the Commons of this kingdom and their representatives in Parliament, it is expedient to give to such places as are greatly increased in wealth and population, and are not at present adequately represented, the right of returning members to serve in Parliament.

" 3. That a select committee be appointed to consider to what places, according to the principle of the foregoing resolution, it may be advisable to extend the right of returning members to serve in Parliament, and of the best method of effecting that measure without an inconvenient addition to the members of this House.

" 4. That it be referred to the same committee to consider further of a mode of proceeding with respect to any boroughs which may hereafter be charged with notorious bribery and corruption, in order that such charges may be regularly and effectively inquired into, and if proved, that such boroughs may be disabled from sending burgesses to serve in Parliament for the future."

Mr. Whitemore seconded the resolutions; Mr. Bathurst opposed them. The discussion was brief and tame, none of the leading members of either party taking part in it, and few of them even being present. The first resolution was lost by a majority of 155 to 124. The other resolutions were negatived without a division.

It may here be noted, however, that although the House was most unwilling to enter upon the general subject of reform, there was not the same objection to proceed to the disfranchisement of any of the boroughs LORD A.
HAMILTON'S
MOTION.1821. proved to be guilty of gross corruption, and instances occur about this time of this procedure having taken place.

On the day following the debate on Lord John Russell's resolution, May 10, 1821, there was a series of resolutions with reference to the amendment of the Scotch representation moved in the House of Commons by Lord Archibald Hamilton.

"1. That it appears by a certified copy of the roll of Resolutions
proposed. freeholders of every county in Scotland as last made up, laid before this House in July, 1820, that the total number of persons having a right to vote in all those counties together did not exceed 2889.

"2. That by the same return it appears that the greatest number of persons having a right to vote in any one county did not exceed 240, viz. for the county of Fife, and that the smallest number did not exceed 9, viz. for the county of Cromarty.

"3. That it further appears from the same return, that the same persons have a right to vote in several counties, and consequently that the total number of voters for all the counties in Scotland is considerably less than 2889.

"4. That it further appears to this House, that the right of voting for a Scotch county depends not on the possession of the *dominium utile* of a real landed estate in that country, but on holding the superiority over such estate; which superiority may be, and frequently is, disjoined from the property, insomuch that of all the persons qualified to vote for a Scotch county there may not be one who is possessed of a single acre of land within the county, while the whole of the land may

LORD A.
HAMILTON'S
MOTION, 1821.

belong to, and be the property of persons who have not a single vote for the representation.

" 5. That this House will early in the next session of Parliament take into its most serious consideration the state of the representation of counties in Scotland, with a view to effect some extension of the number of votes, and to establish some connection between the right of voting and the landed property of that country."

There was an important debate expected, but the attendance was so scanty that Lord Archibald Hamilton did not enter into any wide discussion. The House divided—41 Ayes and 57 Noes, leaving an adverse majority of 16.

Lord J. Russell's motion, 1822.

In 1822 there was a lively debate in the House of Commons, and the result was of importance in showing that some real progress was being made with the cause of reform. Petitions on that subject having been presented from a number of towns, and from the counties of Middlesex, Devon, Norfolk, Suffolk, Bedford, Cambridge, Surrey, Cornwall, and Huntingdon, Lord John Russell, on the 29th April, moved "that the present state of the representation of the people in Parliament requires the most serious consideration of this House." This motion he supported in an exceedingly long and

His speech.

elaborate speech. The foundation of his argument was a comparison of the state of the House with the condition of the people. "If I can show," he said, "that the state and condition of the people has materially changed, and that the change in the state of the House has not been agreeable to that change in the state of the people, but of a very different and opposite tendency, then it must be allowed that the House and the people have no longer that accordance which they ought to have, and that some remedy is required; but if I further show that this dis- LORD JOHN RUSSELL'S MOTION,1822 crepancy has made itself evident by acts which the House has done, and which the representatives of the people never could have sanctioned, then it must be admitted not only that there are abuses to be reformed, but that the duty and love of our country command the House immediately to begin the work." In the course of his speech he made an analysis of the manner in which certain votes had been given in the House of Commons, in order to prove that it was an unfit engine of government. In forming his estimates he considered all those as ministerial who had never voted for the reduction of the public establishments, and put down as opposition mem- His speech. bers all who had voted three times in favour of popular measures, even though they were, in general, supporters of ministers. From the members of the boroughs under 500 inhabitants there was one member in favour of reduction and 19 against it. From the members of the boroughs containing from 500 to 1000 inhabitants there were 12 for and 33 against reduction. From the members of the boroughs containing more than 1000 and less than 2000 inhabitants, 17 were for and 44 against reduction. From the members of the boroughs containing more than 2000 and less than 3000 inhabitants, 19 were for, 46 against reduction. From the members of the boroughs containing 5000 inhabitants there were 25 for and 44 against reduction; and from those of the boroughs containing more than 5000 inhabitants there were 66 for and only 47 against reduction. Thus it was evident that the proportion in favour of ministers diminished as the size of the places increased; for the proportion was in the first class as 19 to 1 in their favour; in the second as 3 to 1; in the third as 2 to 1; in the fourth

E

LORD JOHN
RUSSELL'S
MOTION,1822. as 4 to 3, and in the fifth as 3 to 5. These were facts which ought to convince the most incredulous that the small towns did not represent the interests of the people as well as the large towns. His proposal was to take 100 seats from the small boroughs and give 60 over to the counties, and devote the remaining 40 to the towns and commercial interests of the country. Several members spoke, but there was an impatience to hear Mr.

Mr. Can-
ning's
speech. Canning. "The plan of reform," he said, "now proposed is to make an addition of 100 members to this House, to be returned by the counties and larger towns; and to open the way for this augmentation by depriving each of the smaller boroughs of one half of the elective franchise which they now enjoy. This plan the noble lord has introduced and recommended with an enumeration of names, whose authority he assumes to be in favour of it. Amongst those names is that of Mr. Pitt. But the House must surely be aware that the plan brought forward by Mr. Pitt differed widely, not only in detail but in principle, from that propounded on this occasion by the noble lord. True it is that the object of Mr. Pitt's plan was, like that of the noble lord's, to add 100 members to this House, but this object was to be attained without the forcible abolition of any existing right of election. Mr. Pitt proposed to establish a fund of £1,000,000, to be applied to the purchase of franchises from such decayed boroughs as should be willing to sell them. This fund was to accumulate at compound interest till an adequate inducement was provided for the voluntary surrender by the proprietors of such elective franchise as it might be thought expedient to abolish. There was throughout the whole of Mr. Pitt's plan a studious avoidance of coercion, a careful preservation of vested interests, and

a fixed determination not to violate existing rights in accomplishing its object. It was hoped that by these means every sense of injury or danger would be excluded, and that the change in view would be brought about by a gradual process, resembling the silent and insensible operation of time. Here then, I repeat it, is a difference of the most essential kind between the two propositions of Mr. Pitt and of the noble lord—a difference not superficial, but fundamental, as complete, indeed, as the difference between concession and force, or between respect for property and spoliation.

Lord John Russell's motion,1822.

Mr. Canning's speech.

"The plan now brought forward, dangerous and violent as it was, would never satisfy the genuine reformers. If the House looks only to the various plans of reform which have at different times been laid upon its table, not by visionary speculatists, but by able and enlightened men, some of the ornaments of this and the other house of Parliament, how faint and flat is the noble mover's present plan in comparison with them. Let us take, for example, that one of the plans which had the greatest concurrence of opinions and the greatest weight of authority in its favour. A petition was presented to this house in 1793, which may perhaps be considered as the most advised and authentic exposition of the principles of parliamentary reform that ever has been submitted to the consideration of this House or of the public. Those principles are developed by the petitioners with singular clearness and force, and expressed in admirable language. It was presented in 1793 by a noble person, now one of the chief lights of the other house of Parliament, as the petition of the 'Friends of the People, associated for the purpose of obtaining a Reform in Parliament.' In that petition certain propositions are laid down as the basis

LORD JOHN
RUSSELL'S
MOTION, 1822. of a reform, which, to my recollection, have never yet been disclaimed, either on the part of the petitioners or of those who have succeeded them in the same pursuit. The petitioners complain, in the first place, that there is *not an uniform right of voting;* secondly, that *the right of voting is in too small bodies;* thirdly, that *many great bodies are excluded from voting;* and fourthly, they complain of the protracted duration of parliaments. Does the noble lord believe that all these notions are forgotten; that no persons still cherish them as the only means of effecting the salvation of the country? or does he subscribe to them all, although he may not think this the time for Mr. Canning's speech. pressing them upon the House?

"For my part, sir, I value the system of parliamentary representation for that very want of uniformity which is complained of in the petition; for the variety of rights of election. I conceive that to establish one uniform right would inevitably be to exclude some important interests from the advantage of being represented in this House. At all events the noble lord's plan does not cure this objection. The rights of voting would remain as various after the adoption of his plan as before; and a new variety would be added to them. Even of burgage tenures, the most obnoxious right of all and the most indignantly reprobated by the petition of 1793, the noble lord would carefully preserve the principle, only curtailing by one-half its operation.

"A change in the constitution of the House of Commons is the object of the present motion. That such a change is necessary the noble lord asserts, and I deny. I deny altogether the existence of such practical defect in the present constitution of this House as requires the adoption of so fearful an experiment. The noble lord has attempted to show the necessity of such a change by LORD JOHN RUSSELL'S MOTION,1822. enumerating certain questions on which this House has, on sundry occasions, decided against the noble mover's opinion, and against the politics and interests of that party in the state of which the noble mover is so conspicuous an ornament. But if such considerations bo sufficient to unsettle an ancient and established form of political constitution, how could any constitution—any free constitution—exist for six months? While human nature continues the same, the like division will arise in every free state, the like conflict of interests and opinions, the like rivalry for office, the like contention for power. A popular assembly always has been, and always Mr. Canning's speech. will be, exposed to the operation of a party feeling, arraying its elements and influencing its decisions—in modern as in ancient times; in Great Britain, in this our day, as heretofore in Athens or in Rome. No imaginable alteration in the mode of election can eradicate this vice —if it be a vice—or can extinguish that feeling, be it good or bad, which mixes itself largely in every debate upon the public affairs of a nation—the feeling of affection or disfavour towards the persons in whose hands is the conduct of those affairs. I am not saying that this is a proper or a laudable feeling. I am not contending that partiality ought to influence judgment; still less that when judgment and partiality are at variance, the latter ought, in strict duty, to preponderate. I am not affirming that in the discussion of the question 'What has been done?' the question 'Who did it?' ought silently to dictate or even to modify the answer, that the case should be nothing and the men everything—I say no such thing. But I do say, that while men are mere popular assemblies, get them together how you will, they will be liable to such influence—I say, that in discussing the particular acts of a government in a popular assembly the consideration of the general character of that government, and the conflicting partialities which lead some men to favour it and others to aim at its subversion, will, sometimes openly and avowedly, at other times insensibly even to the disputants themselves, control opinions and votes, and correct or pervert, as it may be, the specific decision. I say that, for instance, in the discussion upon the Walcheren expedition, which has been more than once selected as an example of undue influence and partiality, there was notoriously another point at issue besides the specific merits of the case; and that point was—whether the then administration should or should not be dismissed from the service of their country? Never, perhaps, was the struggle pushed further than on that occasion; and that vote substantially decided the question, 'In what hands should be placed the administration of affairs?' I am not saying that this was right in the particular instance. I am not saying that it is right in principle. But right or wrong, such a mode of thinking and acting is, I am afraid, essentially in the very nature of all popular governments, and most particularly so in that of the most free.

"The noble lord has himself stated that, in the instance of the Revolution, the Parliament did wisely in setting at nought the immediate feelings of its constituents. There cannot, indeed, be the slightest doubt that, had the nation been polled in 1688, the majority would have been found adverse to the change that was then effected in the government; but Parliament, acting in its higher and larger capacity, decided for the people's interests against their prejudices. It is not true, therefore,

that the House of Commons is necessarily defective LORD JOHN
because it may not instantly respond to every impression RUSSELL'S
of the people. MOTION,1822.

"In the year 1811 I myself divided, in a minority of
about forty, against an overwhelming majority on the
question relating to the depreciation of the currency.
It would be idle to deny that the majority, which sturdily
denied the fact of the depreciation, then spoke the sentiments of the country at large. They certainly did so;
but who will now affirm that it would have been a misfortune if the then prevailing sense of the country had
been less faithfully represented in the votes of the
House? What a world of error and inconvenience should Mr. Can-
we have avoided by a salutary discrepancy at that time ning's speech.
between the constituent and the representative ! Eight
years afterwards—but unluckily after eight years' additional growth of embarrassment—in 1819, the principles
which had found but about forty supporters in 1811
were adopted unanimously, first by a committee of this
House and then by this House itself. But the country
was much slower in coming back from the erroneous
opinions which the decision of this House in 1811 had
adopted and confirmed. In 1819, as in 1811, if London
and the other principal towns of the kingdom had been
canvassed for an opinion, the prevailing opinion would
still have been found nearly what it was in 1811. Yet
is it necessary to argue that the decision of the House in
1819, against the opinion of the country, was a sounder
and wiser decision than that of 1811, in conformity to it?
Never, then, can I consider it as a true proposition that
the state of the representation is deficient because it
does not *immediately* speak the apparent sense of the
people—because it sometimes contradicts, and sometimes

goes before it. The House as well as the people are
liable to err; but that the House may happen to differ in
opinion from the people is no infallible mark of error.
And it would, in my opinion, be a base and cowardly
House of Commons, unworthy of the large and liberal
confidence without which it must be incompetent to the
discharge of its high functions, which having, after due
deliberation, adopted a great public measure, should be
frightened back into an acquiescence with the temporary
excitement which might exist upon that measure out of
doors.

"Upon another great question which I have much at
heart—I mean the Roman Catholic question—I have not
the slightest doubt that the House has run before the
sense of the country, which is now, however, gradually
coming up to us. I have no doubt that in all our early
votes on this most important question we had not the
country with us; but I am equally confident that the
period is rapidly advancing when the country will be
convinced that the House of Commons has acted as they
ought to have done. If on such questions as these—
questions before which almost all others sink into insignificance—the House of Commons have been either
against or before the opinions of the country, the proposition that the representative system is necessarily imperfect because it does not give an *immediate* echo to the
sentiments of the people is surely not to be received
without abundant qualification. On this ground, therefore, there is no foundation for the noble lord's motion
unless the free expression of an honest and conscientious
opinion when it may happen to differ from that of its
constituents be inconsistent with the duty and derogatory
to the character of a representative assembly.

" If this House is adequate to the functions which really belong to it—which functions are, not to exercise an un- divided supreme dominion in the name of the people over the crown and the other branch of the legislature, but, checking the one and balancing the other, to watch over the people's rights, and to provide especially for the people's interests—if, I say, the House is adequate to the performance of these, its legitimate functions, the mode of its composition appears to me a consideration of secondary importance. Persons may look with a critical and microscopic eye into bodies physical or moral till doubts arise whether it is possible for them to perform their assigned functions. So, in considering too curiously the composition of this House, and the different processes through which it is composed—not those processes alone which are emphatically considered as pollution and cor- ruption, but those also which rank among the noblest exercises of personal freedom—the canvasses, the con- flicts, the controversies, and (what is inseparable from these) the vituperations and excesses of popular election —a dissector of political constitutions might well be sur- prised to behold the product of such elements in an as- sembly of which, whatever may be its other character- istics, no man will seriously deny that it comprehends as much of intellectual ability and of moral integrity as was ever brought together in the civilized world. Nay, to an unlearned spectator, undertaking for the first time an anatomical examination of the House of Commons, those parts of it which, according to theory, are its beauties, must appear most particularly its stains, for while the members returned for burgage-tenure seats or through other obscure and noiseless modes of election pass into the House of Commons unnoticed and uncriticised, their talents unquestioned and their reputation unassailed, the successful candidate of a popular election often comes there loaded with the imputation of every vice and crime that would unfit a man not only for representing any class of persons but for mixing with them as a member of society. The first effect of a reform which should convert all elections into popular ones would probably be to ensure a congregation of individuals against every óne of whom a respectable minority of his constituents would have pronounced sentence of condemnation. And if it be so very hard that there are now a great number of persons who do not directly exercise the elective franchise, and who are therefore represented by persons whom others have chosen for them, would this matter be much mended when two-fifths of the people of England should be represented not only without their choice but against their will, not only by individuals whom they had not selected, but by those whom they had declared utterly unworthy of their confidence.

"Again: Should we have no cause to lament the disfranchisement of those boroughs which are not open to popular influence? How many of the gentlemen who sit opposite to me, the rarest talents of their party, owe their seats to the existence of such boroughs? When I consider the eminent qualities which distinguish, for instance, the representative of Knaresborough, Winchelsea, Higham-Ferrers, I never can consent to join in the reprobation cast upon a system which fructifies in produce of so admirable a kind. No, sir. If this House is not all that theory could wish it, I would rather rest satisfied with its present state than, by endeavouring to remedy some small defects, run the hazard of losing so much that is excellent. Old Sarum, and other boroughs, at which the finger of scorn is pointed, are not more under private patronage now than at the periods the most glorious of our history. Some of them are still in the possession of the descendants of the same patrons who held them at the period of the Revolution. Yet in spite of Old Sarum the Revolution was accomplished and the house of Hanover seated on the throne. In spite of Old Sarum did I say? No. Rather by the aid of Old Sarum and similar boroughs, for the House has heard it admitted by the noble mover himself, that if the House of Commons of that day had been a reformed House of Commons the benefits of the Revolution would never have been obtained."

Mr. Canning then contended that all who wished for a reform of Parliament must proceed upon one of two principles—either to construct it anew or to bring it back to the state in which it existed at some former period. If the latter branch of the alternative were adopted he showed that there was no date in our history when the structure of the legislature coincided in any degree with the ideas of democracy—none at which every alleged abuse in the composition of the House of Commons was not as prevalent as at present; and to enliven this part of his subject he quoted various curious instances of aristocratical interference in the elections in the reign of Henry VI., Edward IV., Elizabeth, Charles II., and William III. " Thus," said Mr. Canning, " I have endeavoured to dispel the idle superstition that there once existed in this country a House of Commons in the construction of which the faults that are attributed to the present House of Commons, and attributed to it as a motive for inflicting upon itself its own destruction, did not equally exist, and not only exist equally, but exist in wider extent and more undisguised enormity. I have been showing that if the present House of Commons is to be destroyed for these faults, it has earned that fate not by degeneracy but by imitation; that it would in such case expiate the misdeeds of its predecessors instead of suffering for any that are peculiarly its own. I have been endeavouring to prove that of the two options—do you mean to restore or to construct anew?—no reformer who has carefully examined the subject can in sincerity answer otherwise than 'to construct anew,' for that to restore the times of purity of election, that is, of election free from the influence, and a preponderating influence, too, of property, rank, station, and power, natural or ac- quired, would be to restore a state of things of which we can find no prototype, and to revert to times which in truth have never been.

"That the proposition to construct anew is the much more formidable proposition of the two is tacitly admitted by the very unwillingness which is shown on all occasions to acknowledge it as the object of any motion for reform. Yet to *that* must the reformers come. To that I venture to tell the noble lord, he, with all his caution and all his desire to avoid extravagance and exaggeration, must come, if he consents to reform *on principle*. By 'reforming on principle' I mean reforming with a view, not simply to the redress of any partial practical grievance, but generally to theoretical improvement. I may add that even 'on principle' his endeavours to reform will be utterly vain if he insists upon the exclusion of influence as an indispensable quality of his reformed constitution. Not in this country only, but in every one in which a popular elective assembly has formed part of the government, to exclude such influence from the election has

been a task either not attempted or attempted to no pur- LORD JOHN
pose. While we dam up one source of influence a dozen RUSSELL'S
MOTION,1822.
others will open, in proportion as the progress of civilization, the extension of commerce, and a hundred other
circumstances better understood than defined, contribute
to shift and change, in their relative proportions, the prevailing interests of society. Whether the House of Commons in its present shape does not practically, though
silently, accommodate itself to such changes with a pliancy
almost as faithful as the nicest artifice could contrive, is
in my opinion, I confess, a much more important consideration than whether the component parts of the House
might be arranged with neater symmetry or distributed in Mr. Canning's
speech.
more scientific proportions.

"Our lot is happily cast in the temperate zone of freedom, the clime best suited to the development of the
moral qualities of the human race; to the cultivation of
their faculties, and to the security, as well as the improvement, of their virtues; a clime not exempt, indeed, from
variations of the elements, but variations which purify
while they agitate the atmosphere that we breathe.
Let us be sensible of the advantages which it is our
happiness to enjoy. Let us guard with pious gratitude
the flame of genuine liberty, that fire from heaven of
which our constitution is the holy depository; and let us
not, for the chance of rendering it more intense and more
radiant, impair its purity or hazard its extinction!

"That the noble lord will carry his motion this evening
I have no fear; but with the talents which he has shown
himself to possess, and with (I sincerely hope) a long
and brilliant career of parliamentary distinction before
him, he will, no doubt, renew his efforts hereafter.
Although I presume not to expect that he will give any

LORD JOHN
RUSSELL'S
MOTION,1822. weight to any observations or warnings of mine, yet on this, probably the last, opportunity which I shall have of raising my voice on the question of parliamentary reform, while I conjure the House to pause before it consents to adopt the proposition of the noble lord I cannot help conjuring the noble lord himself to pause before he again presses it upon the country If, however, he shall persevere, and if his perseverance shall be successful, and if the result of that success shall be such as I cannot help apprehending, his be the triumph to have precipitated those results; be mine the consolation that to the utmost and the latest of my power I have opposed them."

Motion lost. After a short reply from the mover the House divided —ayes 164, noes 269.

Mr. Canning never spoke on the subject of reform in the House but once, for although a debate took place some years later he took no part in it. It is interesting to read the speech of such a man on such a subject, with all the light of the present day thrown upon it; to see how lightly he deals with the question of a relation between the opinion of the country and the votes of its representatives, and to notice his assertion that with a reformed House of Commons the Revolution settlement would never have been carried!

There is nothing done for reform over the next four years. There was a revival of trade—discontent died down, agitation greatly diminished. There was a considerable reduction in the public expenditure—many Combination laws. taxes were removed, and the ministry made important concessions to the demands of the people. There was one concession of considerable importance to the working-man in an age when manufactures and commerce were about to make a prodigious expansion. This was the acrifice of the combination laws. The lawyers and LORD JOHN RUSSELL'S MOTION,1826. politicians of the period had invented a crime from naterials in which it was difficult to find it, and they alled it "conspiracy." It meant that while an action vas quite legal in itself, yet if two or more combined to lo it the action became a crime. The general law struck gainst a combination of workmen to raise wages or essen time or work, but it received an interpretation in 819, in the trials of *Watson* and *Moss*, which made it ery obnoxious. In his charge it was laid down as law y Baron Wood that "it was very true that a labouring veaver might refuse to work, might be idle, or go to nother master, but he may not advise, excite, or encourage others to do so" (*Annual Register*, 1819, p. 244). This law was removed from the statute-book at the intance of Mr. Hume, and, along with other circumstances, his soothed the country for a time.

After an interval of four years, viz. in 1826, Lord Lord J. Russell's motion, 1826. John Russell again brought forward the general subject f parliamentary reform, in the form of a proposed reolution, to the effect "That the present state of the epresentation of this country in Parliament requires he most serious consideration of the House." After a engthy speech, in which similar arguments were used, His speech. nd the same proposal as to the disfranchising the small oroughs and giving the seats to the large towns, was nade as on a previous occasion, Lord John concluded by noving his resolution in the words of Mr. Fox, "not to ull down, but to work upon our constitution, to examine t with care and reverence, to repair it where decayed, to mend it where defective, to prop it where it wanted support, to adapt it to the purposes of the present time, as ur ancestors had done from generation to generation, and

LORD JOHN
RUSSELL'S
MOTION, 1826.

always transmitted it, not only unimpaired but improved to posterity." Mr. Denison opposed the motion, but it was supported in an excellent speech by Mr. Hobhouse. He said: "The effects of the system on the votes of that House furnished irrefragable answers to every pretence of its voice being that of the country. He had an analysis of the majorities on the great questions which had been discussed in 1821 and 1822, which showed that these majorities were wholly made up of the eighty-nine place-

Mr. Hobhouse's speech.

men, and of members intimately connected with the government, and if it were not unparliamentary he would read their names. He had also an analysis showing the divisions on thirty-six great questions which had taken place in those years, the result of which was rather curious, and which he would take the liberty of reading to the House to show how the state of the representation really stood:—Of the 40 counties of England, 25 members voted for the government and 37 against; of the 24 counties and towns of Wales, 13 members voted for and 9 against the government; of 89 cities and boroughs, where the election was open, 57 members voted for the government and 107 against; of the 99 cities and boroughs in which the election was confined, 151 voted for the government and 12 against; of the 33 counties and boroughs in Scotland, 25 members voted for and 11 against the government; of the 65 counties and boroughs of Ireland, 45 voted for and 21 against the government; of the remaining 112 members, making up a total of 658, they either did not vote at all or voted occasionally on either side. Even the vote which the other night had prevented the creation of a new placeman, proved thoroughly the corrupt state of the representation. The majority in favour of ministers on that occasion consisted of 38 gentlemen who enjoyed places and salaries; of 10 LORD JOHN RUSSELL'S MOTION,1826 more who were intimately connected with them, and only one county member voted with them. Such was the system by which ministers ruled Parliament, and Parliament the country; and of which Mr. Pitt had declared in the days of his youth, that under it it was impossible for a minister to be an honest man."[1] Neither Mr. Canning nor Mr. Brougham took any part in the discussion, and it ended in the motion being rejected by a majority Motion re- jected. of 247 to 123.

In 1830 it was obvious that the battle of reform was soon to recommence. For some years previously the agitation had died away; meetings had ceased to be held; there were no riots; even petitions fell entirely away. In 1821 there had been 19 petitions for reform; in 1822 there were 12; in 1823 there were 29; during the next six years there were none. But a stimulus was given to the movement by the French Revolution of 1830, and the flight of Charles X. This set the whole machinery of political life once more into motion. Meet- Agitation renewed. ings began to be held, petitions were prepared, and the press resumed its activity. In addition to all the former appliances for raising and maintaining popular excitement, there now began to be organized associations of a permanent character, which were termed "political unions," and which immediately began to exercise a great amount of influence. They had a regular constitution with defined objects, a council to advise and direct, and an army of officials to push on the business of the associations.

Action also began to be taken in Parliament. The Marquis of Blandford's motion,1830. Marquis of Blandford had brought a measure before the

[1] *Annual Register*, 1826, p. 97.

F

MARQUIS OF
BLAND-
FORD'S MEA-
SURE, 1830 House of Commons in 1829, and he brought another
forward in 1830. Both were of a general character, and
both dealt with the personal franchise and with the system of decayed boroughs. Lord Blandford was not a
reformer on principle, and was perhaps more desirous of
devising a way of keeping the Roman Catholics out of
Parliament than of remodelling the House of Commons.
There was, therefore, little interest felt in the discussion.

Sir F. Bur-
dett's
speech. It was supported, however, by Sir Francis Burdett, who
contributed some information to the House on the working of the electoral system. He said: "Look at myself.
I have gone through the whole process under the present system of representation, and a most ruinous one it
has been. Early in life I came into this House in order
to defend the constitution of England. I purchased my
seat of a borough-monger. He was no patron of mine.
He took my money, and by purchase I obtained a right
to speak in the most public place in England. With my
views and with my love of the liberty of my country I
did not grudge the sacrifice I made for that commanding
consideration. If I had abused the right I had thus purchased, and passed through corruption to the honours of
the peerage, I should not enjoy the satisfaction I now feel."
His object was to expose the prison system of England.
The motion was negatived without a division, as was also

Motions by
Lord   Al-
thorp and
Lord J. Rus-
sell. an amendment proposed by Lord Althorp to the effect
"that, in the opinion of this House a reform in the
representation of the people is necessary." There was
more skirmishing before the great fight began. Lord
John Russell tried to bring in a measure for conferring
the franchise on Leeds, Birmingham, and Manchester,
but the motion was negatived by a majority of 180
against 40. Mr. O'Connell then moved for leave to

bring in a bill to establish triennial parliaments, univer- MR. O'CON-
sal suffrage, and vote by ballot, whereupon Lord John NELL'S BILL.
Russell took occasion to introduce certain resolutions of
his own, proposing to confer the franchise on a number
of large towns, and embracing a much more comprehensive scheme than any which he had proposed before. He
opposed O'Connell's motion, and so did Lord Althorp
and Mr. Brougham. Mr. O'Connell's motion was rejected by a majority of 319 against 13, while Lord John
Russell's resolutions were negatived by a majority of 213
against 117. Afterwards Mr. Brougham gave notice of
his intention to bring up the subject of reform, but. before this could take place he was called to the House of
Peers as lord chancellor. On the whole, the year 1830
was busy with sporadic efforts at reform, all preparatory
to the conflict that was soon to open and to produce the
first breach in the close system of the three Estates.
There were also during this year a good many changes.
There was the death of George IV., the ascension of
William IV., a dissolution of Parliament and the election
of a new one, the fall of the Wellington administration,
and the accession to power of Earl Grey and the reform
party.

The campaign opened on March 1, 1831, by the First Re-
introduction of the measure. Lord John Russell was form Bill
of 1831.
not a cabinet minister, but in consideration of his previous efforts in the cause the bill was intrusted to his
care. After some preliminary explanations his lordship
laid it down as one principle on which he and his colleagues agreed, that the question of right was in favour Lord J. Rus-
of the reformers, for the ancient constitution of the coun- sell's speech.
try declared that no man should be taxed for the support
of the state who had not consented by himself or his

FIRST RE-
FORM BILL
OF 1831.

representative to the imposition of the taxes. The statute *Tallagio non concedendo* spoke the same language, and although some historical doubts had been thrown upon it, its legal meaning had never been questioned. It included "all the freemen of the land," and it provided that each county should send to the Commons two knights, each city two burgesses, and each borough two members. About a hundred places sent representatives, and thirty or forty others occasionally enjoyed the privilege; but it was discontinued or revived as they rose or fell in the scale of wealth and importance. No doubt, at that early period, the House of Commons did

Lord John
Russell's
speech.

represent the people of England; but, added his lordship, there is, likewise, no doubt that the House of Commons, as it presently subsists, does not represent the people of England. The right being thus in favour of reform the House would find that the result would be the same when they looked to what was reasonable, for it would be impossible to keep the constitution of the House as it at present existed. Who had not heard of the fame of this country, that in wealth it was unparalleled, in civilization unrivalled, and in freedom unequalled in the history of the empires of the world? Now supposing that a foreigner, well acquainted with these facts, were told that in this most wealthy, most civilized, and most free country the representatives of the people, the guardians of her liberties, were chosen only every six years, would he not be very curious and very anxious to hear in what way that operation was performed, by which this great nation selected the members who were to represent them, and upon whom depended their fortunes and their rights? Would not such a foreigner be much astonished if he here were

taken to a green mound and informed that it sent two
members to the British Parliament? if he were shown a
stone wall, and told that it also sent two members to the
British Parliament? or if he walked into a park without
the vestige of a dwelling, and learned that that too sent
two members to the British Parliament? He would be
still more astonished were he to go into the northern
part of the country, and were to see flourishing towns,
containing immense manufactories, and depositories of
every sort of merchandise, and be informed that these
places sent no representatives to Parliament. He would
be still more astonished were he to be taken to a great
and opulent town—Liverpool, for instance—and were to
observe the manner in which general elections were there
conducted. He would see bribery prevail to the greatest
extent; he would see men openly paid for their votes; and
he would be astonished that a nation whose representatives
were so chosen should be at all competent to perform the
functions of legislation. The people called loudly for
reform, saying that whatever good existed in the constitution of this House, whatever confidence was placed in
it by the people, was completely gone. Whatever might
be thought of particular acts, the confidence of the country in the constitution of the House had long ceased; and
so long as towns like Leeds and Manchester elected no
representatives, while such places as Gatton and Old
Sarum did, it was impossible to say that the representation
was fairly and properly carried on. From these premises
his lordship arrived at this conclusion: if the case was
one of right, it is in favour of reform; if it be a question
of reason, it is in favour of reform; if it be a question of
expediency, expediency calls loudly for it. His lordship
then stated the plan by which ministers proposed to

FIRST RE-
FORM BILL
OF 1831.
meet and satisfy the demand for reform which they averred themselves to believe could no longer be resisted. The plan had been so framed as to remove the reasonable complaints of the people, and these complaints again were principally directed, first, against nomination by individuals; secondly, election by close corporations; thirdly, the expenses of elections. In so far as concerns the first two grounds of complaint, the plan of ministers consisted, first, of disfranchisement, in order to get rid of places which had hitherto sent members to Parliament; secondly, of enfranchisement, in order to enable places which had hitherto been unrepresented to elect members; thirdly, of an extension of the franchise, in order to in-

Lord John
Russell's
speech.
crease the number of electors in those places which were to be allowed to retain in whole or in part their existing privilege of sending members to the House of Commons. The part of the plan which related to disfranchisement proceeded on a very plain rule, viz. to disfranchise all boroughs whose population did not exceed a certain number. Lord John Russell allowed it would be an extremely difficult task to ascertain the wealth, trade, extent, and population of a given number of places. We have therefore been governed, said he, by what is a public record—the population return of 1821—and we propose that every borough which at that date contained fewer than 2000 inhabitants shall be deprived entirely of the privilege of sending members to Parliament. This would utterly disfranchise sixty boroughs, and get rid of 119 members. This, he was perfectly aware, was a bold and decided measure. He knew that, on ordinary occasions, no interest, however trifling, should be touched; but this was no ordinary occasion, and the interests to be touched were not private interests but public trusts.

But disfranchisement was not to stop here; there were boroughs which should be blotted out altogether. There were others which, although more flourishing in point of population, were too low to have any good title to retain their present privilege of sending two members to the House of Commons. It was, therefore, further proposed that all boroughs whose population, according to the cen- sus of 1821, though it exceeded 2000, was under 4000, should in future send only one member instead of two. The number of these boroughs was forty-seven, and thus forty-seven members more were disposed of. Wey- mouth, likewise, which had hitherto sent four members, was in future to send only two.

This process of disfranchisement proceeded on the simple fact of numbers, and was necessarily utterly arbi- trary in its very principles, having deprived the House of Commons of 168 members. Then began the work of enfranchisement by giving members to places which had hitherto been unrepresented, and giving more members to other places which had always enjoyed them. In the first place it was proposed that each of seven considerable towns should send two members, and twenty others one member each. This restored thirty-four members. Next were selected twenty-seven of the largest counties, includ- ing Yorkshire, each of which was in future to return four members instead of two, with this exception, that York- shire already possessing four, was now to return an additional member for each riding. The representation of London, likewise, was to be more than doubled. The Tower Hamlets, containing a population of 28,000 in- habitants, were to return two members; the district of Holborn (218,000) two members; Finsbury and its dis- trict (162,000) two members; Lambeth and the places be-

yond the river (128,000) two members; and the parish of
Marylebone two members. The most important part of
the ministerial new constitution still remained behind.
. The cities, boroughs, and counties which were to send members, and the number of members to be elected, being thus
ascertained, the existing right of franchise in all of them
was to be altered, and a new franchise introduced, extending equally to those which remained untouched, with the
declared purpose of increasing the numbers of electors and
having but one uniform right of election throughout the
empire. That right was to be as follows:—The elective
franchise was to be extended to all persons paying a rent

of £10 per annum, whether they occupied the premises
or not. Existing resident electors were not to be deprived of their right during their lifetime, but no non-
resident elector was to be allowed to retain his franchise.
Copyholders whose property was of the yearly value of
£10 and all householders to an equal amount, were to
be electors for counties. All holders of leases for twenty-
one years, which had not been renewed within two years,
were to have the privilege of voting in towns, and all
leaseholders for twenty years of property worth £50 per
annum were to vote for counties. In the towns to be
named to send members to Parliament the property
which entitled a man to vote for the town was not, likewise, to entitle him to vote for the county, so that where
the towns had representatives chosen by themselves they
would not interfere with the county representatives, and
the two classes of voters would be kept as distinct as
possible. No alteration was to be made in regard to the
forty shillings freeholders.

His lordship next gave a general outline of the changes
to be introduced into the representation of Scotland and

Ireland. In the former the existing county franchise,
which depended not on the possession of land, but on a
mere feudal right of superiority over lands belonging to
others, was to be annihilated; the election of members
for boroughs was to be taken from the town-councils and
vested in the citizens at large; and both in counties and
in boroughs the new English franchise was to be introduced. Every resident owner of lands or houses worth
£10 yearly, and every tenant under a written lease for
nineteen years and upwards, paying £50 a year, was to
have a vote in county elections. In towns the franchise
was to attach to the occupancy of a dwelling-house rented
at £10 per annum. To some of the larger towns, which
hitherto had elected only in conjunction with others, as
Glasgow and Aberdeen, or which, not being royal
boroughs, had enjoyed no share in the representation, as
Paisley and Greenock, separate or new members were
conferred; while the Fife district of burghs was annihilated and thrown into the county, and some counties
were conjoined. The detail of these arrangements belongs more properly to the history of the Scottish bill,
but the result of them was to have fifty members instead
of forty-five. In Ireland the principal alterations were
to be the introduction of the £10 qualification, and that
in towns the franchise should be taken out of the hands
of the corporations and given to all qualified resident
citizens. Belfast was to return one member, and Limerick and Waterford two each, thus making an addition of
three members to the representation of Ireland. The
general result of the whole measure, his lordship said,
would be to create a new constituency of about 500,000.
The increase for the towns already represented would be
about 110,000; for the new towns, 50,000; for London

95,000; for Scotland, 60,000; and for Ireland, perhaps 40,000. In counties 100,000 at least would be entitled to vote under this bill who never had the advantage of voting before, and, upon the whole, the constituency of the Commons House of Parliament would certainly be increased by half a million of persons; and half a million of persons, be it observed, connected with the property of the country, persons having themselves a valuable stake in the country, and upon whom it would depend in any future struggle which this country might have to sustain to support Parliament, and to support the throne in carrying that struggle to a successful termination. It

was true that the necessary result of the arrangements which he had detailed was to diminish the total number of members in the House, but that was not a result which ministers considered as a disadvantage. The present number of members was 658; of these 168 were to be struck out by disfranchisement, while there would be added 34 for English towns and 55 for counties, 8 for London, 1 for Wales, 5 for Scotland, 3 for Ireland—in all 106, leaving an absolute diminution of 62, which diminution was inflicted exclusively upon England. Lord John Russell, however, stated the opinion of ministers to be, that this reduction in the number of members would only enable the House to transact the public business more effectually and conveniently.

The bill contained no provision regarding the ballot or the duration of Parliament. It was debated for seven nights, and from seventy to eighty speeches were made

on the subject. The debate was opened by Sir Robert H. Inglis, member for Oxford. He contended that the whole essence of the scheme was not reform in any common or sensible meaning of the word; it was revolu-

tion. It forgot the immense power which public opinion
had been gaining by the press. It forgot that the people were daily becoming more intelligent, and the sympathy between them and their representatives greater, and that all public men were infinitely more under the control of public opinion than at any former period. He believed that in the history of civilized man there was not to be found any system of representation so completely popular as that now proposed, co-existing with a free press on the one hand, and a monarchy on the other;—there was no instance upon record of a free press being placed in juxta-position with a monarchy, and a system of representation such as that which the noble lord had just explained.
Before ten years had passed away all the institutions of the country would sink under the effects of the present measure. An attempt at such an experiment as this had been made by the National Assembly in France. Something of the same sort had been attempted in Switzerland also, and a similar trial was now being made in France. In France it was too obvious to escape observation, that the attempt to produce a purely popular representation had interrupted that country in the fairest course of liberty, arts, domestic trade, and foreign commerce to which she had ever attained; and he entertained not the slightest doubt, that were the calamity proposed by the noble lord to be inflicted on this land, a similar result would ensue. When the noble lord from whose govern-ment the present measure proceeded forty years ago, made a proposition in that House for a much more mo-derate reform, he did not conceal that the very moderate reform involved a fundamental change in the government of the country. What, then, was he not bound to admit with respect to a reform which went at a blow to sweep

away one-third of the House of Commons? Were it agreed to, the House of Lords before ten years would have but a nominal existence. If the representation of the people was complete and perfect in all parts, nothing could withstand its power and authority. An unreformed House of Lords would not for a moment be tolerated by a reformed House of Commons. Mr. Canning more than once had expressed his full conviction that the House of Lords could not continue as at present constituted, if the measure of reform were once carried with reference to the House of Commons; and yet the ministry which proposed the present measure contained the men who had been called, and had held themselves out as being Mr. Canning's chosen disciples and peculiar friends.

Lord Althorp, the chancellor of the exchequer, maintained, on the other hand, that there was no symptom or appearance of agitation in the country; but there was wide-spread dissatisfaction with the state of the representation, and a loudly-expressed desire that it should be reformed. These opinions were universal among the great body of the middling classes; and if the middling classes in this or any other country were hostile to the form of government under which they lived, that government would never be safe, whatever the state of the representation might be. Neither ought the proposed bill to be regarded as merely a first step, as something which was not to be final. In so far as he was concerned he did propose it as a final settlement.

Mr. Hume frankly declared that, radical reformer as he was, the plan proposed much exceeded what he had expected; that with all his disposition to put confidence in ministers, he was not prepared to find them come forward with so manly a measure. They had fully redeemed

their pledge, and though, ~~in his own opinion, the omission~~
to ~~shorten the duration of parliaments and to introduce~~
~~the ballot were deficiencies,~~ yet as these were points on
which a large portion of the members had not been able
to make up their minds, ministers had acted wisely in
not encumbering the present measure with them, as they
could be brought forward at any time as entire questions.

Mr. Macaulay stated that he supported the measure
because he was opposed to universal suffrage, because he
looked with horror on the thought of anything in the
shape of revolution, and believed that the proposed
change was the best security against all possibility of
revolution. If he wished to set before the House in the
strongest light the evils of the present system of representation he would refer to the northern part of this city.
If he wished to make that foreigner who had been introduced first into the debate by the noble lord who opened
it, fully sensible of the peculiar evils of our system he
would conduct him to that great city which lies to the
north of Oxford Street and the west of Russell Square.
There he could show him a city exceeding in size the
capitals of many kingdoms, and even superior in intelligence and knowledge to any city on the face of the
globe. He would there show him long lines of inter-
minable streets, and spacious squares filled with well-
built magnificent houses, inhabited by opulent and intelligent men, some of the first citizens of the state. He
would show that stranger the magnificent shops, the
splendid apartments, he would like to carry him to the
palaces that stretch along each side of Regent's Park,
and he would tell him that the rental of these palaces
and houses exceeded the rental of all Scotland at the
time of the Union; and then he would tell the stranger

that all this wealth and intelligence were unrepresented. He should not need to refer him to Leeds, or Manchester, or Macclesfield, or to tell him that Scotland had only the shadow of a representation. The principle of the pro-perty-tax was that no income below a certain amount per annum should be taxed, and he doubted, should he include only the property assessed to that tax, if he should find one half of the persons who paid that tax had any votes for representatives. One-fiftieth part of those persons returned a greater number of representatives than did the other forty-nine parts. Ours, then, was not a govern-ment on the principle of property; it was only a govern-ment founded on some fragments of property, and no principle whatever presided over its formation. It had been said that it was never better than at present; but the House was there to inquire into what it ought to be, not into what it had been. They were legislators, not antiquaries. They could not possibly think it right that the seat of government should be transferred from London to York, because York was the capital of the country in the time of Constantius Chlorus? Was the representa-tion of the country adapted for two millions of people to be kept now as it had been in the thirteenth century? New property had been called into existence; society had assumed a different form, much wealth and much capital which were formerly unknown were now unre-presented. Some towns had sunk into villages; others had remained stationary, but many had risen from vil-lages to be as large as London in the time of the Plan-tagenets. Society had grown; the form of govern-ment must be renewed to make it accord with that on which it depended, and it was time that our old institu-tions should be new modelled.

If it were true, as has been said on the other side, that a House of Commons reformed according to the proposed plan would destroy our king and peers in ten years— that the property and intelligence of the middle-classes could not be adequately represented without the result being to pull down the majesty of the throne, and the dignity of the aristocracy—if that were a true represen- tation it spoke volumes against the monarchy and the peerage. Monarchy and aristocracy were not valuable in themselves; they were only means to an end; and if the bill should produce a republic by improving the represen- tation—though he was convinced it would have no such effect—what did that imply, but that the peerage and the crown were opposed to the welfare of the nation? If the subversion of the king and peers were the only objections to the measure then there was no ground for opposing it. But the people did not forget what was due to the king and what was due to the peers; it was against the House that the popular voice was raised. They had not lost their respect for the king; they had not lost their respect for the aristocracy so long as the aristocracy remained in its proper sphere; but they had lost their respect for the representative system of the country, and there was good reason why they should, for *corruptio optimi pessima.* Further, it was said that many great and eminent men had been returned for nomination boroughs. True; but in estimating such facts you must look at general tendencies, not at accidents. It would scarcely be possible to hit on any mode of election which would not bring some able men into the House, and if the boroughs were done away with able men would still find their way into it. If one hundred of the tallest men in the kingdom were to be elected members of Parliament some among them would be eminent. If one hundred men of a tawny complexion were to be representatives, men of eminence too would be found amongst them. In ancient times a king was chosen by the neighing of a horse, and though nobody would recommend that mode of election it might happen that one so chosen might be a good king. In Athens public officers were chosen by lot—not a rational mode of election—yet it once caused Socrates to be chosen. Whatever might be our system of representation, clever men would find their way into the House. They might not be the same men as would come in under the borough system, but they would be men of talents, and no one man was indispensably necessary. Give a country good institutions, and it will

be sure to find good and great men. The feeling of the people which could not be denied was said to be temporary—to have sprung from the events which had taken place in France and Belgium. On the contrary, it possessed all the symptoms of a deeply-rooted malady, and had been growing for two generations. The legislature had tried every means in its power to put an end to it. Was it to be supposed that any probable measure of cure had escaped the subtlety of Burke or the sagacity of Wyndham? Had not every species of coercion been tried by Lord Londonderry? Had not laws been passed to put down public meetings and to enthral the press? and was not the evil still in existence increasing from day to day? What new palliatives could they try? Now, then, when everything was alarming around us, when the spirit of the age had just crushed the proudest crown in Europe, and the palace of our monarch was supplying an ignominious asylum to the expelled heir of forty kings; but while the heart of England was yet sound; while the

national feelings of many old associations were yet retained bound to the honour and character of the country,
and which might soon—too soon—pass away, now was
the accepted time—this was the day of our salvation—
when if we acted with a due regard to the signs of these
portentous times the great debt due from the aristocracy
to the people should be paid; and if it were paid, the
deed would never be forgotten by the people whose happiness it would ensure.

Lord Palmerston in the course of his speech remarked
that public opinion called for a change in the constitution,
and for proof of this he need merely refer to himself and
his colleagues now sitting as ministers on the benches so
recently occupied by the present opposition. It was his
firm opinion that nothing but the unbending notions of
a few men in power on the subject of reform had been
fatal to the late ministry. The present measure was said
to go too far, to be pregnant with danger; and those who
had formerly proposed or supported more partial measures were now taunted with extravagance and inconsistency. But he would tell such persons that if they fore-
boded danger, it became them, three years ago, to have
looked forward to the consequences of resisting those
moderate and necessary reforms which at that period more
particularly lay within their power. If they had convicted
the corrupt boroughs which were then brought under the
cognizance of the House; if government, admitting the
principle, had agreed to carry it further as circumstances
might arise, and had transferred the franchise to large
manufacturing towns, the more general reform now introduced would not have become necessary.

Sir Robert Peel strongly opposed the bill, and said
that he could see in it only the instrument of men endea-

vouring to retain power. If ministers had felt it necessary to propose a safe and moderate measure of reform of
some branches of our representation, he would most probably have acted on the views taken by some other members of the danger to be apprehended from all resistance
to change, and had given it his support as a private individual, though he might not have thought it fit to originate it in an official capacity. He would not have
objected to a measure for extending the elective franchise
to some places not at present possessing it. But he
could not consent to a measure which, in the words of its
very mover, went to reconstruct that House; and be the
consequences what they might, so wholly did he despair
of being able to modify the noble lord's bill into a kind
of moderate measure less objectionable, that he would
oppose the plan altogether. To the convincing facts that
the close boroughs were advantageous by bringing in men
who had nothing but ability to recommend them, nothing
like an answer had yet been given, though two had been
attempted. The answer of Mr. Hobhouse was that it was
not desirable that men of splendid talents should be members of that House, that in a reformed Parliament solid
sense and integrity would be more highly valued. Now, on
the other hand, he maintained nothing tended more to fos-
ter the public respect for that House than its being the
great arena of talent and eloquence, and that nothing would
lower it more in public estimation than that it should be
below the average ability of educated gentlemen. Mr.
Macaulay, again, argued that the introduction of able and
useful men was only an accident, and you must judge of
the fitness of institutions, not by their accidents, but by
their tendencies. Now he was content to judge by the
tendency, and not by the accident of the close-borough

system, and would maintain that the tendency was essentially favourable to the entrance of men of ability into
that House. He had that morning turned over the names
of from twenty to twenty-five of the most distinguished
men that had graced that House for the last thirty or
forty years, and he found that with three exceptions they
were all returned for boroughs which the present bill
would wholly disfranchise. There was Mr. Dunning,
Lord North, J. Townsend, Mr. Burke, Mr. Flood, Mr.
Pitt, Mr. Fox, Lord Granville, the Marquis Wellesley,
Mr. Perceval, Lord Plunkett, Mr. Canning, Mr. Wyndham, Mr. Horner, Mr. Huskisson, Mr. Brougham, Sir S.
Romilly, Lord Castlereagh, Mr. Tierney, Sir W. Grant,
Lord Grey, and the late Lord Liverpool, all first returned
for close boroughs, and but three of them ever members
for counties. Nor was the mere facility of admission the
only benefit. The introduction, by affording them an
opportunity of displaying their legislative ability, recommended them at a more mature age to places enjoying a
more extended franchise; and when, again, from caprice,
from the loss of popularity, a loss so easily, and how often
most honourably incurred, they were deprived of these
latter seats, the close boroughs secured to the country the
continuance of their invaluable services. Burke had been
repelled from Bristol to take refuge in Malton; when
Sheridan was defeated at Stafford he found shelter at
Ilchester; Mr. Wyndham, having failed at Norwich, sat
for Higham-Terrers; Lord Castlereagh lost his election in
the county of Down, and was returned for Oxford. Mr.
Tierney when he lost Southwark was returned for Knaresborough; and Lord Grey for Tavistock when defeated in
Northumberland. And yet this system, working so ad-
vantageously for the public weal, so fostering of talent

First Reform Bill of 1831. and statesmanlike ability, was to be destroyed for the sake of a new theory and an untried experiment.

Mr. Stanley, secretary for Ireland, maintained that it was a mere abuse of words to call the measure a revolution, and charged Parliament with having systematically ignored all reform. He saw that by selecting, one after Mr. Stanley's speech. another, the most notorious cases of delinquency, not as technically proved, but those great cases in regard to which moral conviction prevailed, though legal evidence could not reach them, they might have shown a desire to reform by degrees the abuses of the system, and then the public would have been satisfied with a less sudden change than was now contemplated. But let the House look back on the few last years and mark the time, the money, and the talent which had been wasted in discussing useless questions regarding boroughs charged with malpractices, inquiring, for instance, whether one voter received one guinea and another five, when it was notorious that boroughs were bought and sold by their proprietors. And after all this labour and minute inquiry, what had been gained for the cause of reform? Not one great town, not one great district had been added to those represented in that House, not one corrupt borough had been deprived of the means of corruption.

Lord Jeffrey's speech. Mr. Jeffrey, lord-advocate for Scotland, remarked that much had been said of the advantage conferred by the present system in so far as the hereditary aristocracy and the democracy were beneficially blended in the House of Commons. Now he conceived, in the first place, that the hereditary aristocracy in their individual capacity possessed no prerogatives or privileges at all, except that of being hereditary legislators and magistrates, and these privileges they could not exercise anywhere but in their own House. But even of the peers, it was only the rich proprietors who enjoyed this influence in the Lower House—peers who had no boroughs had no such influence. This influence, therefore, did not belong to the peerage: it belonged merely to wealth. Wealth, again, undoubtedly ought to possess influence; but were all wealthy persons proprietors of boroughs? Were the landed and mercantile interests possessed of this influence? A man of small property might lay out his money in this way, and manage, by the purchase of a borough, to get a kind of stock-in-trade; but whatever was done in this way ought to be done openly. If it was desirable that peers should have boroughs, as some of them had at present, not because they were peers, but because they were rich men who had laid out their money just as a commoner might do, it would be better to pass an act that every peer with a certain income should have a member, or, with a certain larger income, a couple of members in that House. Then there would be insured a proper appendage to their rank, instead of a monopoly conceded to those among them who were wealthy. To the question, therefore, which had been so often put, what practical good was to result from the intended reform, he would answer at once that it was the only means of averting the danger he had described, of discontent graduating into disaffection, and disaffection into insurrection. Another advantage of a reformed Parliament would be the great practical influence which it would exercise on the minds of the people, in opening their eyes to a conviction of their best interests, and this it would acquire from its affording greater facilities for the conveyance to it of the feelings and wants of the people. He did not mean by this that the House should be a mere

FIRST RE-
FORM BILL
OF 1831.
ccho of the popular will, that its discussions and decisions
should be guided by every enthusiasm, indignation, or
zeal of the public mind, but that the public mind should
possess a ready audience within its walls. Would any man
tell him that such was the case under the present system?
Had not abuses been habitually persevered in, on account
of the tardy influence which public opinion had on the
acts of the legislature? Was it not true that wars had
been protracted for years after the people had been sick of
them and were pining after peace? Was it not true that a
system of official misapplication of the public money had
been persevered in for want of an efficient popular control?
Was it not true that the slave-trade had been persevered
in for years after public opinion had held it up to scorn
and indignation? Was it not true that abuses in the
criminal law were persevered in till the feelings of the
people, long awake to their enormity, were roused to
such a pitch that a remedy could not be longer withheld?
Were not all these facts true of the present system, and
were they not incompatible with a reformed Parliament?

Mr. Robt.
Grant's
speech.
Mr. Robert Grant said that if any other influence than
that of the people was exercised in that House it could
not be said, constitutionally speaking, that the members
of Parliament were the fair and legitimate representatives
of the people. What was the theory of our constitution?
what its practice? Decidedly different, and he regretted
it; but the House might rest assured that the time had
now gone by when the people of England were unacquainted with the nature and value of their rights and
interests. Where could any authority be found for the
dictum that other influences than those of the people
should be admitted into the House? Neither in Blackstone nor De Lolme. On the contrary, they both con-

tended, in the beautiful theory of our constitution, that First Re-
the House of Commons was to be nothing else than the form Bill of 1831.
direct representatives of the people. By the express
terms of our constitution, by the regulations and orders
of this House, peers were not allowed to interfere in the
election of members of Parliament. The people out of
doors knew this as well as the members of the House.

Mr. O'Connell, in the course of a long speech, asked if Mr. O'Con-
it was not the first order of the House, even before the nell's speech.
king's speech was delivered, that it was a breach of privilege for any peer or prelate to interfere with the freedom
of election, and could they be told in the face of this
that the Duke of Newcastle had a right of appointing a
member of the Commons House of Parliament? Would
gentlemen tell him, in the teeth of that House, that the
giving that power to a lord was "the old constitution?"
Yet these were the gentlemen who denied hypocrisy.
The hypocrisy of that resolution was theirs or they were
parties to it. If any gentleman attempted to violate the
resolution clandestinely it was the duty of the Speaker
to defeat the attempt. But if the violation of it was, as
gentlemen insisted, the "old constitution," let the question be regularly brought before the House and let the
resolution be rescinded.

Lord John Russell made a reply in which he summed Lord J. Rus-
up answers which had already been given to objections sell's reply.
which had already been stated. To the charge that ministers had not acted with consistency even on their own
principles, in so far as they gave a town of 14,000 or
15,000 inhabitants no more members than a borough of
3000 or 4000, his lordship answered that he had never
intended his bill to be a measure of symmetry by which
the House was to be reduced to a certain number of

members for each county. Such a plan of reform might be better or it might be worse, but it had not been intended to go by it. Westminster, with 180,000 inhabitants, returned no more members than St. Albans, or Reading, or other places containing not one-tenth of the population. That was an anomaly with which he did not interfere; as he found it, so he left it. The measure of dividing the county into districts and apportioning to each district a certain number of persons might be a great and a wise scheme, but it had not been thought so; and if the honourable members opposite thought otherwise let them bring that measure forward and show themselves more extensive reformers than the present ministers.

The motion for leave to bring in the bill into the House of Commons was not resisted, and on March 14 it was
read a first time *pro forma*. After this public excitement became daily on the increase, and the cry went forth from the reformers that the ministerial measure should be their standard,—"The bill, the whole bill, and nothing but the bill." Petitioning was carried on to an enormous extent. Menaces were publicly uttered of an unmistakable character; the chairmen of large public meetings openly declared that they could supply whole armies, if necessary, and send them on to London to enable the ministers to fight the borough-mongers. The newspaper press was quite as active as the rest of the community.

The second reading of the bill was moved in the House of Commons on March 21 and lasted two days. It was opposed by Sir R. Vyvyan, member for Cornwall, who contended that it would lead to a pure democracy which would not stop short at what it had gained, but would labour to make Parliament the mere speaking-trumpet of

the multitude.   He contended that the Revolution of First Re-
1688 was a revolution effected by the aristocracy, and form Bill
of 1831.
was regular and orderly; but what was now wanted was
a revolution of the democracy.   He had no objection, he
said, to give representatives to large and flourishing
towns, though he would not go the length of disfranchis-
ing at once sixty boroughs, nor would he adopt the arbi- Sir R.
Vyvyan's
speech.
trary rule of disfranchisement which ministers had intro-
duced; and it was his intention, so soon as the bill was
rejected, to move a resolution which would give an assurance to the country that the House was willing to
strengthen the representation.

    Mr. Shiel, in reply to arguments about the prosperity of Mr. Shiel's
speech.
the nation and its security amid the revolutionary tem-
pests that disturbed other countries, answered, that there
existed within itself a settled and general discontent
which was derived from causes of permanent creation,
and which, instead of being the mere ebullition of transi-
tory passion, flowed out of a deep and constant source.
It was idle to say that it had not long existed, because
it had only recently appeared.   The sudden force with
which it had burst forth was a proof that the materials of
eruption had been long accumulating.   It was of little
avail to say that it was connected with the events on the
Continent.   Were we to omit to strengthen our own
institutions because this island had felt the tremor of
that great shock which had levelled the governments of
France and Belgium to the ground?   It was equally
nugatory to say that the press had done all this.   Would
the press relinquish its natural vocation? and was it not
much wiser to consider, instead of inveighing against its
influence, the materials, in the shape of abuses, upon
which it exerted its powerful operations?   Was the dis-

FIRST RE-
FORM BILL
OF 1831.

content well-founded? That was the main question, almost the only one. This single broad fact was, in his mind, sufficient to call forth the national repudiation of the House of Commons, that its majority was returned, not by the people, but by 150 individuals. Some four or five great proprietors of boroughs were enabled to control the minister, and by their oligarchical coalition to dictate to their sovereign and to lord it over the people. That such a system should exist was a great calamity in itself, but the evil was heightened by many sordid accompaniments. Seats in Parliament were made the subject of bargain and sale, and an almost open mart, a common staple, a parliamentary bazaar, was established for the vendition of the franchises of the people. A parliamentary broker was a customary phrase; nay, matters had been carried to such a pitch that boroughs had been made the subject of marriage settlement, and had been put, by the ingenuity of conveyancers, through all the diversities of matrimonial limitation.

Mr. C.
Grant's
speech.

Mr. Charles Grant argued that the people complained that their rights were invaded, that the interference of the two other branches of the legislature was directly condemned by the standing orders of the House of Commons, yet that the constitution was rendered a dead letter by the habitual violation of those rules—an infraction of which was nevertheless held to be a high contempt of the privileges of the Commons. What answer but one could they offer to an unanimous and indignant nation thus expostulating at their bar?

Mr. Ward's
speech.

Mr. Ward, on the other hand, one of the members for the city of London, the common council of which had petitioned in favour of the bill, strenuously opposed it. He had been intrusted with a petition signed by 600 merchants, bankers, and others against the bill. The signatures to it, he said, were those of men qualified to judge, independent, and having much at stake in the country. He agreed with them that there was no one practical good to be accomplished by this measure, to atone for all the positive mischief and certain danger which it would produce; and unless it could be shown that the Parliament to be called into existence by the new scheme would minister to the wants of the people in a greater degree than that which now existed, everything which had been said in its favour must fall to the ground. He had passed the earlier years of his life principally in two close boroughs, and among the representatives of those boroughs had been, during his remembrance, Mr. Fox, Mr. Pitt, Mr. Canning, Mr. Perceval, the noble lord at present at the head of foreign affairs, and the Duke of Wellington. Such had been the representatives of those close boroughs, and he very much doubted if by a re-formed system more able members would be given to that House; indeed, the country would be fortunate if as good were returned. Still, it was said, however eminent and useful may be the members returned for close boroughs, they are not the representatives of the people. But what was meant by the term representative? Was the physical force of the country to be represented, or was the good sense of the country to be represented, or were the passions of the people to be represented? On the good sense of the country he had great reliance, on the passions none. And if there was a moment when the passions of the people were more liable to excitement than another, that moment was the period of an election. If upon such an occasion the passions were moved in behalf of a par-ticular candidate, whatever might be the character of his

pretensions, up he went to the top of the poll. A person
so returned was not at liberty to exercise his own judgment. He was necessarily but the echo of the passions
of those who had sent him there. Philosophers had
found out that by certain mixture of metals a compound
was formed which was perfect to all known uses; but he
had yet to learn that anyone had ever discovered what
proportion of the feeling and the passions of the people
ought to be represented in that House, or to be allowed
to act upon it. He objected to the bill, therefore, upon
these grounds.

Division   At length a division took place, there being 608 members present, the largest number that had ever divided
on any question in the House of Commons. The num-

Majority of
1 for the
Bill.
bers were (exclusive of speaker and four tellers), for the
second reading, 302—against, 301—a majority of 1.

It was plain that the bill was lost. It was necessary,
however, the ministry should proceed, and accordingly

Bills for
Scotland
and Ireland.
they brought in separate bills for Scotland and Ireland
on similar lines to the English bill. They proposed to
give an addition of five members to each of these two
countries, and this gave rise to considerable debate, not
only among the English but the Irish members. At this
stage Lord John Russell announced that if the House
manifested a strong feeling against reducing the absolute
number of the House below 658, the government would
not consider a resolution of that kind as fatal to the bill;
but it was afterwards explained by Mr. Stanley that this
did not mean that the small boroughs were to escape disfranchisement, but on the contrary that all boroughs below a certain standard would lose their franchise, which
would be conferred on the large towns.

On April 18 Lord John Russell moved that the House

go into committee on the bill, and stated a number of alterations which he proposed to introduce. It was then moved by General Gascoyne as an instruction to be given to the committee: "That it is the opinion of this House that the total number of knights, citizens, and burgesses returned to Parliament for that part of the United Kingdom called England and Wales ought not to be diminished." His motion, he said, was not founded on any superstitious attachment to a particular number, but was directed against the principle of the reduction. Neither was it founded on any hostility to an increase of the representation of Ireland and Scotland, but to their aggrandizement at the expense of England. Let Ireland and Scotland obtain their additional members, but let it not be at the expense of England. The proposed reduction of the English representation could not be defended on any principle of necessity, or justice, or expediency. It could not be defended on the ground of the population of Ireland having increased so much as to warrant such an increase of the relative number of its representatives in that House; for if population were taken as the basis of the Irish representation it ought also to be taken as the basis of the Irish taxation.

This was opposed by the chancellor of the exchequer, who declared that he was quite sure that the object of the amendment was "to destroy the bill." The proposition now made was not merely, he said, that the members of the House should be kept as they were, but that they should either be increased, or that Scotland and Ireland should not receive the additional members proposed to be given them by the bill. It was impossible to misunderstand the nature of this amendment. It was the first of that series of motions by which it was intended

FIRST RE-
FORM BILL
OF 1831.

to interfere with the progress of the committee, and which, if agreed to, would be fatal to the bill, or, at least, so detrimental to it as to render it impossible it should be proceeded with.

He was succeeded by a number of members who offered different items of advice; but Mr. Stanley declared that this discussion would decide the fate of the bill, without uttering one sentence to show how it ought to have that effect. He described it as being concocted in a spirit of hostility to the bill, brought forward to embarrass "the great measure" cautiously framed after much deliberation so as to catch the greatest number of votes, and continue to defeat, under the flimsy pretext of a discussion of the relative proportions of the English, Scotch, and Irish representatives, a proposition which they did not dare to oppose openly.

Majority
against
ministers.

When a division took place it was found that there was a majority of eight against ministers—the number for the motion that the original clause stand being 291—for General Gascoyne's amendment, 299.

The division took place on April 19. Nothing occurred on the 20th to show what resolution the government had come to, except what might be inferred from a remark of Mr. Hume, that he would offer no opposition to the ordnance estimates, because after the vote of last night he was anxious to assist ministers in getting through the necessary business in order that a dissolution might take place. Running neck and neck as parties were in the House, it was a delusion to suppose that the Reform Bill could pass in the present Parliament.

Great con-
fusion.

There was now great confusion in the Houses of the two Estates. The government made up their mind to dissolve Parliament, and the opposition were determined

to prevent it if they could. The opposition saw plainly
that they had nothing to gain, but a deal to lose, by a
dissolution. Questions were put in both Houses as to the
intention of the ministry, but nothing could be elicited
further than that they had resolved to proceed no further
with the bill. Lord Wharncliffe then gave notice in the
House of Lords on April 21, that he would next day
move an address to the king, praying that his majesty
would be graciously pleased not to exercise his royal prerogative of dissolving Parliament. The Houses met on
the 22d, and were soon in a tumult. In the Commons
the speaker lost all authority for a time, but ultimately
Sir Robert Peel was allowed to be heard. In speaking
of the rules of the House under which he had a right to
be heard, he said that these were the rules under which
that House had hitherto acted, although they might not
be the rules that would suit a reformed Parliament. He
for one would never agree to set at defiance that authority
(as had that day been done) to which the House of
Commons had long been accustomed to bow. He did
not, he was happy to say, share in the desponding feelings of his honourable friend the member for Cornwall. He
did not desire the people of England to sit quietly with
their hands before them patiently expecting the confiscation of the funds and the destruction of tithes. He had
that confidence in the power of the property and the intelligence of this country, that if they would unite in the
support of a just and an honest cause he did not despair
of a successful and prosperous issue to their joint exertions.
If their reformed Parliament was to be elected—if "the
bill, the whole bill" were to be passed—it did appear to
him that there would then be established one of the worst
despotisms that ever existed. They would have a Parlia-

ment of mob demagogues, not a Parliament of wise and
prudent men.   Such a Parliament, and the spirit of jour-
nalism, to use a foreign phrase, had, as they must have
seen, brought happy countries to the brink of destruction. At that moment society was wholly disorganized
in the west of Ireland, and that disorganization, he was
grieved to say, was rapidly extending elsewhere.   Landed
proprietors well affected to the state and loyal to the
king, anxious to enjoy their property in security, were
leaving their homes to take refuge in towns, abandoning
the country parts as no longer affording a safe residence.
At this critical conjuncture, instead of doing their duty
and calling for measures to vindicate from the visitation
of lawless and sanguinary barbarians the security of life
and the safety of property, his majesty's ministers, anxious
only to protect themselves and fearful of the loss of
power, were demanding a dissolution of Parliament.
Alas! he already perceived that the power of the crown
had ceased. It was no longer an object of fair ambition
with any man of equal and consistent mind to enter into
the service of the crown.   Ministers had come down
there, and had called on the sovereign to dissolve Parliament in order to protect themselves.   But they had first
established the character of having shown, during their
short reign of power, more incapacity, more unfitness for
office, more ignorance of their duties, than ever was exhibited by any set of men who had at any time been called
on to rule the proud destinies of this country.   After
having accused their predecessors during the last two
years of having done nothing, of having expended much
time in useless debates, not one single measure had they
themselves projected.   What had they done in the last
six months? They had boasted much of the good which

by acting on liberal principles they would produce. But what had they done? where were their works to be seen? They had laid on the table certain bills, the Emigration Bill and the Game Bill for instance, founded on their so much boasted liberal principles, and what then? Why, there they had left them.

At this moment the Commons were summoned to the House of Peers to hear the king's speech proroguing Parliament with a view to its immediate dissolution. Next day the proclamation appeared announcing a dissolution, directing a new election, and making the writs returnable on the 14th June.

The popular excitement was intense all through the course of the election contest, passions on both sides were aroused to a pitch of frenzy, and many breaches of the peace were committed. It was an election for a special purpose, and a direct pledge was the only passport to a vote on either side. The consequence was that there were many changes. General Gascoyne could make no headway at Liverpool. Sir R. Vyvyan was expelled from Cornwall. Sir Edward Knatchbull resigned the county of Kent. And so on throughout the opposition ranks, there was defeat at many points.

On June 14, 1831, the new Parliament met, and on the 24th Lord John Russell moved for leave to bring on a bill to amend the representation of the people of England. Sir Robert Peel rose and stated that he did not wish to divide the House on the first reading, that he wished still less to have a long debate without a division, and that the discussion would take place most conveniently on the second reading. The second reading was moved on 4th July, and the debate was continued on the 5th and 6th. It consisted of a repetition of the arguments

Side notes:
First Reform Bill of 1831.
Parliament dissolved.
Great excitement.
Second Reform Bill of 1831.
Sir R. Peel's speech.
Second reading carried,

SECOND RE-
FORM BILL
OF 1831.

Committee.

Amend-
ments.

used on former occasions, with not much that was new. The vote for the second reading was 367 against 231. Majority, 136. This was a vast change.

The committee was fixed for July 12, and in the first stage of the bill through committee a number of questions were discussed and settled. The case of the borough of Appleby was the one first raised, and Lord Maitland, alleging an error in the matter of population which caused it to be wrongfully included in Schedule A of the bill, moved that the constituency be heard by counsel at the bar, but on the opposition of ministers this proposal was rejected by a majority of 97. There was thereupon a device resorted to, that has been amazingly popular of late years, that of obstruction. There were many motions for adjournment, and motions that the speaker leave the chair; and the obstructionists were defeated over and over again, but after it reached seven in the morning a compromise was effected, and the House adjourned. On the 13th a motion was made that the consideration of claims declaring that the boroughs contained in Schedule A should cease to return members be delayed till the claims which bestowed members on places hitherto unrepresented should have been settled, but this was lost by a majority of 113. Sir Robert Peel then made an amendment on one of the clauses, which was negatived by a majority of 97. A vast number of other amendments, great and small, were afterwards moved, with more or less success, among others the Chandos clause, giving a vote to the farmers who paid £50 of rent. The only two motions that were afterwards made of any significance were for universal suffrage, and also that the £10 qualification be reduced to £5. Neither of them found a seconder, and this

showed unmistakably how far the reform party in Parliament were prepared to go. On September 7 the bill
had passed through committee and was reported to the
House.

The third reading was formally carried by a majority
of 55; but on the motion that the bill do pass a discussion
again arose, that lasted three days, beginning on the
19th and ending on the 21st of September. In the
course of the debate Mr. Macaulay spoke at some length.
He denied that the framers or supporters of the bill had
ever held out that it would remove the burdens which
affected the working-classes, by giving them high wages
while it materially lowered the amount of their taxes.
This was a mere artful assertion of the sworn foes of
reform, and had no foundation in fact or reason. Neither
ministers nor the unofficial supporters of the bill
attempted to delude the people into its acceptance by
such an unworthy artifice. No; they knew too well
that no ministry—no legislative measure—could accomplish such results, and were too honest in their purpose
to pretend to acts beyond their capacity. The end of
government was not to make the people rich by irregular
or illegal means, but to protect them in the acquisition
and possession of their riches, and to remove all unnecessary obstacles to that acquisition. No honest government could affect to do more. No honest government
could affect to do less. No ministry could presume to
do more than direct and provide for the general weal,
and could not take upon them the office of the pro-
phet in the wilderness, and by their official wand to
make water to flow from the rock to ease the burdens
of the people. It was never, then, pretended that the
Reform Bill would necessarily of itself do away with the

burdens which oppressed the working-classes and industry of the country; all that was asserted was the unde-
niable fact, that had we had a reformed Parliament
fifty years ago the national embarrassments would not
have been a tithe of their present amount. He believed
the present bill would ultimately improve the physical
condition of the people, because its first result would be
a more equal and judicious distribution of the public
burdens than at present existed. To reproach it for
not doing more was to reproach it for not accomplishing
what no constitutional legislative measure nor any ministry in the world could accomplish; and any ministry or
legislature that professed to do more, by the very fact of
profession proved themselves to be arrant quacks. The
supporters of the bill had been much taunted with having
shut their eyes on facts and experience, and been guided
solely by the mere abstractions of theory. The very
reverse was the truth; facts and experience were the
groundwork of the bill, while hypothetical assertions
were the only weapons with which its opponents had
condescended to oppose it. For example, look at all
their bugbear assumptions with respect to the dangers—
democratic dangers—of enabling the inhabitants of a
large town—Manchester to wit—to return their own
representatives. Were they not all in the very teeth of the
facts and experience for neglecting which those members
opposite were so loud in charging ministers? No public
man, it was said, whatever his pretensions, can have a
chance under the bill to represent a large town; the
representatives of the populous towns will be chosen on
exclusively local considerations. Now, what said "facts
and experience" on this point? Let Nottingham, let
Leicester, let Chester answer the question. To come

nearer home, the representation of the metropolis was a clear proof that non-resident public men had a chance in populous districts, and that local considerations were not the sole guide in these places. Did honourable members recollect the great men who, within all or most of their recollections, had represented Westminster and South-wark?—Mr. Fox, Mr. Sheridan, Mr. Tierney, Sir S. Romilly—surely no mob orator, no hustings demagogue. The dangers which it was apprehended would flow from passing the bill were chimerical, but those which would result from a different course were real. He had supported the bill on a former occasion, because he had believed there was danger in refusing it in the then state of public opinion; and he supported it still more cordially now, because that danger had been augmented. It was deplorable infatuation to suppose that the public mind had cooled, or would cool, on this subject, till the object had been achieved. The people, having given vent to their joy when the reform measure was first introduced, became tranquil and contented, as natural to those who anticipated a triumph. After this, General Gascoyne's motion evinced to them their danger, and again were they aroused, and they showed their senti-ments in every possible manner. Again did they triumph gloriously as far as they were concerned, and as far as reform depended upon their representatives. They placed the bill in security, and again did they return to their repose. At this moment the people were, as they had been on the very eve of General Gas-coyne's motion, waiting with anxious interest and reso-lution the result of the measure; but because they were not violent, they were again told that there was a re-action in the public mind. Those who thought that

there could be any such reaction were utterly ignorant
of the public mind, they were utterly unacquainted with
the very nature of that people whom they aspired to
govern. The measure of Catholic emancipation had
broken the last link of attachment on the part of the
people to the Tory leaders, and reform became the first
question that occupied the minds of all men. The
people of England had long been disposed to move in
its favour upon the slightest impulse; and he should as
soon think of seeing them revert to the drowning of
witches, or to the burning of heretics, as to find a re-
action in favour of Old Sarum. It was as probable that
the people should go back to their attachment to Thor
or Odin, as that they should revert to any attachment to
the old system of representation. Revolutions produced
by the excitement of feelings would produce reactions,
but the victories of reason once gained were gained for
ever. The calmness of the people of England was not
the calmness of indifference—it was the calmness of confident hope, and in proportion to the confidence of hope
was the bitterness of disappointment. In that House,
continued Mr. Macaulay, the dread of disappointment
was gone; but members who opposed the measure expressed their hope that the barons of England would
interfere to curb the career of what they termed this
democratic frenzy. If the Peers valued the voice of
example and experience, let them look to the long line
of deserted halls and desolate mansions of a certain
quarter of a neighbouring capital. From those mansions
and castles of the aristocracy of France, as proud and as
powerful a body of nobles as ever existed were driven
forth to exile and to beggary, to implore the charity of
hostile religions and of hostile nations. And why did

such destruction fall upon them? Why were they swept away with such utter destruction? Why was their heritage given to strangers, and their palaces dismantled, but because they had no sympathy with the people? Because they reviled those who warned them of their danger, when they might have been saved; and because they absolutely refused to make any concessions until all concessions were too late. Those who would tell the aristocracy of England to keep the body of the people from power, would place them in the exact situation in which the aristocracy of France had been placed. It was the duty of that House to treat with respect the privileges of the House of Peers; but it was likewise their duty not to neglect their own. Many who heard him thought that the rejection of the bill would be the means of their being restored to power. Dark was the day of their flight from power, and darker for England would be the day of their return, for they would return in triumph over the people of the British Empire, united as firmly as when the armada had sailed up the Channel, or as when the army of Napoleon was encamped at Boulogne. They could sustain themselves only in the utter scorn of public opinion, and if they fell, they might involve in their fall the whole frame of society. It would be the duty of that House to convey the wishes of the people to a patriot king. The place of that House was in front of the nation, and whatever prejudices might exist elsewhere, in that House, when freely elected, would be found the virtue, the wisdom, the energy, and courage that would save the country.

Mr. Croker thought that the boldness of Mr. Macaulay in teaching the peers of England what they ought to do, was only equalled by the magnanimous disregard of his-

tory and fact on which the lesson had been founded.
The nobility of France fell, forsooth, because they refused
concessions till concessions were too late. All men knew
that precisely the reverse was the truth of the case. The
French nobility made extravagant concessions to the
people, and it was those concessions which had involved
them in ruin. Was not the honourable member aware
that the peers of France had conceded the point of join-
ing the *Tiers Etat?* Was he not aware that it was a
Montmorency who proposed the abolition of nobility,
and a Noailles that moved for the destruction of seignorial
rights, whilst the Archbishop of Paris brought forward
the plan for yielding up the tithes—a measure so strong
that even the Abbé Gregoire considered it too bold for
him to support? The French noblesse may have fallen
because they yielded too far to democratic intimidation,
or they might not have stood if they had refused to yield;
but to tell men who could read history that they fell because they refused concessions was a mere disregard of
all facts for the purposes of rhetorical declamation. A
similar disregard of fact was manifested in setting forth
that modern abuses had converted the House of Commons into a mockery of representation for all practical
purposes. It was still that system under which, from its
first regular establishment, the country had become what
it was; for it was not even pretended that there had been
any change in the constitution of the House of Commons
since the Revolution. Not a single county, not one
rotten borough, had been added to the representation.
Not a hint had been given that the power of the crown
had increased in that House, and the very majority now
arrayed in favour of the Reform Bill proved that the bill
was unnecessary, for it was difficult to conceive of an

intellect so framed as to look at the majority now ruling
the House, returned, too, as they were told it had been
returned, by the mere constitutional action of popular
sentiment, and yet maintain that popular sentiment was
so utterly incapable of being represented under the existing system that the government had been turned over,
in defiance of the people, into the hands of an oligarchy.

Mr. Crampton, Solicitor-general for Ireland, said: If
ever there was a bill with which the Lords should feel a
delicacy of interfering, and on which they should not
even exercise a severity of criticism, it was this bill. It
should be viewed by them as a money bill on which they
ought to make no alteration. In any question affecting
the rights of Peers, the Peers alone had the right to interfere. In any question affecting representation in the
Commons, the Commons had the right to interfere without any control by the other House. He maintained
that by the common law and the usage of Parliament
the King and the House of Commons, without any interference by the other House, had the right to make
regulations respecting the representation. Undismayed
by the loud expressions of amazement which these doctrines called forth, Mr. Crampton proceeded to a still
more tangible application of these his ideas of the constitution. "The House of Lords have, no doubt, a constitutional right to reject this bill; but if they do, one of
its main objects may still be attained without their concurrence. The disfranchisement of all the boroughs in
Schedule A, with the exception of those whose right to
send members has been granted or confirmed by Act of
Parliament, might be effected without legislation—and
this I state as a lawyer, and do not expect it will be
controverted by any legal authority. The House of

Commons may address the Crown to dissolve Parliament,
and not to issue writs to the decayed boroughs, but in
lieu of them to issue writs to the large, populous, and
wealthy towns which were now unrepresented. This
does not apply to the representation of Scotland and
Ireland, which has been fixed by Acts of Union, and can
be altered only by an Act of Parliament; but, with regard
to the decayed boroughs of England, if they do not send
representatives by virtue of any local statute, I repeat,
that the Crown, on an address of this House, has power
to issue or withhold writs, and that in this respect the
concurrence of the House of Lords is not necessary. At
the same time he thought the Crown should not refuse
writs to any borough which was free and independent in
character, containing large manufactories and a numerous
population, but only to decayed places, to rotten and
nomination boroughs," which necessarily meant that the
Crown was to issue writs where it chose and to refuse
them where it chose.

Mr. Wynn's
speech.   In reply, Mr. Wynn stated that it was absolutely
necessary to know whether the doctrines now started
were the doctrines of his majesty's ministers and constitutional advisers, because if they were so all other
business must stop until it should be settled whether the
Crown did or did not possess the prerogative now claimed
for it. It was purely a question of prerogative, for every
man must know that an address of the House of Commons, though it might administer advice as to the mode
of exercising a prerogative, could neither give one nor
take it away. No question of such importance had been
raised since the vote of a certain House of Commons,
that the House of Lords should be abolished as a nuis-
ance. He felt the more alarmed on this point, because

he could not but remember that something not very dis
similar from what the solicitor-general now maintained had formerly fallen from the law officer for England.

Sir Charles Wetherell brought the matter to a point
at once by moving that the present debate be now suspended. He did so because one of the king's law officers in that House had asserted, not merely that the House of Lords ought not to criticise the Reform Bill, but that all the places enumerated in Schedule A might be legally and constitutionally disfranchised by the crown merely by withholding their writs. The House had only the choice of two modes of proceeding—either to put an end to its present piece of legislation, which, if the doctrines now stated were correct, was altogether superfluous and unnecessary; or to vindicate the rights of the Commons of England from the insult and disgrace of the attack which was now made upon them. Ministers were involved in the legal statements of their law officers, and were bound to declare their opinion. If they would disavow the doctrines of their legal adviser as illegal and unconstitutional, he was content to go on with the debate; but if they did not, he would move that the words of the solicitor-general be taken down, and that the debate be adjourned.

Mr. Crampton endeavoured unsuccessfully to explain. He complained that what he had stated had been misrepresented. "I am ready to abide," said Sir C. Wetherell, "by the decision of any one member present, whether I have or have not stated correctly the learned solicitor's proposition. He said in plain terms that 'if the House of Lords should reject the bill, ministers had nothing to do but dissolve Parliament, and the Crown might withhold the writs from the boroughs in Schedule A.'" No

answer being given to the challenge, Lord Althorp rose
and disclaimed the doctrines which had been put forward.
He could not, he said, admit that because an individual
connected with the government expressed an opinion on
a point of law, a pending discussion should be stopped
until ministers declared whether they concurred in that
opinion. The appeal which had been made to government was not according to the usages of the House. The
opinion expressed by the Solicitor-general for Ireland had
been propounded without the slightest communication
with any of the ministers, and was an opinion on a legal
rather than a constitutional case. He would have great
diffidence in expressing an opinion on the point of law;
but if he were called upon to say whether the course

pointed out by the Solicitor-general for Ireland was a
constitutional course, he was perfectly ready to say that
he thought it was not. Sir Robert Peel admitted that
in ordinary circumstances it was not usual to make
members of the government responsible for the opinions
of subordinate officers; but the question in the present
case was a question of prerogative and constitutional law,
advanced by one of the persons to whom the crown would
refer for legal advice. As, however, to the explanation
so properly demanded, ministers had equally properly
given an answer by declaring that the doctrines of their
legal adviser were unconstitutional, there was no reason
why the debate should not proceed. Sir C. Wetherell
accordingly withdrew his motion.

Lord Althorp, on behalf of the government, said that
the arguments which had been used by many gentlemen
in this debate tended to prove that there was no use in
representation at all. Those arguments were, that the
constitution of that House contained a sample of every

class in the community, and that every interest found a SECOND RE-
FORM BILL
OF 1831. representative in that House. But did it follow that because there were in the House samples of every class, and
members of every interest, those persons were the representatives of the interests with which they were connected? If they were to ask an individual whether he
would have his interest represented merely by a man of
his class, or whether he would himself choose a representative for that class, he thought that the individual would
reply that he thought it preferable to be represented by
a man of his own choice than by a person who found
his way into Parliament through a borough over which
he had no control. Even supposing the people to have
formed extravagant and unfounded hopes of the good to
be effected by this measure, would they not be less dis- Lord
Althorp's
speech. contented when they had confidence in members elected
by themselves than they would be when represented by
men over whom they had no control? It had been assumed, continued his lordship, in the course of the debate, that by this bill they were going to establish a
democracy and entirely change the constitution. Now,
the constitution of the country would stand, after this
bill, as it did at present, in all its relations with the
country. It would still consist of King, Lords, and
Commons; and as to the just influence of property and
the aristocracy, there was nothing in that bill, or in any
other bill, which could diminish that due influence. Undoubtedly it would spread that influence more over the
body of proprietors than it was spread at present; for
at present the influence of property over that House was
only exercised by such proprietors as were also proprietors of close boroughs. By the bill it was proposed that
the latter influence should be destroyed, and that the

SECOND RE-
FORM BILL
OF 1831. influence of property should be exercised by the mass of proprietors—not by an oligarchy of them.

The debate was wound up by Sir Robert Peel, who felt it his duty to continue, at the last stage of the bill, the opposition which he had offered to it at the commencement. He continued his opposition on precisely Sir R. Peel's
speech. the same grounds, with no increased predilection for changing the constitution of his country. Popular opinion had been sufficiently demonstrated in favour of the measure to induce him to treat that opinion with the utmost respect, and to consider maturely whether he was justified in opposing it. He regretted to say that his deliberative judgment was against the measure. He did not think that it would conduce to the permanent interests of the country. On that ground, and that ground only, and not for the purpose of maintaining the interests of peers or other persons, he felt himself bound to oppose the wishes of the people. "I cheerfully submit to pay the penalty to which that difference of opinion subjects me. With reluctance I surrender the hold which I may have on the people's esteem. That is a penalty which they have a right to inflict, but they have no right or power to compel me to acquiesce in their error—for I believe them to be in error. I will not involve myself in the responsibility of the measure, and being with others a life-renter only in the admirable constitution which has hitherto secured the peace and happiness of my country, I will not be instrumental in cutting off the inheritance of those who are to succeed me."

Bill passed. On the House dividing, the majority in favour of the motion for passing the bill was 109, the ayes being 345, and the noes 236.

The Reform Bill was now to approach the House of

Lords <u>for the first time.</u> It was taken up by Lord John Russell, attended by about a hundred of his supporters, and on the motion of Earl Grey was read a first time, and the second reading was fixed for the 3rd of October.

In moving the second reading Earl Grey argued that the system of nomination not only was no part of the British constitution, but was absurdly inconsistent with its acknowledged principles. In every session it was a standing order that the interference of peers in the election of members of Parliament was unconstitutional. There was a statute of the realm declaring that no taxes were to be levied on the people except such as were imposed by their representatives, and the House of Commons was so jealous of its privileges in this respect that it would not suffer the interference of the Lords to cor- rect the most trifling mistake. Such was the principle of the constitution. As to the practice, was it not the fact that it had ever been the prerogative of the Crown to summon members to Parliament for such towns as it deemed competent to the power of election? How, then, could it be said that to do away with decayed boroughs was a course unknown to the constitution? The disfranchisement of certain boroughs had been described as spoliation and robbery. But the right to send representatives to Parliament was a trust, and there could be no greater mistake than to confound the obligation of a trust with the right of property. A trust is ever confided upon certain conditions, and may be resumed if they be broken. There was no lapse of time, no prescription of abuse, which could convert that which was originally a trust for the people into a property. But if the resumption of a trust after manifest abuse was an act of spoliation, had it not taken place over and over again?

There are now forty-four boroughs and one city which formerly sent representatives to Parliament, but which, in consequence of the discontinuance of the writs, do not now send members. This was disfranchisement nearly equal in amount to that of schedule A, and effected by .the ordinary process of the constitution. The Union with Scotland reduced the number of representatives of boroughs in Scotland from sixty-five to fifteen, and the Irish Union struck off at one blow a hundred boroughs returning two hundred members. Was this spoliation and robbery? Oh, but compensation was given, and interests in those boroughs were thus treated as a right of property! That compensation was scandalous bribery and corruption; but twenty-eight of these boroughs were
struck off without compensation. The disfranchisement of the boroughs in schedule A, therefore, was merely the exercise of a constitutional power in the resumption of a trust which was no longer beneficially exercised. The system, it was said, had worked well; and were we to do away with that under which the country had attained its present high degree of power and prosperity? It had not the confidence of the people, and if that were most essential to the support of every government, then, so far from working well, the system had worked very ill. Earl Grey next proceeded to consider how far the system of nomination boroughs contributed to the real weight and influence of the House of Lords. In the first place, he said, it is to be considered that the power of nominating members to sit in Parliament is not enjoyed by this House in general, by your lordships as a body in the state, but by a few wealthy individuals amongst you, who exercise the power for their own separate interests. The power, therefore, is exercised and enjoyed only by a

few, whilst the odium falls upon the whole body; so that SECOND RE-FORM BILL OF 1831. by getting rid of the system you remove the odium, and the peerage as a body loses nothing. Then the power of nomination is liable to continual transfer and change. "It may leave your lordships' hands altogether, or it may accumulate in an individual to such an extent as to be not only odious to the country, but inconvenient to the government, by rendering it in a great degree dependent upon the person who possesses this power. Though I am the last man to propose to retain the influence which enables any member in this House to interfere in the elections of members of the House of Commons—an interference that cannot be too strongly condemned—yet do I propose that your lordships should be deprived of any part of your legitimate power or influence? God Earl Grey's speech. forbid! The respect due to your rank, and the influence which, from property, you necessarily possess, will belong to you after the passing of the bill as fully and in as great a degree as they now do. The odious power which is possessed by some of you does not help to increase that legitimate influence; but if you resolve to maintain the nomination boroughs the whole voice of the United Kingdom will be raised against you. You are asked only to give up that which is odious, unjust, and unconstitutional, and by retaining which the security of this House may be shaken. The influence which your lordships possess in the representation of sixty-five old boroughs may be taken from you by this bill, but the peers and the landed interest are not thereby deprived of their influence in the representation; on the contrary, that influence is increased." He next contended that this measure had received the approbation of the country. He was one of the last men in that House who

I

would grant anything to intimidation. He would say, "Resist popular violence; do not give way to popular commotion!" but here there was no violence, there was no commotion. The opinion of the people was, however, fairly and unequivocally expressed; no government could turn a deaf ear to it, and least of all could a government founded on free principles take such a step. He flung aside all idea of menace and also intimidation; but ho conjured them, as they valued their rights and privileges, and wished to transmit them unimpaired to their posterity, to consider well before they came to a decision on this question, with reference to which nine-tenths of the people had expressed their opinion in a tone too loud not to be heard, and too decisive to be misunder-

stood. Let not their lordships think that if this measure was rejected a more mitigated and less comprehensive one might be substituted in its place with safety. The time was past for taking half-measures. They must either adopt this bill, or they would have, instead of it, something infinitely stronger and more extensive. The measure thus brought forward in the first instance at the recommendation of the Crown— (Cries of order from Lord Wynford and several other noble lords.) He was not aware that he had said anything out of order; he had alluded to the speech from the throne, and to which he was perfectly justified in alluding, as a matter on the journals of the House. He would speak of it, then, not as the recommendation of the Crown, but as the speech from the throne; and though he admitted that even in this sense it must be considered as the production of ministers, yet still it was not to be supposed that it would be delivered by the sovereign, unless it had previously received the sanction of his private opinion. The measure was one which had been carried by an overwhelming majority of the other House; it was supported by the prayers of millions who respectfully knocked at their lordships' door, and asked for that which they considered to be the restoration of their just rights. Were their lordships prepared to reject a bill so supported, and that, too, on its second reading? He did not believe that the rejection of the bill would be productive of a civil war; still he could not conceal his apprehension that the result of its rejection would be most dangerous to the best interests of the country. He would venture for a moment to address himself to one part of their lordships' house, the right reverend prelates on the benches near him; and while he assured that body that no man was more sincerely attached than he was to the maintenance of all the rights and privileges of the Church, no man held in higher veneration the purity of its doctrines and discipline, no man was more ready to admit the zeal, and learning, and piety of those who presided over it; let him at the same time respectfully entreat those right reverend prelates to consider, that if this bill should be rejected by a narrow majority of the lay peers, and if its fate should thus, within a few votes, be decided by the votes of the heads of the church, what would then be their situation with the country? Those right reverend prelates had shown that they were not indifferent or inattentive to the signs of the times. They had introduced measures for effecting some salutary reforms in matters relating to the temporalities of the church, and in this they acted with wise forethought. Let them, he implored, now follow up the same prudent course. The eyes of the country were now upon them. He called upon them to *set their house in order*, and prepare to meet the coming storm, to consider

SECOND RE-
FORM BILL
OF 1831.

Earl Grey's
speech.

Lord
Wharn-
cliffe's
speech.

seriously what would be the opinion of the country should a measure, on which the nation had fixed its hope, be defeated by their votes. They were the ministers of peace; earnestly did he hope that the result of their votes would be such as might tend to the tranquillity, peace, and happiness of the country. As regarded the whole of their lordships, spiritual and temporal, he hoped that the consequences of the rejection of the bill would be seriously considered, for its consequences could be no other than serious. As to the effect which the rejection or adoption of the measure might produce to him, or the administration of which he formed a part, it was not necessary for him to say much, for that was perhaps a matter of insignificance. He would only say that by this measure he was prepared to stand or fall. The question of his continuance in office for one hour would depend on the prospect of being able to carry through that which he considered so important to the tranquillity, the safety, and the happiness of the country.

Lord Wharncliffe defended nomination, not because it was made by peers or other influential individuals, but because its effect on the House of Commons was, that it acted as a check on those places that were popularly represented. It prevented the ebullitions of popular feeling from having too great an influence on the decisions of a deliberative body, and saved it from being merely an assembly of delegates sent only to express the opinions of the people as they dictated from without. The nomination might in itself be irregular, but had not the whole system worked in that which made it worth preserving? He moved that the bill be read a second time that day six months.

The Duke of Wellington spoke at length, and concluded by saying that if this measure should be carried SECOND RE-FORM BILL OF 1831. the influence to which he had referred would become so predominant in the House of Commons that it would render the conduct of the government of the country absolutely impossible; and force, or something like it, would be necessary to carry the ordinary operations of the executive into effect. A small step taken in this matter could never be retraced. In taking a single step they might go too far; but if they once took that step they must proceed in a course, which, after exposing them to all the horrors of a democratic revolution, would most Duke of Wellington's speech. probably terminate in the establishment of a military despotism, with all the evils attendant upon that system of government. There was no country in the universe in which so much happiness, so much prosperity, and so much comfort were diffused amongst all the various classes of society; none in which so many and such large properties, both public and private, were to be found as in England. Such was the condition of this country under that system which was now so greatly condemned. We enjoyed under that system the largest commerce, and the most flourishing colonies in the world. There was not a position in Europe in any degree important for military purposes, or advantageous for trade, which was not under our control, or within our reach. All those great and numerous advantages we possessed under the existing system; but it would be impossible that we should any longer retain them if we once established a wild democracy, a complete democratic assembly, under the name of a House of Commons.

The Lord Chancellor Brougham spoke thus:—It had Lord Brougham's speech been said that the members returned under this bill will be delegates. In the first place, a member might happen

to be a delegate although there was but one delegator. Surely there could be no more mischief in a person being delegated by 4000 persons than by one or fourteen. A noble lord, an attorney, or a Jew jobber and loan contractor who sent a member through a rotten borough was as much a delegator as any constituency could by possibility be. A member returned by a real constituency, if a delegate, was still honest; whereas the nominee of an individual was returned under false and hypocritical pretences, for he was called the representative of the people and the guardian of their interests, while, in fact, he was only a representative and guardian of the particular
interests of the individual who had delegated him. It was monstrous to suppose that the same law would apply to Parliament at the present time as formerly. Formerly seats in Parliament were a burden, but now they were sought after, and bought and prized. Circumstances had changed, and the real innovators were those who proposed to maintain the laws unaltered, and not those who wished to adapt them upon old principles to altered circumstances. But their lordships had been told that great men, under the present system, found their way into the House of Commons. Because a way was dirty, and people from necessity crossed it while dirty, was that a reason why it should not be swept? If he could not get into the House of Commons by a direct, open way, he took a by-way. He got in with as little dirt as he could. He bribed not—he corrupted not— but still the way was dirty; and knowing it to be dirty from experience, that very fact made him the more desirous to cleanse it. But it was said the system worked well. Did the people think so? If it worked well their lordships would not at this moment have been called

upon to alter it, and there would not have been political
unions throughout the country. It had been asked,
What benefit might be expected to result from the
change? He could enumerate many. A noble earl (Winchelsea) had pronounced a long and severe invective
against the licentiousness of the press, and had said that
the worst tyranny that was experienced in the present
day was the tyranny exercised by the press. There
certainly could be no doubt that the press exercised a
great sway over the opinions of the people. But he was
convinced that if the people were represented by their
legitimate organs, namely, parliamentary representatives,
the press would lose the objectionable portion of its
ascendency. When the people obtained proper channels
of representation, then, and not until then, their lordships might expect to see the press, instead of exercising, as it did, an unlimited sway, solely engaged in
correcting the errors of the people, the errors of the
government, and the errors of the representatives of the
people. All that was unwholesome would be destroyed,
while all that was desirable would be preserved. The
learned lord concluded a speech of brilliant rhetoric by
emphatically calling on their lordships not to disappoint
the anxious expectations of the people, but, by allowing
the bill to go into a committee, to give themselves an
opportunity of judging more leisurely of its probable
effects.

He was followed by Lord Lyndhurst, who, in speaking
of the position of the House of Lords in the constitution,
remarked that their lordships were placed there as a
barrier against the crown, and bound to protect it against
its own imprudence and folly, if such qualities should
unfortunately ever be exhibited. They were placed there

SECOND RE- as a barrier against the ministers of the crown in case
FORM BILL they should betray the sovereign, or seek to subvert the
OF 1831. liberties of the people, or attempt any invasion of the
rights of any other order of the state. They were placed
there as a barrier against rash, dangerous, and hasty
legislation, whenever attempted by the other House of
Parliament. This was the crisis of their fate. If they
now timidly abdicated their trust they would never be
able to resume it. The rights and liberties of the people,
together with their own properties and titles, would be
trampled in the dust. Their properties and titles they
had received as a trust, and if they suffered them to be
disgraced in their hands they would be degraded for
ever. Perilous as their position was, he felt that they
stood upon a pinnacle before the face of the world, and
if they did their duty as became them, they would receive
the approbation of their own conscience and the applause
of an enlightened and honourable community.

There was a vast deal of commonplace discussion that
would be tiresome to notice. The House divided, with
the following result:—

Contents.		Non-Contents.	
Present,	. . 128	Present,	. . 150
Proxies,	. . 30 = 158	Proxies,	. . 49 = 199

Bill lost. Majority against the bill, 41. Two bishops voted for
the bill, and 21 against it.

The Lords had now thrown down the gauntlet to the
reformers, and it was at once taken up. On Monday, the
10th, when the House of Commons met, Lord Ebrington
brought forward a motion, the object of which was to
prevent the ministry from resigning, by pledging the
House to support them, and which plainly meant that

no one else would have their confidence. A discussion SECOND RE-FORM BILL OF 1831. took place. Lord Althorp declared that the present motion had been brought forward without any suggestion on the part of the ministers. For himself, unless he felt a reasonable hope that a Reform Bill equally efficient would be brought forward and carried, he would not remain in office a single hour. He did not mean to say that, after discussion, modifications might not be made, which, without diminishing the efficiency of the measure, might make it more perfect. But he would not be a party to any measure which he did not in his conscience believe would give a full, fair, and free representation of the people in Parliament, and effect all the objects which Motion that ministers do not resign. would have been effected by this bill. Having said this, he need not say that government did not contemplate making any other proposition to the House. The opponents of reform had certainly gained a great triumph, and might doubtless rejoice in their success; not that he thought that any great triumph would eventually be gained, for he was confident that the measure was only postponed. If the people of England remained firm and determined, but peaceable, he hoped and believed that there was no doubt of their ultimate and speedy success. There was only one chance of failure—if their disappointment led them into acts of violence or to unconstitutional measures of resistance.

The motion was carried by 329 votes against 198, Motion carried. being a majority of 131.

Now that the Lords and the reformers were brought face to face on this great question it set the nation a thinking on what was to be the solution. For the What was to be done? Commons to stop the supplies, as some called for, was to disorganize the king's service and not to punish the

Lords. In early times it was a mode of concussing the sovereign, but here the sovereign was quite on the side of the people. This was an absurd suggestion. Another mode of dealing with the difficulty was to summon another House of Commons by issuing writs to new constituencies, and refrain from calling upon the nomination boroughs to return representatives, as the crown had been in the practice of doing for many centuries before the time of Charles II. This, however, would not answer the purpose—it was difficult to give the new electors a constitution in this way. The only other course open—and one that was quite constitutional as well as quite adequate for the purpose—was to create a sufficient number of new peers to overcome the majority of 41. This was the course that the ministry resolved on.

Great indig-
nation.
As soon as it was noised over the land that the Lords had thrown out the bill there was raised a perfect blaze of indignation, and never perhaps in its whole history has the country been so near a revolution. The extreme danger lay in the fact that it was not confined to a district here or there, but the excitement was everywhere. The members of the two Houses who had made themselves conspicuous by their opposition to the bill were, many of them, mobbed, and ran the risk of their lives. Their houses were pillaged, and in many cases burned to the ground. There were parading everywhere noisy processions and immense assemblages of men such as had never been seen before. The more respectable class of reformers counselled order and self-control to the multitude, but this was difficult to maintain. In various places there was unfortunately both rioting and bloodshed, the worst of them being Derby, Nottingham, and Bristol. The last-mentioned town was for a time completely taken

possession of by the mob. The jail was burst open and the prisoners let free; then the jail and governor's house were burned. The military were repeatedly called out, and a vast amount of life and property was sacrificed. There were over one hundred killed and wounded. The country by and by settled down to comparative quiet once more on the tacit assurance that the government would get the king's consent to the creation of peers so as to obviate the difficulty in the way of the bill.

The Parliament was prorogued on October 20, 1831, but met again on December 6. On the 12th Lord John Russell for the third and last time moved for leave to bring in the Reform Bill, subject to a few amendments that had been made upon it.

Sir Robert Peel, for his own part, was willing to take the decision on the second reading; but in one thing there must be, without discussion, one unanimous feeling on all sides, that of gratitude at the great escape which the country had had from the bill of last session, a danger which he had never fully appreciated till now. The new bill, now about to be introduced, was a full and complete answer to the calumnies of which they had heard so much in the last session against the factious delays, as they were then called, of those who sought to introduce some of those very modifications now adopted by the noble lord who brought forward the former measure. The advantage of those much-maligned delays and objections was now visible in many parts of the new bill. He for one rejoiced at the delay which had taken place, not only on account of the amendments which had been made in the details of the bill, but be- cause if the House should determine, on the second reading of the bill, to adopt the principle of the measure,

and to make so extraordinary and extensive a change in
the frame and constitution of the government of this
country, he could not help thinking that when they ap-
proached the discussion of the details there would be a
disposition on the part of the majority of that House to
follow the course of the king's government, and to introduce more amendments into the measure. Another and
a great advantage arising from the delay was, that they
would now have an opportunity of discussing this important question in a state of greater calmness, influenced
by less excited feelings, and altogether under circumstances better calculated to enable them to arrive at a
wise and dispassionate conclusion.

Lord Althorp, on the other hand, could not recollect
that a question had been moved from the opposition side
of the House with respect to any of the alterations which
had since been made in the bill. Ministers had certainly
given their attention to every reasonable suggestion with
regard to the details of the bill; and many of those alterations which were now proposed might have been pressed
upon their consideration; but he did not remember that
an opportunity had been given them from the other side
of the House, during the last session, to adopt such alterations. When ministers brought forward the measure
objections were raised to some of its details, and various
improvements were proposed in it. The bill having been
thrown out, they employed the interval which had since
elapsed in endeavouring to remove all reasonable objections to the details of the measure, and in introducing
such improvements as were consistent with its great principle; and because they had thus attempted to render the
measure as perfect as they could, the right honourable
baronet now taunted them with their conduct. Would it

have been the conduct of men of sane minds, when time for THIRD RE-
consideration with regard to a measure of this description FORM BILL OF 1831.
had been forced upon them, not to employ it in endeav-
ouring to remove all the reasonable objections which had
been raised to the bill? The main principle of the bill
remained precisely the same as it was before, and in all
points of material consequence the present bill would be
precisely similar to the late one.

On the 16th the motion was made that the bill be read Lord Por-
a second time, when an amendment was moved by Lord chester's motion.
Porchester that it be read a second time that day six
months. His lordship contended that so long as the
national institutions were in harmony with the property
of the country he was not apprehensive of any disorganization of the constitution; but if that constitution
were made more democratic than it now was, a contest
would ensue between property and numbers, in which
either property would break down the representative institutions opposed to its safety, or these institutions
would break down property. To separate power from
property was the secret motive of the revolutionary impulse in so many states of Europe. In the natural progress of the democratic institutions of America the Federal
or Conservative party, once so powerful, was now nearly
annihilated.

The debate was continued on the 17th. In the course
of a long speech Mr. Macaulay remarked that at present Mr. Macau-
there were two parties in the country—a narrow oligar- lay's speech.
chical power above, which exhibited all the vices that
arose from abuse of power, and an infuriated multitude
below, which equally developed all the vices that originated from distress and destitution. The one party sought
to hallow a system of corruption with the same sacred

character which a civilized community ascribed to the right of property, and the other was clamouring against property itself. He feared not a collision, for between these extremes was a third party infinitely more powerful than either which, though vilified by both, would save both from the consequences of their own infatuation. This was the party which had supported the first Reform Bill, and which he hoped would be found to rally with equal zeal and readiness around the second.

The debate was almost entirely a repetition of former debates. It closed early on the morning of Sunday the
18th, and the second reading was carried by a majority of 324 to 162, a majority proportionally greater than on the occasion of the second reading of the former bill. The House then adjourned till the 17th January, 1832.

At the meeting of the House on the 17th it went into committee on the bill, and during this stage there was much discussion of details and many amendments were made. No attempt was made in the direction of annual parliaments, universal suffrage, or vote by ballot. The nearest approach to the Radical platform was a motion by Mr. Hunt that everyone paying taxes should be entitled to a vote, but only eleven members voted for the proposal. He put it then in another form—that all persons who would not possess the elective franchise under the new bill should be exempted from paying rates and taxes, from being balloted for the militia, and from impressment as seamen; but this was negatived without a division. On March 22 a division showed 355 for the third reading, and 239 against it; majority, 116; and on the 23d the bill finally passed the Commons.

It had now to pass a second time the final ordeal of the House of Lords. It was read a first time on March 26, and the debate on the second reading commenced on April 9, THIRD RE-FORM BILL OF 1831. and was continued on the 10th, 11th, and 13th. There was not much new matter in the debate, but much temper. In moving the second reading Earl Grey took oc- Second reading in House of Lords. casion to remark that all change was not revolution, and least of all such a change as was proposed in the present bill. It was to be effected, according to the acknowledged principles of the constitution, by an act of Parliament passed by the united will of King, Lords, and Earl Grey's speech. Commons. It infringed on none of the ordinary authorities of the land, it violated none of the ordinary forms of the constitution, it invaded not the privileges of their lordships, it interfered not with the prerogatives of the crown. He knew of no way of effecting a reform in Parliament—a measure which presupposed the existence of defects—except by one of three modes: either by disfranchising decayed and inconsiderable boroughs, which was the ancient practice of the constitution; or by giving the right of representation to large and populous towns which had risen into importance, and that too was the practice of the olden times; or by a great extension of the right of voting, which had also been done in the good old times. These were the principles of the present measure; in none of them was there anything which strayed beyond the ancient limits of the constitution or partook of a revolutionary character.

Lord Ellenborough moved the rejection of the bill, and Lord Ellenborough's speech. contended that if the present bill passed, Parliament must be prepared to go farther. It would be impossible to resist the demands of the most numerous and most necessitous class in the state, and concession must proceed until universal suffrage was established. He knew that by rejecting the bill inconveniences might be created; but

THIRD RE-
FORM BILL
OF 1831.

he believed that none would be created which might not be met by a firm government, and certainly none equal to the danger which would, in his opinion, follow the establishment of the proposed system of representation.

Lord Had-
dington's
speech.

The Earl of Haddington said that it appeared to him that this great question must be settled by a compromise, and he could see no reason why any one of their lordships, who admitted that they must now have a reform embracing enfranchisement, disfranchisement, and an extension of the right of voting, could hesitate to come to a compromise of that kind.

Lord Gage's
speech.

Lord Gage likewise declared that he had changed his opinion, or at least would now act differently. The only ground, he said, on which the second reading could be resisted was that a reaction had taken place in the public mind. Would to God that such had been the case! but he lamented to say that it had not. It was impossible to prevent the people from having a reform, and by refusing to go into committee on this bill now, their lordships might deprive themselves of the opportunity of introducing such amendments as they wished into this bill.

Lord
Shrews-
bury's
speech.

He was followed by the Earl of Shrewsbury, a Catholic peer, who did not think that the British constitution, which had been so much lauded, worked at all miraculously in practice. Under its protection we had courted unjust and expensive wars, we had experienced civil strife, rebellion, and revolution, we had suffered under commercial embarrassments unknown to other nations, and were surrounded with a crowded population, poor, unemployed, starving in the midst of abundance. Notwithstanding its blessings, crime had multiplied upon us in atrocity no less than in quantity, the reins of government were consigned to profligate keeping, and they had seen

governments supplying want of capacity by venality, and
retaining, by the profuse distribution of treasury largesses,
an army of occupation in both Houses of Parliament. The
exasperated nation had at length risen, determined to be
no longer oppressed, and here was the consequence, a bill
which would establish independence in every branch of
society, and annihilate the foul corruptions generated by
a long dominant oligarchy. The rule of this oligarchy
had cramped the energies of every order in the state, and
checked the growth of liberty and intelligence. It had
been carried on to the destruction of their lordships
themselves, and the legislature had ceased to be the depository of power. Their unnatural estrangement from
the great body of the community, their contemptuous
disregard of the interests of the country, their absolute
tyranny over the people of Ireland, had sown seeds, the
bitter fruits of which they were now reaping. In all this
they had found willing coadjutors in the bishops.

The Earl of Harrowby, who had hitherto strongly
opposed the bill, was now to support it. He said that
the present state of the public mind, with reference to
this bill, betokened a state of things which no honest
man could contemplate without alarm, evincing, as it did,
a want of that confidence on the part of the people in the
institutions of the country, without which there could be
no effectual and beneficial co-operation between the
nation and the government. The people had no confidence, and after the two records of its own condemnation
could have no confidence, in the House of Commons.
Had not the House of Commons, by large and increased
majorities, declared that it was unworthy of the confidence of the people whom it professed to represent?
And if so, was it for their lordships to turn round and
K

gainsay a decision thus solemnly pronounced and repeated.

The Duke of Wellington declined to follow the Earl of
Harrowby. He said that ministers had found a Parlia-
Duke of
Welling-
ton's speech.
ment prepared to pass a measure of moderate reform; but
instead of proposing such a measure, they had dissolved
that Parliament, and a new Parliament was called under
a degree of excitement in the public mind such as had
never before been witnessed. The consequence was that
the excitement had continued ever since, and it had been
kept up by the strong opinion put forward and entertained, that it was the king who wished for parliamentary
reform in the manner proposed by this bill. He did not
believe that it was so. His opinion was that the king
followed the advice of his servants; but it was the idea
thus engendered which rendered it difficult that there
should not be some reform.

Lord
Wharn-
cliffe's
speech.
Lord Wharncliffe, who had moved the amendment
which threw out the former bill, had now adopted the
course followed by the Earl of Harrowby, and he explained
and justified it on the same grounds, that the danger of
rejecting the bill was greater than that of taking it into
consideration; that by going into committee they might
get rid of those parts of it against which a strong objection was felt, and at all events would be enabled more
thoroughly to weigh its provisions.

Bishop of
Exeter's
speech.
The Bishop of Exeter opposed the bill, and set forth
an argument that was new. He stated that with regard
to the influence of peers in the other House of Parliament,
he denied it was exercised to the extent generally stated,
maintained that it was no usurpation of the rights of
Parliament or of the commonalty, because the nomination
boroughs had been originally created in order that the

influence given by them should be exercised by the great proprietors; and asked whether there had been no usurpation on the part of the commonalty and of the public on the influence of their lordships and on the rights of Parliament. The publication of the proceedings of Parliament and of the debates of both Houses was a usurpation upon the rights of Parliament which had been far greater in its results, and far more important in its operation, than any usurpation that had been charged upon their lordships or upon any of the proprietors of nomination boroughs. So far from lamenting this change, he was of opinion that no more salutary and wholesome measure could have been adopted, no better or more complete reform of Parliament could have been effected, no more admirable remedy could have been devised against any abuses which might exist in our legislative system, than that all that they said and did should be made known to the public. While the people possessed so large, so great, and so direct an influence over their representatives, there could be no doubt that everything would be done by them to "keep their House in order." But if in addition to that great means of influence which the people already possessed over the Parliament, those checks should be removed which were to be found in the system of nomination boroughs, the result would be that the public would exercise such an overwhelming influence, particularly over the other House of Parliament, as to render it impossible to carry on any regular system of legislation.

The Marquis of Lansdowne supported the bill, and remarked that the Bill was said to be a violation of the constitution inasmuch as it was founded on a spoliation of prescriptive rights. But what was this prescription?

THIRD RE-
FORM BILL
OF 1831.

The value of a right by prescription depended upon acquiescence in that prescription. That was to say, acquiescence made prescription, as it had been justly observed that obedience made the law. With respect to private property, there was no doubt that prescription was as good a title as any other, for it was no man's interest to question such a title, because he could not thereby appropriate such property to himself. But when prescription applied to a trust created for the benefit of others, and those for whose benefit it was created questioned the propriety of the prescription, and conceived that the trust was misplaced, the title by prescription lost its force and value.

Lord
Durham's
speech.

Lord Durham made a vigorous speech in favour of the bill. He said that till the Revolution the object of all political struggles had been to prevent the sovereign from becoming despotic. The contest was carried on between the crown and the higher classes. The people did not interfere or demand political privileges, because they felt themselves, for want of education, incompetent to exercise them. But they had long ago reached a very different point in skill, talent, and political intelligence. The middle-classes were as competent, if not more so, for the discharge of political duties as the higher orders of the state. All the scientific institutions, the literary societies, the associations tending to the advancement of arts and letters, were supported by the middle-classes. The gentry, living apart in the country, followed the amusements and enjoyments of their class, leaving to the inhabitants of towns to be the supporters and patrons of the liberal arts; and when any political matter brought the gentry and the inhabitants of the towns together the superiority of the former was no longer manifest. The middle-classes had

thus become entitled to a share in the government be- THIRD RE-
FORM BILL
OF 1831. cause they were fitted to exercise it; and they were the
more resolved upon attaining it in consequence of the
misgovernment to which their exclusion had led. It had
burdened the nation with an enormous debt; had increased extravagantly the annual expenditure; it had
augmented the poor-rates sevenfold; it had lavished our
wealth in unnecessary wars and in subsidizing foreign
princes.   They now demanded to be admitted to a share
in parliamentary representation, and concession alone was
the path of safety.   All history taught that ill-judged
resistance to public opinion invariably led to disaffection
and resistance on the part of the people—next to a bloody
struggle—and finally to unlimited compliance.   What
means were there now of resisting popular opinion? If
their lordships, by rejecting the bill, pronounced a sentence of national excommunication, were they prepared
to contend with an indignant people?

Lord Eldon opposed, and said that he had heard much LordEldon's
speech. of an exercise of the royal prerogative by which the passing of this bill was to be secured. He did not deny the
right of the sovereign to the free exercise of that prerogative.   He would admit that at the next recorder's report
of persons condemned at the Old Bailey the sovereign
possessed not only the right to grant a free pardon to
any number of such convicts, but to make peers of them
if he pleased. At the same time no censure would be too
severe, no punishment too great, for any minister who
should advise his sovereign to destroy the independence
of the House of Lords by such enormous creation of new
peers. What caused the Revolution of 1688, which hurled
James II. and the whole race of Stuarts from the throne
of this country? Was it not the power which he claimed

of dispensing with the laws and of setting his own will above the will of his two Houses of Parliament? Now, if the crown were to exercise its power of creating peers to carry into execution an act of Parliament which that House deemed unfit to be carried into execution, would it not be a stretch of the prerogative in legislation quite as dangerous as the dispensing power of James II.? His lordship further contended that the House had no more right to take away the elective franchise from the present holders of it than they had to deprive them of the house or land which conferred it. The elective franchise was a vested right which could not be forfeited without some proof of delinquency. This interest in boroughs was a species of property which had been known in England for centuries; it had been over and over again made the subject of purchase and sale in all parts of the kingdom; and Parliament might as well extinguish the right of private individuals to their advowsons as their right to exercise the privileges which they derived from the possession of burgage-tenures.

Lord Tenterden followed on the same side. He admitted that the expressed wishes of the people deserved consideration; but, at the same time, it was the duty of their lordships to consider whether the fulfilment of their wishes might not be pernicious to themselves, and if they were convinced that it would it was their duty to prevent the realization of their hopes. He admitted also that the opinion of a majority of the House of Commons was entitled to respect from their lordships; but it ought to have no other influence over their judgments, and certainly ought not to induce them blindly to pass a bill of which they could discover neither the merits nor the necessity.

The lord-chancellor (Brougham) argued that on the THIRD RE-
FORM BILL
OF 1831. delicate considerations involved in the consequences of rejecting the bill he would not enter, though much had been already said. But if there was any one feeling more than another which he would carefully guard Lord
Brougham's
speech. against—any one enemy which he considered more fatal than another to the security of all establishments in church and state—that feeling was an alienation on the part of the middle and lower classes from those above them in wealth, in station—in fact, anything which would tend to increase the distance which separated the higher orders from the body and bulk of the people. Their lordships had now an opportunity not only to regain any ground they might have lost by the unfortunate decision of last session, but to raise themselves infinitely higher than ever in respect of the people of England. "Do not flatter yourselves that their interest in this measure has subsided. It has stood the test of disappointment and of long delay; but it is as strong and as intense as ever; and you may rely on it, that from one end of this land to the other the people—the intelligent, the thinking, the rational, the honest people, and that, too, not merely of this metropolis, but of every town, village, and hamlet in England, and, if possible, still more in Scotland—hang with breathless suspense upon your decision this night."

Lord Lyndhurst contended that in the scheme of the Lord Lynd-
hurst's
speech. constitution of this country it was generally admitted that the sovereign, or those who represented him, joined the conservative mass in order to keep down the democratic power. It never was imagined that the crown would throw itself into the democratic scale against the conservative body. Lord Bolingbroke in his essays, as well as another very able writer, had stated that if such an occurrence took place it would inevitably lead to the overthrow of the constitution. From the time the measure had first been brought into the other House of Parliament ministers had been challenged to point out any sufficient reason for so extensive a change, and he had heard nothing in the discussions either of the last or of the present Parliament which could in any respect justify it. The measure intended to have been proposed by the noble and learned lord on the woolsack would, he believed, have been approved by all parties; but it was a measure that would have been less extensive and sweeping than that now called for. They were told that they

ought to have strictly independent representatives in the House of Commons. Taking the meaning of the word independence as those who advanced the argument used it, he would maintain that if the principle were conceded there would be an end to the other two powers in the state. Never in any part of the world had such a system existed. It had been tried in more instances than one, and constantly failed. Fifty years ago Mr. Hume wrote a treatise on this very point, and the result of his inquiry was that the scheme was wholly impracticable. In our own times, a learned lord, a member of the other House of Parliament, had canvassed the same subject in a quarterly publication, and had arrived at the same conclusion. Lord Bolingbroke had also considered the question, and he thought the plan impracticable unless it was accompanied by another change in the constitution. And what was the remedy he proposed? An extension of the prerogative of the crown. Under this bill the House of Commons would be so constituted that no government could be carried on with it, unless in such a way as the House itself should dictate, and by ministers who would implicitly obey its commands.

In winding up the debate Earl Grey stated that this measure of reform was introduced, and was received with satisfaction by the whole country. In the progress of the feeling of reform it was strongly directed to those injurious systems, annual parliaments, universal suffrage, and vote by ballot. Those "I have declared on other occasions, even when I was most eager for reform, to be in opposition to my principles; but this measure, founded on the satisfaction of the public—and without it I admit the measure would be good for nothing—was no sooner propagated than all agitation became silent, and a unanimity manifested itself to a degree which was hardly conceivable." On the subject of the threatened creation of peers which had been so frequently and so pointedly alluded to, his lordship said that the best writers on the constitution maintained that the best way to prevent a collision between the two branches of the legislature was to put in requisition the prerogative of the crown for the creation of peers. That the crown had the right to use this prerogative for such a purpose he was prepared to maintain. More than that he would not say at the present moment.

The House divided at seven o'clock in the morning of the 14th of April, when the second reading was carried by a majority of nine. The numbers were:

Contents.........Present, 128; Proxies, 56	184
Non-contents...Present, 126; Proxies, 49	175
Majority for the second reading, ...	9

It was felt on all sides, except among the Radical party, as a relief that the bill was to go into committee.

THIRD RE-
FORM BILL
OF 1831.

It was also felt as a relief that as yet no creation of peers had taken place. It was not known whether the ministry had got a *carte blanche* for that purpose or not. There was therefore much excitement, because there was much danger. It was shrewdly guessed that the whole crisis was at the command of the king, and that a word from him would convert the Tory majority into a minority at once. It was all but certain that the House of Lords was not prepared to consent to the double sacrifice of having the bill passed and of having their House degraded.

Committee

Parliament met on May 17, and the House of Lords went directly into committee on the bill. It was plain at the outset that the spirit of the House was not broken. The danger was not exactly near enough. Lord Lyndhurst immediately moved that the disfranchising clauses be postponed, and around this motion there was much fighting. The government let it be distinctly understood that this motion, if carried, was fatal to the bill. Nevertheless it *was* carried by a majority of 151 to 116, and Earl Grey immediately moved that the House resume, when he proposed that the further consideration of the bill be delayed till Thursday, the 10th.

Creation of
Peers.

Earl Grey proceeded to the king and stated that he must be armed with the necessary authority for the creation of peers, otherwise the ministry must resign. The king informed Earl Grey on the following day that he was prepared to accept their resignation. The ministers

Ministers
resign.

immediately resigned, and the king sent for Lord Lyndhurst, who put himself in communication with the Duke of Wellington and Sir Robert Peel. The king's message to the party was not to form a cabinet at all hazards, but to form one prepared to carry on the government, and likewise to carry through an "extensive measure of reform."

THIRD RE-
FORM BILL
OF 1831.

Meantime the House of Commons met, and Lord Ebrington moved on May 10, "That an humble address be presented to his majesty, humbly to represent to his majesty the deep regret felt by this House at the change which has been announced in his majesty's councils by the retirement of those ministers in whom this House continues to repose unabated confidence.

Address by
the Com-
mons.

" That this House, in conformity with the recommendation contained in his majesty's most gracious speech from the throne, has framed and sent up to the House of Lords a bill for a reform in the representation of the people, by which they are convinced that the prerogatives of the crown, the authority of both Houses of Parliament, the rights and liberties of the people are equally secured.

" That to the progress of this measure this House considers itself bound in duty to state to his majesty that his subjects are looking with the most intense interest and anxiety, and they cannot disguise from his majesty their apprehension that any successful attempt to mutilate or impair its efficiency would be productive of the greatest disappointment and dismay.

" This House is, therefore, compelled, by warm attachment to his majesty's person and government, humbly, but most earnestly, to implore his majesty to call to his councils such persons only as will carry into effect, unimpaired in all its essential provisions, that bill for the reform of the representation of the people which has recently passed this House."

In support of his motion, Lord Ebrington added that it would be worse than madness to suppose the House could ever be weak enough to support an administration

Lord Eb-
rington's
speech.

composed of persons who, throughout the whole discussion, had been either obstinately contesting all the vital principles of the measure or cavilling at its details. The House would never consent to trust the management of this bill to those who had proved its determined enemies, or had shown themselves its reluctant and wavering supporters.

Mr. Baring, in opposing the motion, said he was convinced that a majority in the House of Peers would have agreed to the disfranchising clauses, not from any conviction that the destruction of the small boroughs would contribute to the public prosperity, but from the stress which had been laid upon them out of doors, and as essential to the peace of the country. Why, therefore, did not Earl Grey wait a couple of days to ascertain whether this was not the course intended to be pursued? for that brief period would have sufficed to test the sincerity of his opponents, and, as a consequence, to have saved the king and the country from the present embarrassment. Mr. Baring added that it was highly necessary that the House knew the nature of the advice which Earl Grey had given to the king, upon which Lord Althorp replied that he had no objection to state plainly that the advice which ministers had given the king was that he should create as many peers as would enable them to carry the Reform Bill through the House of Lords in all its efficiency.

A debate followed upon the motion. Mr. Hume said that the expectations of the country had been raised to the utmost pitch, and it was the duty of the House to take a step on this occasion before the people to counsel his majesty how they thought he ought to act, and in case he would not take that counsel, to exercise that

control which legitimately belonged to them. He con- THIRD RE-
FORM BILL
OF 1831. tended that ministers had done right in pressing upon the king the necessity of making peers to carry the proposed disfranchisement. They had a right to say to his majesty, "You have guaranteed to your people the success of this measure, and we now call upon you to take the only step which can secure it. Let us therefore create sixty peers." Less than that number, he admitted, would have done no good; but he would not have objected to creating even 100 peers. Knowing what he did of the House of Lords, and of the motives which influenced the conduct of its members, he had no hesitation in saying that if his majesty had given a *carte blanche* to Earl Grey, the creation of ten peers would not have been required. The reason why the anti-reforming peers were so bold was, that some silent word had been whispered to them that no peers would be created. They had acquired this knowledge somehow or other. He thought that ministers had acted rightly and wisely in bringing this matter at once to a speedy conclusion, instead of allowing it to linger on for months, delaying all public business and keeping the public mind in a state of perpetual ferment.

Mr. Macaulay argued that the constitution afforded the Mr. Macaulay's speech means of dealing with a factious and perverse opposition on the part of the House of Commons; for the king could dissolve the Parliament and appeal to the people at a time when he might think that appeal would stand the best chance of success. Again, that House was a check upon the king, for it could refuse the supplies. But was there to be no check at all upon the House of Lords? There existed, moreover, a strong necessity for counterbalancing by a creation of peers from the Whig party, the number of peers which, during the last thirty or forty

years, had been made from the Tory party. He did not
think that there could be a strong objection, under such
circumstances, to the creation of fifty peers in one day,
when no objection had been raised to the creation of 200
in the course of a generation by the one party that during
that period held power. They should redress the balance
by throwing in a number from themselves. He therefore heartily concurred in the advice which, it was stated,
ministers had given to the king, and he deeply regretted
it had not been taken. Unless the present ministers
returned to office the Reform Bill was lost.

The resolutions were carried by a majority of 80.
This made it plain that the House of Commons would
not give any support to another ministry. Meantime,
the political unions became active and threatening. Many
gave out that they would pay no taxes, as the House of
Commons had declared itself not to be representative of
the people. The common council of London petitioned
the Commons to stop the supplies, and appointed a permanent committee to support Earl Grey and continue
their sitting until the Reform Bill, brought in under his
administration, be passed into law. During this crisis the
excitement through the country was intense.

The duke and his friends failed to form a cabinet.
The people's battle was won! The king again sent for
Earl Grey, and gave him assurance that when the power
of creating peers became necessary it would be given.
The ministry then re-entered into office. In the House
of Lords Earl Grey explained that the advice "we ten-
dered to our sovereign was absolutely required by the
circumstances of the case. Under these circumstances it
was constitutional; and I can refer the noble and learned
lord to books on the constitution, in which he will find

that this prerogative of creating peers was given to the crown in order to counteract the serious evils that might arise from this House placing itself in opposition to the remaining estates of the realm. My lords, but for the existence of this prerogative your proceedings would be without control, while upon all other branches of the legislature salutary checks are imposed. The Commons possess a check upon misconduct in the crown, in its power of stopping the supplies; a check upon factious conduct in the Commons resides in the king's power to dissolve the House. Were the Lords alone to be exempt from control? Should this House combine, in some purpose adverse to the crown and House of Commons, and should it be able to hold out in its determination, no power existing to check its proceedings, then is this no longer a government of King, Lords, and Commons, but an oligarchy ruling the country. On the grounds stated we gave the advice which we conceived we were bound in duty to offer, and are prepared to take the consequence of its rejection by resigning office."

It was obviously not the king's wish, nor that of the ministry, to proceed to the creation of peers, if that step could be avoided. On May 18, therefore, Earl Grey moved that the committee on the bill be taken on Monday, and this was agreed to. Meantime a royal circular was ordered to be sent to the opposition peers in the following terms:—

"St. James's Palace, May 17, 1832.

"My Dear Lord,—I am honoured with His Majesty's commands to acquaint your Lordship that all difficulties to the arrangements in progress will be obviated by a declaration in the House to-night from a sufficient number of peers, that, in consequence of the present state of affairs they have come to the resolution of dropping their

THIRD RE-
FORM BILL
OF 1831.

further opposition to the Reform Bill, so that it may pass without delay, and as nearly as possible in its present shape.

"I have the honour to be,

"Yours sincerely,

"HERBERT TAYLOR."

This was decisive; there could be nothing but submission. A few amendments were proposed, which the Commons agreed to, and the great Reform Bill was passed —106 voting for it and 22 against it—on the 4th June, 1832: and on the 7th of June it received the royal assent and became law. The passing of the Scotch and Irish bills possess no historical interest in this place, for the conflict ended with the passing of the English bill.

Bill carried in the House of Lords.

And now, for the first time in English history was the House of Commons to undergo an organic reform, and for the first time was the country to get a direct control over the House. It was, of course, not by any means a complete control, for it will be seen by and by that the absolute numbers enfranchised were not very large, but nevertheless it was a great change. It did not bring the working-class within the constitution, but it brought the middle-class, and that was a considerable step. It was the first break, too, in the great political "ring"— the "close corporation" of the three Estates which had reigned over the country for a hundred and forty-four years. And there can be no doubt that it was the firmness of King William IV. and his personal sympathy with his subjects generally, that made this break possible,

Remarks on the Bill.

at least without a civil war. There can be little room for doubt that if he had thrown in his lot with the Peers the whole estates of King, Lords, and Prelates would have tumbled to the ground—at least, there was the

choice before them of an immediate appeal to the sword.
But the lessons of the French Revolution were much too
recent to admit of *that* as the issue!

It might be asked why it was that it took fifty years
—the period from the time of Pitt's first Reform Bill till
1832—to effect the change that was then completed.
In the first place, it is tolerably clear that at the outset
the people as a whole were not fitted for the use of political power on a large scale. Even in 1832 it is very
questionable whether the reform was not quite sufficient.
There can be little doubt that the working-classes were
ignorant and poor and impulsive—as classes. They were
at first merely a mob, and the "combination laws" contributed largely to keep them so. They had no organization, they had no principle of association, no cohesion.
They were easily corrupted, easily bribed, and had little
confidence in one another. They were not united in
clubs or friendly societies, they had no trades-unions, no
political associations. They were not accustomed to act
together as classes, and consequently were unfitted for
self-government. They lacked that unity which was
necessary to enable them to break up that political con-
cert of the three estates which was the cause of their
oppression. There were other circumstances that delayed reform for many years. There were foreign wars
kept-going during almost the entire period. Then there
were the horrors of the French Revolution, which frightened all Europe, and prevented anyone from breathing
reform. And lastly, there was much division among the
people themselves on many questions, which helped to
keep them weak and disunited on the question of reform.
There were the questions of Catholic emancipation, the
Test and Corporation Acts, and free-trade—questions

L

that split them up into Protectionists and Free Traders, Churchmen and Dissenters, Catholics and Protestants, instead of having them arrayed simply into the two great orders of Reformers and Conservatives.

The *extent*, generally, of the changes produced by the Reform Acts of 1832, for the three kingdoms, was as follows:—The electorate was raised from a nominal figure up to 931,735 at once. The membership of the House was not altered. It remained as before at 658; but the distribution of seats was different. It stood originally at the following figures:—For England, 513; for Scotland, 45; for Ireland, 100. It was now to stand as follows:—For England, 500; for Scotland, 53; for Ireland, 105. There was thus 13 seats taken from England, of which 8 were transferred to Scotland and 5 to Ireland. The changes otherwise were very great. In England there were 56 boroughs returning one member each disfranchised. 36 other boroughs were disfranchised to the extent of one member each. There were a number of large towns enfranchised, 22 to the extent of two members each, and 20 to the extent of one member each. There was also a rearrangement of counties and boroughs, a division of counties, and certain counties were to return two members each. In Scotland there was also a rearrangement of counties and a grouping of boroughs. There were two members each given to Edinburgh and Glasgow, and one member to each of Aberbeen, Paisley, Dundee, Greenock, and Perth. In Ireland there were similar changes; while the five additional members were conferred upon Limerick, Waterford, Belfast, Galway, and Dublin University. The *effect* of the reform generally will be referred to further on.

SECOND REFORM.

From 1832 onwards there was a course to run of CONSTITU-
thirty-five years before another reform of the House of TION OF 1832.
Commons was to take place. However good at first was
the Act of 1832, the system it introduced soon became
in a great measure non-representative. It was only an
instalment of reform to begin with, for the reformed
House may be said to have only represented property,
not labour. But the arrangement of the electoral system
was fairly good, so that there was something like an
equitable distribution of political power to begin with.
There was, therefore, a good deal of parliamentary busi- Results of
ness done at the outset. There was a vast reduction of Reform Act.
expenditure; there was a great diminution in those taxes
that affected the masses. There was, by and by, the
abolition of the corn-laws. There was likewise the
removal of all those taxes and restrictions upon the
newspaper press and upon paper. The criminal laws
were modified; slavery in the colonies was abolished;
the Factory Acts were passed; the municipal corporations of the country had constitutions given to them;
poor-laws were established, and the various disabilities
upon Dissenters were all removed. Lastly, the qualification of a landed income as necessary to a candidate for
the House of Commons was abolished, the Navigation
Laws were repealed, and Free Trade was declared to be
for the future our commercial policy.

But it began to be found out that the system would Defects.
go no further. It was found, in the course of time, that
the reformed House would not touch education, nor the
Irish Church, nor Irish land. It would not pass the

Ballot Bill, although the electoral system had been most corrupt for more than a century, and was still extremely bad. Nor would it deal with the system of purchase in the army, so that the country would get a control over the army. These were all felt to be matters for dealing with, but to do. this it was necessary to have the reformed House reformed again. Indeed it was found that in regard to some of the measures that had been passed the House would not have taken them up at all, unless it had been from great external pressure—pressure that ought not to have been required, if the House of Commons had been quite representative of the country. There ought to have been no agitation necessary for the repeal of the corn-laws.

It was seen that the constituencies of the country only consisted, immediately after the passing of the Act of 1832, of 931,735, and immediately before 1867 the numbers had only risen to 1,352,970. The electorate of England and Wales rose from 652,285 in 1832 to 1,040,492 in 1867, that of Scotland from 80,271 in 1832 to 107,780 in 1867, and that of Ireland from 199,179 to 204,748. Meantime the population was not what it was; it had increased absolutely over the United Kingdom from 24,392,485 in 1831 to 29,321,288 in 1861. In England it had increased in these thirty years from 13,896,797 to 20,066,224. In Scotland from 2,364,386 to 3,062,294. In Ireland it had decreased from 7,767,401 to 5,798,967. There was a great change of population all over, and besides, there was a considerable shifting of the population, especially from the landward districts into the large towns. All this tended to aggravate the non-representative character of the House of Commons, apart altogether from the fact that the constituencies of the country

did not include, from the outset, the largest class of the Constitu-
population, the working-class. As the interval of the tion of 1832.
thirty-five years, therefore, from 1832 to 1867 began to
lapse, and the defects of the system began to manifest
themselves, so a call for a further reform became louder
and louder until towards the year last mentioned it became irresistible. With these preliminary remarks we
shall proceed with the history of reform between the two
periods we have mentioned.

In 1848 the first motion for general reform was made.
It was a year of revolution throughout the Continent,
and it was felt more or less by every nation in Europe.
It led to a great deal of excitement in our own country;
meetings began to be held, a great Chartist demonstration
took place. Mr. Joseph Hume took a leading part in the Mr. Hume's
movement, and on the 31st June he proposed a resolution motion of 1848.
in the House of Commons in the following terms: " That
this House as at present constituted does not fairly represent the population, the property, or the industry of
the country; whence has arisen great and increasing discontent in the minds of a large portion of the people;
and it is therefore expedient, with a view to amend the
national representation, that the elective franchise shall
be so extended as to include all householders; that votes
shall be taken by ballot; that the duration of Parliament
shall not exceed three years; and that the apportionment
of members to population shall be made more equal." In
the course of his speech he reverted to the Reform Act, His speech.
1832, and contended that it had failed to answer all the
purposes for which it was intended. Parliament purports
to be an engine for governing a constitutional country,
all classes being represented; is that so now? Taxation
and representation should go together. Every man should

have his share in sanctioning the laws by which he is governed, the sole difference between a free man and a slave. The Crown, Lords, and Commons should invent the best method of giving effect to that constitutional government; the House of Commons therefore ought to be invested with the highest authority and influence in the country. No act of the crown ought to be valid without its sanction, and the large classes of the community ought to be represented. But what is the effect? Five out of every six male adults in this country are without any voice in the election of the representatives to that House. The population of Great Britain was 18,500,000 in 1841; out of the male adults above twenty-one, taking the average—some individuals being registered for three, four, or five different places—the number of registered electors does not amount to more than from 800,000 to 850,000. The rest of the 5,000,000 or 6,000,000 adults who have not this privilege are placed in an inferior situation and deprived of that *right* which by the constitution they are entitled to enjoy. At eighteen or even sixteen years of age a man can be drawn for the militia and called out to quell riots, yet classes of workmen distinguished for their industry, intelligence, and ability are excluded from the franchise. He also defined household suffrage to be "that every such person of full age, and not subject to any mental or legal incapacity, who shall have occupied a house or part of a house for twelve months, and shall have been rated to the poor for that period, shall be registered as an elector; and every lodger shall have the right to claim to be rated to the poor, and after such rating and residence for twelve months he shall be registered as an elector." There would be no difficulty in carrying out this object.

Mr. Henry Drummond opposed the motion, and said that if Mr. Hume's assertion were correct, that every man who contributed to the taxes had a right to vote, there was an end to the question, and there was no occasion for the restrictions and qualifications with which Mr. Hume was now going to encumber that pretended right. If every man had that right, what did Mr. Hume mean by now restricting it to all householders? Even under his definition of household suffrage some two or three millions of adult males would be excluded from the representation, and thus the universal content which he wished to introduce would not be obtained. He differed from Mr. Hume as to the basis of his proposed representation. That which every man of full age had a right to was the best possible government and the best representative system which the legislature could form. If universal suffrage would give the best representative system, the best laws, and the best government, the people would have a right to it; but if universal suffrage would not give this, then it was mere idle pedantry to say that every man had a right to a vote and was entitled to share in legislation. In considering this question he could not but recollect that ours was a mixed constitution, that we had a sovereign and a House of Lords, and that they were not evils to be endured, but institutions to be proud of. Tacitus had said that every government was formed of monarchy, aristocracy, or democracy; that a government formed out of the three might be easily conceived, but could not easily be brought to pass, and that if it could be brought to pass it could not be durable. That sentiment had been justified by the experience of all the modern nations of the world save one, and that was England. We, therefore, ought to apply ourselves with the greatest caution and anxiety to any plan which would alter in any way the adjustment of the different powers of the constitution, as this plan would do in regard to our whole representative system. The honourable member then entered into a long argument to prove that a Parliament elected by householders and lodgers would not be a better Parliament than the present. He declined to enter into any long argument as to the vote by ballot, though he was of opinion that it would be no remedy against intimidation. He also declared himself satisfied with the present duration of Parliament, and should not give his vote for any change in it. He then proceeded to defend the Reform Act by showing that since it was passed the House had not been the mere servant of the aristocracy or the bigoted opponent of all plans of amelioration. No one who considered the changes which had been made since 1832 could say that the House of Commons had not responded quickly and readily to public opinion. He had recapitulated the great measures which it had passed in that interval, as, for instance, the abolition of slavery, the opening of the China trade, the commutation of tithes, the remedy of the grievances of Dissenters as to births and marriages, the reform of the municipal corporations in England, Scotland, and Ireland, the alterations in the tariff, the alterations in the postage system, and, lastly, the total repeal of the corn-laws, which proved that the House was not under the rule and dominion of the landed aristocracy. He trusted that the House would not select the present as the time for making are form, which stopped, indeed, short of the Charter, but which must ultimately terminate in it; but that it would think it due to the other branches of the legislature and to that great people of which it was the representative to give a decided negative to this resolu-

Mr. Cobden said that the members of the large constituencies would support the motion, and he appealed
to that fact as a proof that the middle-classes were anxious to open the portals of the constitution to those who
were anxious to come within them.   There had as yet
been no organization in favour of this movement; but it
had already made great way: 130 meetings had been held
in its favour within the last five weeks, and it had already
excited as much feeling in its support as had been acquired by the Corn-law League after five years' agitation.
The present representative system was a sham; but if it
were amended as Mr. Hume proposed, it would once
more be a reality.   He defended at some length Mr.
Hume's scheme of household suffrage, contending that it
would not create a change in the government, but would
only bring the legislature into harmony with the wants
of the people.

Mr. Villiers supported the motion, as it recognized the
policy of extending the basis of the representation; but,
on a vote being taken, there was, for the motion 84, and
against it 351.   Majority against it, 267.

Reform then lay over till 1851, when Mr. Locke King
moved a resolution to the effect that the franchise in
counties should be reduced to £10, and that the two
franchises—borough and county—should be assimilated.
There was considerable discussion.   The government
opposed the introduction of the question this session;
but on a division the motion was carried against the
government by a vote of 100 against 52.   This division
in a small House did not mean much; but, nevertheless,
a bill was brought in to give effect to the resolution of

Mr. Locke King's motion of 1851. the House. The second reading was fixed for April 2, when Mr. Fox Maule on behalf of the government asked for a postponement of the measure. A division took place. For the second reading, 83; against it, 299. Majority against the bill, 216.

Mr. Hume's bill of 1852. In 1852 the Tories were in power with Lord Derby as premier, when Mr. Hume again took up the subject, and again failed. On March 25 he moved for leave to bring in "a bill to amend the national representation by extending the elective franchise in England and Wales, so that every man of full age, and not subject to any mental or legal incapacity, who shall be the resident occupier of a house, or of part of a house as a lodger, for twelve months, and shall have been duly rated to the poor of that parish for that time, shall be registered as an elector, and shall be entitled to vote for a representative in Parliament, also by enacting that votes shall be taken by ballot, that the duration of Parliament shall not exceed three years, and that the proportion of representatives be made more consistent with the amount of population and property." There was a lengthened debate; but on a division the numbers were: for the bill, 89; against it, 244. Majority against the bill, 155.

Mr. Locke King's motion. On the 27th April thereafter Mr. Locke King moved for leave to introduce his measure for the assimilation of the county franchise to the burgh franchise, but was defeated by a majority of 202 against 149.

The next proposal for reform was made two years later.

Lord John Russell's Bill of 1854. On 13th February, 1854, Lord John Russell, a member of the Aberdeen cabinet, moved for leave to bring in a bill. There were, he observed, three main defects in the Reform Act which required the serious consideration of the House. First, although a very large disfranchise-

ment of boroughs was made by the Reform Act, there Lord John
were still several boroughs which had hardly a sufficient Russell's
Bill of 1854.
number of electors to justify their retaining the power of
sending members to Parliament. At the same time he
did not concur in the opinion that there ought to be anything like an equalization of the numbers of electors.
At the passing of the Reform Bill he had thought 300
was the proper minimum; but he found there were several His speech.
boroughs which fell below that number of electors, and
that in others, although the number of electors exceeded
300, yet the population fell below 5000. These boroughs,
amounting to nineteen, and returning twenty-nine members, he proposed to disfranchise altogether. Certain
other boroughs he found had less than 500 electors, or
less than 10,000 inhabitants, and from these he proposed
to take away thirty-three representatives, which, with the
preceding, would give sixty-two seats. Another defect
in the Reform Act consisted in the manner in which the
counties were divided, and this defect he proposed to
correct in the distribution of the sixty-two seats. It was
proposed to take population generally as the rule to be
applied. The West Riding of Yorkshire and the county
of Lancaster it was intended to divide respectively into
two counties, giving to each of the divisions three members; it was proposed to give an additional member to
each county and town having more than 100,000 inhabitants. By the mode in which the votes would be
given four members would be added for the West Riding
of York, and four for the South Lancashire division;
there would be thirty-eight for other counties, making in
all forty-six. To each of nine large towns (including
Salford) which now sent representatives, it was proposed
to give an additional member, and one member to each

of the towns of Birkenhead, Staleybridge, and Burnley; two members to a metropolitan borough formed of Kensington and Chelsea; two members to the Inns of Court, and one to the London University. While discussing this branch of the subject he admitted his belief that there was much truth in the arguments adduced on behalf of the representation by minorities. There were many cases where an electorate of several hundreds, or even thousands, found themselves very narrowly outvoted by their opponents, and justly complained that their votes were swamped and their opinions unrepresented. By way of partial remedy for this injustice, although without appearing to consider it a vital element in his measure, he proposed in cases where three members were returned for any district to give every elector only two votes. By this contrivance he calculated that whenever in such localities the minority of votes on any side did not fall below two-fifths of the numbers of their opponents, they could, if they pleased, return one member out of the three, and thus obtain a proportionate weight in the House and upon divisions. He next adverted to a third defect in the Reform Act. He thought that, in taking the £10 borough franchise and abolishing the intricate franchises then existing, Parliament had confined itself too much to one species, and it was proposed now to make several new franchises common to counties and towns. The new qualifications were £100 yearly salary; £10 a year dividends derived from the Government funds, Bank stock, or East Indian stock; the payment of 40s. a year either to income-tax or assessed taxes; the being a graduate at any university in the United Kingdom; and, lastly, any person having had a deposit of £50 in a savings-bank for not less than three years, would be entitled to vote. Lord John next proceeded to define the fran- chises belonging exclusively to counties or boroughs. First, as to counties, it was proposed that £10 house-holders should have a vote for the county, provided that the building be of the value of £5 a year. As the pro-posed alterations would add forty-six members to the county representation, if £10 householders were included in the constituency there would, he observed, be a great and wholesome mixture of interests therein. With re-spect to the borough franchise, it appeared to him that in taking the £10 franchise so absolutely as was done in 1831 sufficient provision was not made for the admission of the working-classes, and seeing the character of those classes, and how much the wealth of the country de-pended upon them, he thought the door ought to be opened wider than it now was. He did not, he added, shrink from saying that the extension of the franchise, as he had formerly proposed, to £5 householders was not putting it too low; but as this proposition had been met by grave objections, the government had adopted the limit prescribed in an act which passed two or three years ago, and proposed that all persons rated as above £6 a year, with the condition of the municipal term of residence—two years and a half—should be placed upon the register, which would extend the suffrage to working-men, and those most remarkable for steadiness and skill. It was further proposed to abandon the obligation of paying rates and taxes before voting, and to make the register of voters final. Another change of considerable importance was contemplated. Among the complaints of bribery and corruption made against certain boroughs it had been represented that one class of electors, namely freemen, were particularly obnoxious to the charge; and it was proposed that after the expiration of existing interests freemen should have no right to vote. Another change (which would be the subject of a separate bill) was in the Act of Anne concerning the vacating of seats of members of the House of Commons on acceptance of office, which it was proposed to repeal. He then recapitulated the number of seats that would be to dispose of, namely, sixty-two by disfranchisement, and four now vacant, making together sixty-six. Of this number sixty-three were to be filled up in the manner he had stated, and the remaining three would be added to the representation of Scotland.

There was a considerable amount of discussion upon
the bill, principally as to its being brought forward at a time when the country was on the eve of a great war with Russia, and, with much regret, Lord John resolved to abandon it.

As we approach the year 1858 we find that a public interest in Reform was again beginning to manifest itself. At the elections which had been taking place for some years the candidates had been asked for pledges. The Liberal party had now for many years identified themselves with this question, and with popular interests generally, and it was becoming apparent that the Tory party were being stirred up to a little species of rivalry on the subject, and this gave a "party" complexion to some of the Reform movements that took place after this date. It had also become the fashion for members of the House of Commons, with a view to keeping Reform generally alive, to make an annual motion upon some limited section of the question, and raise a discussion upon it. The most conspicuous of those members was Mr. Locke King. In 1858 he brought in a bill for the abolition of the property

qualification required of English and Irish members, and
he carried it. It was not really opposed by either party
in Parliament, and as it was a requirement that did not
apply to Scotland, and was besides understood to be a
sham, the House passed it. He followed this up by
proposing a measure for the extension of the franchise
for counties in England and Wales to occupiers of £10
per annum, but as it was supposed that this would rather
increase than abate the anomalies of the representative
system, it was extensively opposed. It was, however,
read a second time on June 10; but as the House
was busy with the Indian question, and the session was
advanced, the bill was dropped. Then Mr. Caird tried
to get a bill introduced for the purpose of assimilating
the Scotch county franchise with that of England, but
the motion was negatived. Mr. Berkeley brought in his
annual motion for the ballot, but was defeated by a
majority of 294 to 197.

In the following year (1859) it was announced by a ✓
Tory ministry, in the speech from the throne, that Parliamentary Reform was to be taken up as a cabinet question; and shortly after Parliament met the 28th of February was fixed for the first reading of the ministerial
bill. After some general observations Mr. Disraeli proceeded to the consideration of the franchise both in
counties and in boroughs. It was proposed, he said, not
to alter the limits of the franchise, but to introduce into
boroughs a new kind of franchise founded upon personal
property, and to give a vote to persons having property
to the amount of £10 a year in the Funds, Bank stock,
and East India stock; a person having £60 in a savings-
bank would under the bill be an elector for the borough
in which he resided; as well as the recipients of pensions

in the naval, military, and civil services amounting to £20 a year. Dwellers in a portion of a house whose aggregate rent was £20 a year would likewise have a vote. The suffrage would also be conferred upon graduates of the universities, ministers of religion, members of the legal profession and of the medical body, and certain schoolmasters. In considering the county franchise he reviewed the controversy respecting the Chandos clause in the Act of 1832. To terminate the heart-burnings arising from it, and to restore the county constituency to its natural state, and bring about a general content and sympathy between the different portions of the constitu-

ent body, the government proposed to recognize the principle of identity of suffrage between the counties and the towns. They proposed that Boundary Commissioners should visit the boroughs in England, re-arrange them, and adapt them to the altered circumstances of the times. Their appointment would be delegated to the Enclosure Commissioners. The effect of giving to counties a £10 franchise would be, according to the estimate of the government, to add to the county constituency 200,000. Having laid before the House the character of the proposed electoral body, he next proceeded to state how it was proposed they should be registered, and how they were to vote. Overseers of parishes would be required to furnish a list of owners as well as occupiers, which would be a self-acting register. It was proposed that the number of polling-places should be greatly increased; that every parish having 200 electors should be a polling-place; that every voter should vote in the place where he resided, and that those who liked it might vote by polling-papers instead of going to the hustings, precautions being provided against fraud and personation. A

complete representation, he proceeded to observe, did not
depend upon the electoral body; it also depended upon
whether the different interests of the country were adequately represented. Discarding the principle of population, and accepting as a truth that the function of that
House was to represent, not the voice of a numerical
majority or the influence of a predominant property, but
the various interests of the country, the government had
felt it to be their duty to see whether there were interests not represented, and whether the general representation of the country could be matured and completed;
and they proposed to add four members to the West
Riding of Yorkshire, two to South Lancashire, and two
to Middlesex; and that the following towns should be
represented :—Hartlepool, Birkenhead, West Bromwich
and Wednesbury, Burnley and Staleybridge, Croydon
and Gravesend. Assuming that in the opinion of the
House its numbers ought not to be increased, means
must be found for the representation of these interests,
and those means had been found before in similar circumstances and in the same constitutional spirit. He
promised that a schedule of places now sending two
members to Parliament, which was intended should hereafter return only one each, should be laid before the
House this day; but the cry of "Name, name" being
loudly raised, Mr. Disraeli, after a little well-feigned
reluctance, proceeded to mention the names. They were
Honiton, Thetford, Totness, Harwich, Evesham, Wells,
Richmond, Marlborough, Leominster, Lymington, Ludlow, Andover, Knaresborough, Tewkesbury, and Maldon.
With a few words in conclusion, in which he described
the measure as "wise, prudent, adequate to the occasion,
conservative, and framed by men who reverence the past,

M

MR. DIS-
RAELI'S BILL
OF 1859.
are proud of the present, and confident of the future," Mr. Disraeli resumed his seat amidst considerable cheering.

Lord J. Russell's speech.
Lord John Russell said that there were two points in Mr. Disraeli's statement which had filled him with great apprehension. The first was what he understood him to say regarding freeholders in towns, amounting to 90,000 or 100,000, that they were no longer to vote for the county. ' So far from this title to vote being an evil requiring a remedy, it was a very great advantage. ᐧ The other point was a serious omission, namely, that little or nothing was said for the working-classes. Unless more satisfaction was meant to be given to the country it would be better not to change the representation at all.

Mr. Roebuck's speech.
Mr. Roebuck observed that a change of the representation was only justifiable when it led to a better state of things. His objection to the bill was that it would lead to a worse state. It would not give one iota of power to the working-classes. It was a measure of disfrancisement, not of enfranchisement; and it would be opposed in every stage.

Mr. Bright's speech.
Mr. Bright said a government representing a party which had always opposed the extension of political power to the people ought not to have undertaken to settle this question. He took exception to a great many points in the bill, but chiefly to the total exclusion of the working-classes from power. The new franchises were, he said, absurd; they seemed intended merely to make it appear that something was given. He insisted upon the dissatisfaction that would be created by the withdrawal of their county vote by the freeholders in towns. It would have been better, he thought, if Mr. Disraeli had adhered to the ancient maxims of his party, or had

adopted a measure of his opponents, than have introduced a bill which must create anger and disgust throughout the country, which would disturb everything and settle nothing.

A few days after the bill was introduced Lord John Russell gave notice that he should move the following resolution:—" That this House is of opinion that it is neither just nor politic to interfere in the manner proposed by this bill with the freehold franchise as hitherto exercised in counties in England and Wales, and that no readjustment of the franchise will satisfy this House or the country which does not provide for a greater extension of the suffrage in cities and boroughs than is contemplated in the present measure."

In order to remove one of the objections to the measure Mr. Disraeli gave notice of the following clause: "Provided always, that any person who at the passing of this act shall be entitled to be registered as a voter for any county in respect of his ownership of any freehold, copyhold, or leasehold interest in property situate within the limits of any borough, shall, in case he shall think proper to claim the same, according to the provisions hereinafter contained, have the option to be registered in respect of such property for the county within which such borough is situate; but, in order to be so registered, such claim must be sent in to the overseers of the parish in which such property shall be situate not later than the twenty-fourth day of July in the year next but one following the passing of this act; and after such claim shall have been once made and admitted for such county the claimant shall be incapacitated from ever claiming to vote for such borough in respect of the same, or in respect of his ownership of any other freehold, copyhold, or lease-

MR. DIS-
RAELI'S BILL
OF 1859.

hold property in such borough, so long as he shall continue to hold the qualification in respect of which he shall
have so claimed to vote for the county as aforesaid."

Lord   J.
Russell's
speech.

Lord John Russell immediately rose and proposed his
amendment. He strongly objected to the taking away
from freeholders in towns the county vote, and he also
urged that the bill would enable landed proprietors to
flood small boroughs with faggot-votes. He also contended that while the measure of the government destroys
what is ancient, it does not provide for what is new. Since
the Reform Act, which gave the franchise to £10 occupiers in boroughs, the working-classes have made great
progress in knowledge and capacity. "Now the basis on
which the representation should rest is fitness for the
functions in the constituency. Can you say that there
are not persons below the class of £10 householders
thoroughly fit for the suffrage? There are thousands of
persons fit to exercise the franchise who are excluded.
Two questions—Roman Catholic Emancipation and Corn-
law Repeal—were refused to reason and calm petitions,
and granted to noise, clamour, and agitation. It was to
avoid a similar result, and not to gain popularity, that in
1851 the then government proposed an extension of the
franchise. In 1851 I proposed a certain franchise. In
1854 I proposed a modification of that franchise. I will
not say now what that franchise ought to be at the
present day. I hold that it is for the government of the
day to propose the franchise they may think right."

Lord Stan-
ley's speech.

In reply Lord Stanley held that the bill did not exclude the working-classes, but provided for their dis-
criminating admission in the property qualification and
the lodger and savings-bank franchises. He quoted Mr.
John Stuart Mill and Mr. Holyoake, who represent per-

sons of extreme political opinions, to show that the working-classes should not be indiscriminately admitted to the franchise. The principle should be admission by selection, and not admission in the mass, and for that the bill provided. As to the small boroughs, their existence could not be defended upon principle; but if they had been disfranchised the bill could not have been carried. Besides, there was a great difficulty in the redistribution of seats. Therefore ministers only dealt with the subject so far as the exigency demanded.

Mr. Horsman asked, Was this the precise moment when, although we had peace to-day we might have war to-morrow, to transfer political power from the middle-classes to a wider area not up to the mark of education required to make the majesty of the intellect of England confront with effect foreign powers? The bill of the government was emphatically a bill for the middle-class. The cause was theirs down to the verge at which the influence of that class would melt away amidst the necessities of manual labour, and the turbulence of concentrated numbers. " If they of the middle-class," he continued, "like to abandon that cause they abdicated their own power, and with it all which has hitherto made the resources of England unshaken amidst the vicissitudes of commerce and the calamities of war. If they honestly think the time has come when it is safe to accept the counter principle which you advance, viz. that political power should begin to descend to the working-class— not knowing where that principle, once adopted, can stop till it reaches manhood suffrage—then I say with the middle-class the responsibility must rest. Meanwhile, you in this House will determine whether it is your duty thus abruptly to sign away the influence of that class of

MR. DIS-
RAELI'S BILL
OF 1859.
which you are still the representatives and trustees—
whether you really secure the title-deeds of their commerce, and take solid guarantees for the safety of their
old English freedom by accepting an amendment which
commits you to a pledge to the working-class—a pledge
which you can never redeem to their satisfaction until
you have placed capital and knowledge at the command
of impatient poverty and uninstructed numbers."

Mr. Bright's
speech.
Mr. Bright, in a powerful speech, said: "Now, the
people out of doors understand by a Reform Bill a large
enfranchisement, and larger, freer constituencies. The bill
does not meet that demand. It gets rid of the most independent electors from counties, and insidiously proposes to alter the boundaries of boroughs to complete the
work. But not all boroughs. Some boroughs are not
towns at all. Droitwich and Petersfield are examples.
But, if the line is to be drawn between counties and
boroughs, it must be drawn in all cases. The bill, however, would shut out as many as possible in boroughs in
one case and not interfere in the other. I find everything has been done in one direction and one only. The
object is to make the representation of counties more
exclusively territorial. Is that desirable? Why, the
150 gentlemen elected by the territorial interest have
been the chief difficulty in the way of carrying every
measure demanded by the country. Ask Lord Lyndhurst,
ask Sir James Graham, ask Lord Aberdeen, ask Mr.
Disraeli, who in 1852 was turned out because he was
forced to meet the demands of his party with regard to
the malt-tax. Does any one believe that this is the sort
of bill which Mr. Disraeli thinks the best for the country?
He knows that the bill is framed to satisfy the prejudices
of the 150 gentlemen who sit behind him. As to the

small boroughs they are only a refuge for the politically Mr. Dis-RAELI'S BILL OF 1859. destitute—a shelter for what are called 'deserving objects.' What would be the effect of the voting-paper system upon small boroughs? I know no limit whatever to the amount of corruption it may occasion." Mr. Bright exerted himself to show that the bill would exclude the working-classes, telling them they are dangerous; that these are privileges they ought not to share. He pictured their improved mental, moral, and physical condition; and yet, he said, the government tells them they are as dangerous and ignorant as they were twenty-seven years ago!

Sir Stafford Northcote—after suggesting a variety of Sir S. North-cote's speech. reasons in favour of a uniformity of suffrage for all classes of voters, and citing *data* to show that the probable addition to the constituency by the bill would be one-third, or 300,000—observed that the government invited the House to deal with this measure practically, to go into committee and there discuss any definite proposals for the amendment of a bill which contained elements for a settlement of the question.

Mr. Cardwell contended that variety of franchise was Mr. Cardwell's speech. the rule of the constitution, and that, in order not to unsettle ancient prescription, a Reform Bill should deal with the county franchise according to the history of that franchise, and with the borough franchise according to its own peculiar history. If a new great principle was imparted into the British constitution that would become a vital and animated principle, pervading all its parts and affecting all its operations. Comparing the history of this country with that of other countries, it would be found that freedom, not equality, had been the desire of the British people; and equality rather than freedom had

been the desire of other countries. The principle of
uniformity was wholly foreign to our constitution, and
dangerous in its consequences; and as the resolution was
favourable to an alteration both in the county and the
borough franchise, while it was adverse to the principle
of uniformity, he should vote for it and against the
second reading of the bill.

Lord Palmerston said he too was going to give his
cordial support to the resolution moved by Lord J. Russell. Long as the debate had lasted, and as it was likely
to last, he could not say that the time and the attention
which the House had bestowed upon the subject had
been entirely thrown away. At the beginning they had
been led to believe that the identity of the suffrage and
the disfranchisement of the borough freeholders were
fundamental principles of the bill, but he rejoiced to hear
that the government held every part of the bill to be
open to consideration in the committee, including even
the propositions contained in the resolution. When the
present administration applied themselves to the framing
of a measure of Reform they would naturally discern
certain defects and imperfections in the Act of 1832.
The county franchise required to be lowered, and, upon
further considerations, he was of opinion that the borough
franchise should be reduced below £10. Then it would
be a question whether there should be a transference of
seats from small constituencies to unrepresented places.
Upon this point he was not disposed to quarrel with the
government measure; and he assigned reasons why, in his
opinion, small boroughs should be retained. But the
government had inserted in their bill provisions totally
inconsistent with the principles of the constitution, com-
mitting an act of injustice against those county freeholders

who happened to reside in boroughs, and identifying the town and county franchise, thereby destroying an ancient principle of the constitution, which provided for a marked distinction between them, and actually establishing electoral districts. The principles of the bill being so unjust the question was whether the measure ought to be resisted on the second reading, and that had been his first impression; but he had since thought the most expedient course under the circumstances was to propose the amendment, and the government ought to thank Lord J. Russell for relieving them from a serious difficulty. In considering the courses the government might pursue he believed they would neither resign nor resort to a dissolution; and he felt assured that they would not adopt the course of abandoning the bill. They would, no doubt, feel it their duty to go on with it, and would, indeed, be bound, and even compelled, to conform to the decision of the House.

Sir James Graham said he wished not to see the day when it became necessary to reconsider the fundamental principles of the constitution. The measure of 1832 produced an immense change; it had been called a bloodless revolution; it took power from the aristocracy and gave it to the middle-classes, its object being to blend property and numbers. Since that period we had enjoyed better legislation, more prosperity, and less civil discord than at any other period of equal duration. Upon the whole, therefore, the experiment had been successful, and he had hoped that it would have been a final one. In this he had been disappointed; and the object of all reformers should be, when change was required, to prevent the necessity, if possible, of further alterations. In this bill three principles were contained, namely, identity of

MR. DIS-
RAELI'S BILL
OF 1859.

suffrage, electoral districts, and voting papers, which had a direct tendency to consequences most to be apprehended, and it seemed as if the bill—"too clever by half"—had been framed so as to obtain support from every quarter of the House.

Mr. Glad-
stone's
speech.

Mr. Gladstone concurred in nearly everything that had been said against it. "I cannot be a party to the disfranchisement of the county freeholders residing in boroughs. I cannot be a party to the uniformity of the franchise. I cannot be a party to a Reform Bill which does not lower the suffrage in boroughs. I may go a step further, and say it appears to me that the lowering of the suffrage in boroughs is the main purpose of having a Reform Bill, and that unless we are to have that lowering of the suffrage it would be better that we should not waste our time on this subject." He was bound, however, to say that he approved of that portion of the bill relating to the redistribution of seats. He understood Lord Palmerston to approve of it. (Lord Palmerston assented.) The question of redistribution of seats was full half the measure. The bill of 1854 would have failed, because it proposed extensive disfranchisement. Here Mr. Gladstone went into a defence of the small boroughs. He regarded them as the means of supplying the race of men who were trained to carry on the government of the country, the masters of civil wisdom, like Mr. Burke, Sir James Macintosh, Mr. Pelham, Lord Chatham, Mr. Fox, Mr. Pitt, Mr. Canning, Sir Robert Peel, all of whom sat first for small boroughs. If there was to be no ingress to the House but one, and that one the suffrages of a large mass of voters, there would be a dead level of mediocrity. The extension, the durability of our liberty, were to be attributed, under Providence,

to distinguished statesmen introduced to the House at an MR. DIS
RAELI'S BILL
OF 1859. early age. But large constituencies would not return boys, and therefore he hoped the small boroughs would be retained. These facts formed a reason for going into committee.

Mr. Roebuck said they were about to reform the MR. ROE-
buck's
speech. Reform Act, and the questions were—What was it that required reform? and what were the means to attain the end? One great blemish in the Reform Act of 1832 was the exclusion from power of the working-classes. These classes had since been increasing in intelligence, showing themselves worthy of participating in power with the other classes; and the two great objects of any Reform Bill were to extend the suffrage to the working-classes, and to regulate the distribution of the electoral bodies. Did the bill of the government attain either end? He believed that it would be anything but satisfactory to the working-classes; but he believed, in opposition to Mr. Bright, that good could be got from the bill. He proceeded to consider how this could be done, passing under review the merits, as reformers, of Lord Palmerston and Lord J. Russell, expressing no implicit confidence in either; and he asked the government whether, if the bill went into committee, and the House enacted that the borough franchise should be £6, the county franchise being £10, they would accept the alteration? If they would, he said, he was ready to vote for the second reading of the bill.

A division showed 291 for the second reading, and Bill re-
jected. 330 against it. The government resigned—Lord Palmerston took office, and the subject was postponed till the following year.

On March 1, 1860, the ministry of Lord Palmerston

LORD PAL-
MERSTON'S
BILL OF 1860.

professed to deal with reform, but the country was apathetic on the subject, and the ministry was not in earnest. Lord John Russell was intrusted with the bill. Before he entered into the subject he disclaimed entirely a wish to introduce a new constitution; and if he now proposed to amend the representation of the people, it was not, he said, to be understood as a concession that the Reform Act of 1832 had failed; on the contrary, he believed that no measure had so few faults. What the government proposed to do was, in a simple manner, to supply the omissions and remedy the defects of that act. They proposed to add to £10 occupation franchise

Lord John
Russell's
speech.

in counties a security that would make it a *bona fide* franchise; that where the land was attached to a house, not being a dwelling-house, the building should not be of a less annual value than £5. The next question was as to lowering the borough franchise. The Act of 1832 was framed not to exclude the working-classes, but to open the franchise wider to the middle-classes; but it would be a great evil to continue much longer the practical exclusion of a great number of the working-classes, who, by their qualifications and character, were competent to exercise the franchise freely and independently, and in his opinion it would add strength to the constitution if a certain number of these classes qualified for it should be admitted to the franchise. He thought that the legislature ought not to wait for an agitation that would force demands upon Parliament; that if the desire for their franchise by those classes was founded upon a fair appreciation of their own qualities, and it could be conceded with safety to the constitution, the concession should not be delayed because there had not been any agitation. In another respect the government had thought it on the whole better to make the measure as simple as possible; they had not introduced franchises not known to the constitution, or what had been termed "fancy franchises." What they proposed was to extend the borough franchise now enjoyed. One question had been frequently discussed with reference to the franchise —namely, whether it should be a rated franchise. He stated reasons why the government had thought it would not be advisable, but, on the contrary, practically inconvenient, to have a rated franchise. The next question was, what should be the gross annual rental; and Lord John, taking the number of electors in cities and boroughs now on the register at 440,000, showed the respective numbers that would be added if the occupation franchise was reduced to £9, £8, £7, and £6; the latter sum would give an aggregate number of electors in the cities and boroughs in England and Wales of 634,000, which he thought not an extravagant addition. With regard to the character of the persons who would be admitted, the accounts from the different cities and boroughs varied extremely; in some, rents were low, in others high; but he believed that a £6 franchise would include a great number of the working-classes; that the number would not be extravagant, and that their admission would be a great benefit to the constitution. He now came to another question, totally different. He believed it was quite necessary that, besides great counties and large cities and manufacturing towns, smaller places should return members to Parliament; and that, if the government was to be carried on in that House, it was desirable to have more than two classes of representatives for counties and for great cities, and no plan of reform had proceeded upon a different principle. Having laid down this general rule, and treating the subject practically, there was a question which concerned the present state of the House. When the Reform Bill of 1831 was introduced there was no difficulty in abolishing the title to return members enjoyed by certain boroughs with few or no electors. Without going now into the question as to how many small boroughs there ought to be, the government proposed to go only a certain length beyond the bill of last year, which took away one member from fifteen places returning two members. The principle of total disfranchisement was one of very great importance, and ought not to be adopted without some great and palpable public benefit. The government proposed a much milder course—that the following boroughs should return one member instead of two, as at present—viz. Honiton, Thetford, Totnes, Harwich, Evesham, Wells, Richmond, Marlborough, Leominster, Lymington, Ludlow, Andover, Knaresborough, Tewkesbury, Maldon, Ripon, Cirencester, Huntingdon, Chippenham, Bodmin, Dorchester, Marlow, Devizes, Hertford, and Guildford. There would, therefore, be twenty-five seats to be disposed of, and it was proposed that the following counties should return additional members — viz. the West Riding of Yorkshire, two; and each of the following one: viz. the southern division of Lancashire, the northern division of Lancashire, the county of Middlesex, the western division of Kent, the southern division of Devonshire, the southern division of Staffordshire; the North Riding of Yorkshire, the parts of Lindsey (Lincolnshire), the southern division of Essex, the eastern division of Somerset, the western division of Norfolk, the western division of Cornwall, and the northern division of Essex. Thus fifteen additional members would be given to the counties, and with regard to boroughs it was proposed that Kensington and Chelsea (as one borough) should return two members; that Birkenhead, Staleybridge, and Burnley should return one member each; and Manchester, Liverpool, Birmingham, and Leeds three members each instead of two; and the London University one member. This, he repeated, was a simple plan, containing as little novelty as possible. In conclusion, he remarked, that although he had not been successful in the two measures he had proposed upon this subject he was not discouraged, and felt sure that the measure he now offered to the House would strengthen the foundations of the constitution. LORD PAL-MERSTON'S BILL OF 1860.

Mr. Cardwell, as Irish secretary, likewise introduced a measure for Ireland. It reduced, he said, the qualification for voting for counties from £12 (required by the Act of 1850) to £10, and substituted a borough franchise of £6 for £8, and it proposed to give to the county of Cork and the city of Dublin three members each instead of two, supplying the additional members from the four seats in England suspended and unappropriated. He hoped, he observed, that a day might come when Parliament would think it right to give a member to the Queen's University; but, looking at the circumstances of the university, he did not think it right to make such a proposal yet. The bill proposed likewise to remove the disqualification of peers of Ireland to represent Irish constituencies. Irish Bill.

The lord-advocate asked leave to introduce a similar measure for Scotland, which appropriated two of the four suspended seats in England to the Scotch universities, and provided a £10 occupation franchise for counties, and a borough franchise of £6, the basis of franchise to Scotch Bill.

Lord Palmerston's Bill of 1860. be the valuation-rolls. It proposed to reduce the property qualification for counties from £10 to £5, enforcing residence unless the property were of the former amount. The second reading was moved on March 19. Mr.

Mr. Disraeli's speech. Disraeli was the first speaker. With reference to its first principle—the extension of the franchise in boroughs —he remarked that the late government in their bill did not look to numbers but to the fitness of those who were to receive the suffrage. This was not, however, the principle upon which the present government had proceeded. The existing borough constituency of England was 440,000, to which number this bill would add 217,000, and this addition would consist almost entirely of one homogeneous class. It was important to consider how this new constituency must act upon the old. In some boroughs the constituency would be trebled, in others doubled, and about one-half of the boroughs would be under the influence of the new class about to be enfranchised. He wished to put before the House the probable result of these facts. Had the new class shown no inclination to combine, or were they incapable of organization? Quite the reverse. The working-classes of this country had shown a remarkable talent for organization and a power of discipline and combination inferior to none, and to these classes the bill was about to give predominant power. He thought a measure which founded the constituency upon the principle of numbers, not fitness, and which added 200,000 electors, composing one homogeneous class, having the same interest, who would neutralize the voices of the present borough constituency, was not a wise and well-considered one. The next principle was the reduction of the county franchise. In reducing the qualification for this franchise one considera-

tion should, he said, be observed: the constituency should Lord Pal-
be fairly connected with the chief property and the chief merston's Bill of 1860.
industry of the country. This great consideration was
not observed if freeholders in a town, where votes might
be split, were to be allowed to vote for a district with
which they had no local sympathy or connection. Then
the fourth clause, which would disfranchise a great
number of voters for counties, would greatly reduce the
influence of the landed interest; and he objected to the
bill because the reconstruction of the county franchise
tended to diminish that salutary influence. The third
principle of the bill—the redistribution of parliamentary
seats—he objected to on the ground that it went too far
or not far enough, and that it was radically unsound.
Then the question was, What ought to be done? It was
a very bad bill. He knew only two members who approved it—its author and the member for Birmingham.
His opinion was that by the bill of 1859 the franchise
would have been more extended than by this bill; but
he was not prepared to say that he would reject the bill
upon the second reading. He hoped, however, that ultimately this uncalled-for and mischievous measure would
be withdrawn.

Mr. Baxter believed that the extending of the franchise Mr. Baxter's speech.
to the working-classes would strengthen, not impair, the
foundations of our institutions. Those classes were intelligent, and he did not think that the people of this
country were in the habit of voting in classes. The bill
had, he admitted, defects.

Mr. Rolt said, if he rightly understood the measure it Mr. Rolt.
made a large step towards severing the representation of
the people from the property of the country. This he
took to be its true principle. The bill of 1832 did this

N

LORD PAL-
MERSTON'S
BILL OF 1860.
professedly, and it was now proposed to do this a second time in little more than a quarter of a century. He warned the House that they could not stop at this point; they must proceed to household suffrage, and then to universal suffrage.

Mr. Bright's
speech.
Mr. Bright said he was in one respect in the same condition as Mr. Disraeli; he did not desire to reject the second reading of the bill, but he should not endeavour to persuade the House that it was a dangerous and fatal measure; on the contrary, though anxious for a good measure of parliamentary reform, he was ready to make due allowance for the difficulty of dealing with this question. It was evident that the bill met with two kinds of objectors—one who thought it went too far, another who wished it to go further. He did not oppose or advocate it upon either ground. He regarded the measure as the fulfilment of a pledge given by the government. As to the redistribution of seats, he had thought it would be better that the reform should be by steps, and this was a bill for reducing the franchise in counties and boroughs; it did not settle the question of disfranchisement or the transfer of seats, it rather unsettled it. If it passed it would not add more than 160,000 to the borough constituency. And how many of these would be working men? Not more than 100,000; and how could it then be said that they would swamp the other classes? The objection that the measure did not go far enough was more difficult to answer, and was a rational objection. He thought this parsimony on the part of the House was a mistake; that the character of the lower classes would justify a more liberal view of the matter. But if 300,000 or 400,000 were admitted to the franchise, he could not refuse the measure because in his opinion these numbers

ought to be doubled. He thought the bill failed in certain Lord Pal- points. He objected to the ratepaying clauses, to the merston's Bill of 1860. fourth clause, and to other details of the bill. With regard to the ballot, that question would be brought under consideration upon a future occasion, and he was convinced that under this bill there would be a still greater necessity for that measure. Upon the whole he urged upon the other side that under the circumstances of the country it was their duty as well as their interest to accept the bill.

After Mr. Stansfeld and Sir J. Pakington had spoken Sir George Grey urged that the objections to lowering Sir G. Grey. the borough franchise so as so admit the working-classes was, he contended, inconsistent with declarations made by the late government; and he did not believe, considering the character of those classes, that their admission to the franchise would, as Sir J. Pakington alleged, overpower the property of the country. The principle of the reduction of the borough franchise, and, practically, the admission of the working-classes to the franchise, had been in fact assented to by the House since issue was taken upon that question when the resolution moved by Lord J. Russell last year was submitted to the House. Sir George discussed the objections urged to the other parts of the bill relating to the county franchise and the redistribution of seats, and in conclusion observed that there never was a period when – the country being tranquil and prosperous—a measure of this nature was more likely to obtain a calm consideration.

Mr. Newdegate contended that the element of num- Mr. Newde-gate. bers being so enormously increased in the constituency, there should be an increase in the county representation, as proposed in 1854, in order to offer a resistance to

LORD PAL-
MERSTON'S
BILL OF 1860. what he considered a confiscation of real property by
taxation.

Sir E. B. Lyt-
ton's speech. Sir Edward Bulwer Lytton said that the numbers
admitted by the bill to the franchise would be sufficient
to overbear the interests of the existing constituency, and
it would not be a fair representation of the community
upon the theory of numbers. No security was taken for
the fitness of the class to be admitted; it was not required that those who were to have the lion's share in
political power should have a proportionate stake in the
country, and a regard for order, the foundation of property. This bill was designed to amend the representation; but would it improve it in respect to property,
station, and knowledge? It had been argued by Sir G.
Lewis that the time had come for greater progress in the
same direction as the great Reform Act; but this bill
went back in the very direction from which that act departed; it took a long stride towards the old scot-and-lot
voters, giving to the working-classes a preponderating
influence over property and knowledge. He would confer
a fair share of the representation upon the working-
class, but he would have some security for intelligence
and property. If this bill were passed a settlement of
the question would be as far off as ever; it would settle
nothing, and they were asked to pass it when the House
of Lords were making inquiries into an important point
which the House of Commons was expected to take for
granted.

Lord J. Rus-
sell's reply. Lord John Russell in reply said that objections had been
made on the other side to a reduction of the franchise
that would reach the working-classes. It was said that
those classes deserved the care and attention of the
House; but the representation generally was that they

were very poor, very ignorant, and very corrupt. There Lord Palmerston's Bill of 1860.
was a spirit of distrust of the working-classes holding
any political power. [This remark was met with a loud
cry of " No."] What, then, he asked, was the objection
to the admission of those classes? His impression was
that the speakers were of opinion that the working-classes
were not to be trusted; but the late government had
recognized their title to the franchise, and he believed it
would be a dangerous course to introduce a Reform Bill
without admitting the working-classes. Then it was
alleged that the bill was about to confer upon the poorer
classes the whole representation of the country; but this
allegation was without proof, and he showed that the
influence of the working-classes in their electoral functions
would be balanced by that of others.

Mr. Walter did not believe that there was any griev- Mr. Walter.
ance which gave that class a just cause for complaint.
They paid no direct taxes, and they had been relieved of
a great portion of the indirect. Unless some improvement could be attained it was best not to meddle with
parliamentary reform. If the present measure were to
pass, it behoved the House so to improve it as to make
it an honour and not a discredit to its author.

Mr. Du Cane urged that the bill was the most danger- Mr. Du Cane's speech.
ous and one-sided the House had ever had to deal with,
unsettling everything and settling nothing, and in its
consequences revolutionary. He pointed out what he
considered would be its injurious effects upon the county
constituency, in which a predominance would be exercised by house-occupiers, while in the boroughs 330,000
would be admitted at the low franchise, outnumbering the
other classes of voters, whereby the franchise would be
shut up in a narrower compass than by the bill of last

LORD PAL-
MERSTON'S
BILL OF 1860.
year. He urged strenuously what he regarded as a most important branch of the question, and which, he said, had not been sufficiently considered, the danger of making the working-classes, who had shown themselves in the late strike so capable of organization and combination, a preponderating element in the constitution, when about to inaugurate a constitutional change which was to be only the prelude to further changes.

Mr. J. Locke.
Mr. J. Locke argued that there was no danger in admitting the working-classes to a participation in the franchise. He believed that if the Conservatives had continued in power they also would have proposed a £6 franchise. He thought the bill of the government defective in its machinery, but capable of improvement.

Mr. Macau-
lay's speech.
Mr. Macaulay said he assumed that the object of the bill was to rectify defects in the Reform Act, of which, for many years, Lord John Russell had not been sensible. The £10 borough franchise, it was said, did not allow of an adequate representation to the middle-classes, and none at all to the working-classes. This, however, was very much a local question, having reference to the character of the different towns. Lord John Russell had only transposed the error, and this bill would be open to the same objection, in an aggravated form, as the Reform Act. The qualification given by this bill, he complained, had no reference to fitness, and it was uniform in its character; whereas he (Mr. Macaulay) desired a multiform composition of the constituency. The principle of the bill of the late government was selection; the principle of this bill was indiscriminate admission, there being no test of personal fitness except the amount of rent. Another objection was that, in a matter of so

much moment, there should be a fair and reasonable hope that the measure would be permanent; but if he was not greatly misinformed, there was a large party in the House who accepted the bill grudgingly indeed, and only as the commencement of a new agitation. He asked anyone to name a considerable statesman (not in the government) who gave an ostensible countenance to this measure, and he asserted that in society, as well as in that House, it was talked of universally with dislike and suspicion. LORD PAL-MERSTON'S BILL OF 1860.

The motion for the second reading was adopted without a division. The 4th of June was the day appointed for going into committee on the bills, and notice had been given of numerous amendments. Lord John Russell stated that the course which government intended to pursue was to proceed, in the first instance, with the English bill, and leave the Scotch and Irish bills over in the meantime. There then ensued a long discussion, accompanied with a motion for adjournment, which the government defeated by a majority of 21. But as the postponement of the measure for another session was urged by a very large section of the House, Lord John Russell was under the necessity of giving way. He accordingly withdrew the bill on the 11th of June, and even Mr. Bright, in the circumstances, did not blame him for the course he had taken.[1] Read a second time. Bill withdrawn.

Nothing more was done with reform till 1864, when Mr. Locke King brought forward his bill for the assimilation of the county with the borough franchise—the same measure that he proposed in 1858. Lord Palmerston voted for it, but urged that the country was not at present anxious for any change. It was negatived by a Various motions in 1864.

[1] *Annual Register*, 1860, p. 125.

majority—254 against 227. The next motion was by
Mr. Baines of Leeds, whose proposal was to lower the
borough franchise from £10 to £6. Mr. Cave moved
the previous question, and urged that the measure was
not needed. Mr. Gladstone supported Mr. Baines, and
remarked that although there was a general admission
that this was not a time at which it would be advisable
for the government to introduce a comprehensive measure
of parliamentary reform, yet he would not consent to the
amendment, which went the length of denying that there
was any need of reform. The "previous question" was
carried by a majority of 56. The ballot was the subject
of another debate, which was only remarkable as bringing out Lord Palmerston's opinion as to the fiduciary
character of the franchise. Mr. Berkeley, in moving for
leave to bring in the bill, contended that the Corrupt
Practices at Elections Act had proved so complete a
failure that corruption and malversation might be said
to flourish by Act of Parliament. Lord Palmerston remarked, "It deals with the right of voting as if it was
a personal right, which an individual is entitled to exercise
free from any responsibility; whereas I contend that the
vote is a trust to be exercised for the benefit of those
on whose behalf it is held." The bill was lost by a majority of 89.

In the following year—1865—Mr. Baines renewed his
motion for leave to bring in his bill for the reduction of
the borough franchise to £6, and the second reading was
fixed for May 3. Lord Elcho, seconded by Mr. Black of
Edinburgh, moved the previous question. There was a
smart debate, in which Mr. Lowe, though professing to
be still a Liberal, gave the extension of the franchise his
uncompromising opposition. He said, "I am inclined to

think that democracy in the present state of things would be a great misfortune. If driven to it, we must, of course, submit, and it may perhaps be better to do so than to give rise to a great internal commotion or civil war." He observed that the interests of the working-classes were better represented and protected by the House of Commons as at present constituted than if it were elected by themselves, because in these times legislation was a complicated science, requiring men of the highest education and intelligence to put it in practice. Mr. Disraeli admitted that there should be reform, but it should be *lateral* not *radical;* the extension of the franchise, not its degradation. The bill was lost by a majority of 288 against 214.

The session of 1866 opened with the prospect of a parliamentary struggle. Mr. Gladstone was determined to bring the reform question to a crisis. What had taken place up to this time was understood to be party warfare, not the business of reform. The war-note was sounded in the queen's speech, and was well known to mean all that was said. At the outset Mr. Clay, member for Hull, made a frivolous proposal to extend the franchise on the basis of an educational qualification. His bill provided that every man of full age might submit himself to be examined before the Civil Service Commissioners upon the four elementary subjects of reading, writing, spelling, and arithmetic, and upon the examination proving to be satisfactory he would receive a certificate entitling him to the exercise of the franchise. It was contended that the effect of the bill would be to admit the *élite* of the working-classes to the possession of the franchise, whilst it would prevent them from coming in in such high numbers as to counterbalance the claim

Mr. Glad-
stone's Bill
of 1866.
of intelligence and property. Upon the second reading a smart debate ensued, which was adjourned and never resumed. The bill was ultimately withdrawn.

On March 12 Mr. Gladstone, as leader of the Lower House, asked for leave to bring in a bill for reform. He stated that it had been announced by five administrations, in no less than six royal speeches, as time for the national representation to undergo a revision, and yet nothing had been done. The government, in the meantime, would confine themselves to a measure for the alteration of the elective franchise. In 1860 it was proposed to reduce the county franchise from £50 to £10, but in the present case the government proposed to modify that plan, and to reduce the county franchise to £14 of value. This,

His speech. however, would not apply to a house alone, but would apply equally to a house and land, provided the rental of either or both was not less than £14 per annum. This would correspond with a £12 rating franchise, and it was estimated that it would add 171,000 persons to the electoral lists. It was also proposed to recognize the possession of copyhold or leasehold property within the limits of boroughs, and to give them the same privileges as if they were freeholds within the limits of a borough. It was next proposed that all adult males who had deposited £50 in a savings-bank for two years should be entitled to be registered for the place in which they resided. This privilege would add from 10,000 to 15,000 electors to the constituences of England and Wales. An annual claim to be registered would be essentially necessary in the case of savings-bank voters. With regard to towns, there were at present four classes of occupiers, viz. rate-paying householders, compound householders, those who occupied portions of houses without being rated, and those who were the inmates of other people's families. The growth of the constituencies in towns had barely kept pace with the growth of the population generally; but he was glad to find that the infusion of the working-classes in the present constituencies was larger than he expected, being in boroughs 21 per cent. It was intended to abolish the ratepaying clauses of the Reform Act, which, it was hoped, would admit 25,000 voters above the line of £10. Persons who were now in the position of compound householders would in future be treated like ratepayers, and it was believed that votes would thereby be given to 35,000 persons. In showing the evil consequences resulting from the ratepaying clauses the right honourable gentleman said:—"In some places it has been supposed that the local officers, under the in- fluence of particular bias, did not apply for the payment of the rate until the date had passed when the payment of it would avail with a view to the exercise of the franchise. The rates of the two parties of voters are paid by the political agents in the interest of the respective candidates; and one local gentleman who very kindly sent this information, as far as his own place was concerned, hoped that the communication would be considered confidential. There were certain boroughs where, by common consent, the law is overlooked on both sides. In Liverpool I do not overstate the case when I say that there are not less than between 6000 and 7000 persons, probably more, whose rates are habitually and ordinarily collected from the landlord by arrangement with the parish officers, and are therefore disfranchised without any neglect of their own. They are not compound householders, but their rates are collected from the land-lord. We expect that the victims of this class are almost all of them persons who belong to the designation of working-men. We shall admit not less than 25,000 ✓ above the line of £10 by the abolition of this clause. Then we come to the question of compound householders. The principle upon which we go is that they should be treated exactly as ratepaying householders, if the rent of their house is of such a scale that in the judgment of the legislature they are suitable persons to be enfranchised.

"Then comes the third of the classes to which I formerly alluded—that class which is also very numerous in the metropolis, the occupiers of flats or portions of houses not under separate landlords, and not the subject of separate rating. As to these, we can do nothing but leave them as they are. If they can show that the portion of the tenement inhabited by them is of the clear annual value of £10, and if they get themselves rated, as I believe they are entitled to ask, though legal difficulties of this kind form an almost insuperable obstacle, they may by a circuitous process get themselves placed on the list of voters.

"As to lodgers, we propose to place them exactly on the footing of those holding tenements of the clear yearly value of £10, without taking into consideration rates and taxes. These will be entitled, through a claim made from year to year, to be placed on the register."

What the government, therefore, proposed to do was, to take the amount next above £6, namely, a £7 clear annual value, a figure not very far from that apparently fixed by the Small Tenements Voting Act; and it was calculated that the net number of persons enfranchised by this provision would be 144,000. The total number of new voters of all classes would be—

In counties,	.	.	.	.	.	.	.	172,000	Mr. Glad-
In towns,	.	.	.	.	.	.	.	204,000	stone's Bill
Lodger and savings-banks franchises,			.	.	24,000	of 1866.

Total, ...   400,000

Of this number one-half would belong to the working-classes and one-half to what might be termed a new middle-class. The only remaining provision in the bill had reference to the dockyards, and it was proposed to disfranchise the labourers in those places. Such was the scheme of the government.

The bill was received with considerable opposition, and Mr. Laing's speech. gave rise to a division in the Liberal ranks. Mr. Laing declared himself a dissentient from the policy of the government, of which he was usually a supporter. He said that the chancellor of the exchequer had himself shown the impolicy of dealing in a hurried and precipitate manner with a measure which required the most grave and cautious consideration. He was indisposed to re-open a question which he thought had been satisfactorily settled many years since; and he objected to a bill which, while professing to amend the representation of the people, gave as many members to Honiton as to Liverpool, Manchester, Edinburgh, Glasgow, or Dublin. He admitted that he was elected to support Lord Palmerston's policy, but he contended that the present was a measure which that statesman would not have sanctioned.

Mr. Lowe contended that the proposal for increasing Mr. Lowe's speech. the county franchise by 172,000, and the voters in towns by 204,000, would increase the expense of elections and make extensive changes in the distribution of political power. He complained that the chancellor of the ex-

Mr. Glad-
stone's Bill
of 1866.
chequer had not stated a single ground which justified the introduction of the bill. He had not proved that the working-classes were at present excluded from the franchise, for the returns just collected by the government showed that a considerable percentage of them were already voters. For many years past, owing to the discovery of gold in Australia and California, and owing to the great emigration which had taken place, the condition of the working-classes had gradually improved, and the result was that a process of spontaneous enfranchisement had grown up and was going steadily forward. He believed that process would continue, and that the tendency of the present system would eventually be to put the working-classes in the majority. The chancellor of the exchequer appeared to be of opinion that a constituency could not be too large so long as improper people were not admitted to it. Before bringing in a bill to alter the constitution of the House, the government ought to have instituted a minute and careful examination into its present state. If the character of constituencies out of doors was lowered, the members sent to the House would be of a lower class too, and the tone of public men would likewise be lowered. He warned the House, therefore, how it allowed constituencies to become too democratic. Having pointed out what he considered to be the shortcomings of the House of Commons, the right honourable gentleman said that in 1832 there was a practical grievance, but that in 1866 the grievance was altogether theoretical. There was now no pressure from without from the working-classes.

Mr. Villiers'
speech.
Mr. Villiers urged, in reply to the arguments of Mr. Lowe, that Parliament was pledged to deal with the question of reform, and reminded that right honourable

gentleman that he himself had declared that "no reform would be satisfactory that did not reduce the franchise." The present was not, he thought, a fortunate moment to cast a slur upon the working-classes, after the fortitude and endurance which they had recently exhibited in the manufacturing districts. The government had brought in a simple bill to lower the franchise because they were persuaded that under existing circumstances it would not be possible to carry a more extensive measure in the present session.

Mr. Fawcett, remarking on the inconsistency of Mr. Lowe, said he would put to him a simple question; and if he could not answer it satisfactorily, his reasoning, however profound, would not much influence the country. The question was—Did not Mr. Lowe join in that combination which declared that no government was worthy of the confidence of the country unless it reduced the borough franchise? Further, Had he not been a distinguished member of the government which came into office expressly to carry an extension of the franchise? and did he not sit on the treasury bench when an extension of the suffrage was proposed much wider than the present bill? But, so far as Mr. Lowe was concerned, he asked how it was that he had taken office under an administration which had deposed Lord Derby's government because it had not been liberal enough in the matter of reform?

Mr. Bright said: "What is the reason these gentlemen, who had been holders of office, take this course against the government bill? I will not deal in any insinuations, but I will say that, from gentlemen who held office with ministers in this country, but happened to be left out of what may be called the 'daily ministrations,' we had a

right to expect a very minute account of the reasons why they change their opinions before we can turn round and change with them. These are the gentlemen who all at once start up as the great teachers of statesmanship in the House and the country. What I complain of is this, that when place recedes into the somewhat dim past, that which in office was deemed patriotism vanishes with it. Last night Mr. Horsman made an attack upon so humble an individual as myself. He is the first of the new party who has expressed his great grief, who has retired into what may be called his political cave of Adullam, and he has called about him every one that was
in distress and every one that was discontented. The right honourable gentleman has been long anxious to form a party in this House. He has made efforts to bring over many members to his party or cabal, and lastly he has succeeded in hooking Mr. Lowe. A cabinet minister had once said that two men would make a party. When a party is formed of two men so amiable, so discreet, as the two right honourable gentlemen, we may hope to see for the first time in Parliament a party perfectly harmonious and distinguished by mutual and unbroken trust. But there is one difficulty which it is impossible to remove. This party of two is like the Scotch terrier, so covered with hair that you could not tell which was the head and which was the tail. The right honourable member for Calne told us that he had some peculiar election experiences. There are some men who make discord wherever they appear. The right honourable gentleman, on going down to Kidderminster, got into some unpleasing altercation with somebody, and it ended with having his head broken. But I am happy to say, and the House will bear witness, that with regard to his

power now, it is probably as strong as before he took his leave of Kidderminster and went to Calne, a village in the west of England. The right honourable gentleman found on the list of electors about 174 names, of whom, according to the blue-book, about seven were working-men. But the real constituent of the right honourable gentleman is the Marquis of Lansdowne, and he could send in his butler or his groom instead of the right honourable gentleman, to represent the borough. I think, in one sense, regarding the right honourable gentleman as an intellectual gladiator in this House, we are much indebted to the Marquis of Lansdowne that he did not do that."

After some further discussion leave was given to bring in the bill. Earl Grosvenor thereupon gave notice that on the second reading of the bill he would submit an amendment to the effect that the House was of opinion that it was inexpedient for the House to consider the bill for the reduction of the franchise until it had before it the whole scheme of the government for the amendment of the representation of the people. Sir W. Hutt also gave notice that he would move that the bill should not take effect until the Redistribution Bill was passed. There was thus raised the same question that has been raised in more recent times. This last notice of amendment, however, was afterwards withdrawn; but a combined movement of different parties in the House took place to compel the government at all events to disclose their intentions in the first instance with regard to redistribution. Mr. Gladstone, in the course of his reply, stated that the government was not unwilling to give a promise that after the second reading of the bill, and before going into committee, they would state their intentions with respect to redistribution, and likewise with respect to the franchise in Scotland and Ireland.

Agitation.

There was a great deal of discussion both in the press and on the platform throughout the country upon the merits of the bill. It assumed, however, an organic form and was conducted really by the leaders of the people. There was no popular agitation in the rude and unorganized shape that it took in 1831 and 1832. It was kept within bounds, and assumed a sort of representative character, the Liberals taking the lead. There were a great many provincial gatherings in different parts of the country, and Mr. Gladstone was present at one of the Meeting in Liverpool most important of them at Liverpool, along with the Duke of Argyll, Lord Clarence Paget, Mr. Goschen, M.P., and many others. He concluded one of the speeches he delivered on this occasion as follows:—"I am sorry that at this moment immediate danger to the measure that the government has introduced should proceed from a name honoured in the lists of the aristocracy. A notice of motion has been given by Lord Grosvenor for the purpose of defeating the bill; and we are told, and as the announcement has been publicly made without contradiction, we are, I suppose, truly told, that that notice is to be seconded by Lord Stanley. I know not two individuals more entitled to respect and honour in the position they occupy; but I am bound to say that I Mr. Glad-stone's speech. think a more deplorable arrangement was never made. A more gross blunder never was committed than when in the councils of political party, with that kind of cleverness which so often outwits itself, it was determined that the representatives of two of our noblest and most ancient houses should come forward combinedly for the purpose of defeating an act of grace, and what is likewise an act

of justice to the great community of the country. How- Mr. Glad-
ever, gentlemen, much lamenting that unhappy instance, stone's Bill of 1866.
I am persuaded that that is not to be taken as an indica-
tion that there will be a fundamental change in that wise
moderation which has hitherto for the most part distinguished the conduct of the most favoured members of
society, those upon whom the bounties of Providence
have been poured out in the largest abundance. I do not
think that that movement, formidable though it be, is
likely to succeed. We have framed a measure, I think,
in the strictest spirit of moderation. We do not desire, we
should be the first to resist, sudden and violent sweeping
changes; but the progressive enlargement of the popular
franchise—with due regard to the state and circumstances
of the country—we consider not to be liable to the application of any of these epithets. Having produced this
measure, framed in a spirit of moderation, we hope to
support it with decision. It is not in our power to secure Mr. Glad-
the passing of the measure; that rests more with you, and stone's speech in
more with those whom you represent, and of whom you Liverpool.
are a sample, than it does with us; still, we have a great
responsibility and are conscious of it, and we do not
intend to flinch from it. We stake ourselves, we stake
our existence as a government, whether it be worth much
or little is not for us to say, but such as it is we stake it,
and we also stake our political character, on the adoption
of the bill in its main provisions. You have a right to
expect from us that we should tell you what we mean,
and that the trumpet which it is our business to blow
shall give forth no uncertain sound. Its sound has not
been, and I trust will not be, uncertain. We have passed
the Rubicon, we have broken the bridge and burned the
boats behind us. We have advisedly cut off the means

of retreat; and having done this, we hope that as far as
time has yet permitted, we have done our duty to the
crown and the nation. The result, gentlemen, is in other
hands than ours. I beseech you, I beseech all reflecting
Englishmen in whose hands by the well-understood constitution of our country the ultimate settlement of this
great issue is lodged, to consider what the future is to be.
I cannot doubt, from the extraordinary working and
movement of society, that there is on the part of the
masses of the community a forward and onward movement, which will be perfectly safe and harmless and
infinitely profitable if we only deal with it wisely and in
time. But read the signs of the times—the voice that
spoke as man never spoke, rebuked those in authority
who could not read the signs of the times. Does any
man really suppose that the political limit signified by
the number 10 is to be for ever and ever, from generation to generation, the limit within which all are to
enjoy, but beyond which every man is to be deprived of
the enjoyment of the franchise? Certainly not. The
defeat of the bill, what would it procure? an interval, but
not an interval of repose; an interval of fever, an interval
of expectation, an interval for the working of those influences which might possibly extend even to the formidable dimensions of political danger. Let the great English
nation be wise, and be wise in time. Let it not, through
any unwise dallying, through any unwise neglect of an
opportunity as favourable, I believe, as was ever offered
to the legislature, and through the influence of weak, or
cowardly, or selfish apprehensions, refuse the granting of
a boon which, I am firmly persuaded, if granted now, will
be received as a boon in a spirit of gratitude, and tend to
increase the attachment of the people to the institutions

of the country and its rulers. Let them not convert what is for their own advantage into an occasion of danger and of evil; but let them, in regard to the duty of the day and the prospects of the future, rally round us and strengthen us for the task which we have in hand. If they so rally round us, whatever difficulties may lie in our way will soon be surmounted; and the next time we meet in these now crowded halls it will be to congratulate one another on the passing of this measure into law, and on the evident fruits which it may have begun to produce in the augmented contentment, attachment, and loyalty of the people."

The debate began on April 12, and was continued for eight nights. The ordinary opposition was supported by Earl Grosvenor and the "Adullamites" generally, as the Liberal secession was now denominated. In order to justify the resolution of the government to introduce a bill, Mr. Gladstone pointed out that since 1832 Parliament had been engaged in constant efforts, by promoting education, fostering prudential habits, and unfettering the press, to fit the people for political privileges, and asked the House whether it would refuse to complete the work which it had thus been long preparing. He next canvassed the arguments against the bill, beginning with that which objected to the transfer of the government of the country to the class which did not bear the cost of it, asserting that the working-classes, while they only possessed now one-seventh of electoral power, paid five-twelfths of the taxation. He denied that working-men would act together as a class, appealing in proof to the working of the municipal franchise, and to the fact that eight boroughs in which they had now the majority, returned five Liberal and nine Conservative members.

MR. GLAD-
STONE'S BILL
OF 1866.
Under this bill he calculated that they would have the command of 120 seats against 538 elected by the other classes in the community, whereas before the Reform Bill of 1832 they had 130 seats; and from this he drew the conclusion that the bill would not involve any transfer of power, and that it was not opposed to the interests of the Conservative party. He dealt next with the allegation that the working-classes were being gradually admitted to the franchise by a kind of self-acting process, quoting statistics to show that of late years there had been a great slackening in the enlargement of the £10 constituency. Having expressed an individual opinion that a further reduction of the franchise would not be dangerous, though he preferred to adhere to the constitutional course of gradual progress, he explained that though the government, in deference to the representations of some of their supporters, had agreed to explain their views on redistribution before the committee, they would not proceed with any other part of the subject until the fate of the bill was determined, and pointed out that as the new electors could not get on the register until June, 1867, there was ample time for the present constituencies to settle both branches of the question.

Lord Gros-
venor's
speech.
Lord Grosvenor, in supporting his amendment, urged that the present anomalies of the electoral system would be increased by the bill, taken by itself, and lamented that it would delay the complete measure which he, in common with the majority of the House, desired to see passed. Differing from the chancellor of the exchequer, he maintained that the working-classes were gradually and silently finding their way into the electoral body—a process which, by the passing of this bill, would be converted into a precipitate transfer of political power into

the hands of one class. He advocated the withdrawal of
the question from the domain of party, and expressed a
strong conviction that, though many members might not
be able to shake off their allegiance to their leaders on
this occasion, his amendment had the sanction of the
great bulk of the Liberal party.

Lord Stanley seconded the amendment, animadverting
strongly on the distrust of the House of Commons shown
by the government in refusing to disclose their views on
the redistribution of seats until they had pledged the
House on the extension of the franchise, although they
now allowed that the two branches must be considered
together. He predicted that such a transparent device
would not conciliate any opposition, and warned the
House that even if it saw the government plan of redistribution before passing this bill, there would be no
security that the identical plan would be produced next
year, or that this Parliament or this government would
be in existence to pass it.

Sir E. Bulwer Lytton argued against the predominance
of the democratic element in the House; while Mr. Mill
supported the other side. Mr. Laing and Sir Hugh Cairns
were also in the opposition. Sir Hugh contended that
the bill would give the working-classes the representation
of the majority of boroughs, and that in a balanced state
of parties this would give them the command of the legislature. While admitting that working-men might differ in
their politics like other classes, he believed that on questions affecting their special interests they would band together, and particularly whenever motions might be made
for a further extension of the suffrage—in fact, the bill
was a measure for the attainment of universal suffrage by
easy stages. The redistribution of seats, he maintained,

MR. GLAD-
STONE'S BILL
OF 1866.
was the key of the whole question, and the House could not understand the effect of what it might do in passing this bill until they saw the interpretation which now with so much want of confidence was withheld from it.

Lord Elcho's
speech.
Lord Elcho objected to the bill because it said one thing and would do another, and because it dealt only with one branch of the subject. It would, in the course of a few years, give the entire preponderance to the working-classes, and this he objected to—not from any hostility to the working-classes, which he earnestly repudiated, but because the balance of the constitution would be endangered by the preponderance of any class.

Mr. Bright's
speech.
Mr. Bright, in a vigorous speech, urged that the reason why the House was now called on to deal with reform was the sense entertained in the country that the number of electors was too small for a fair representation of the people; and as another proof of the predominant importance of the extension of the franchise, he instanced Mr. Disraeli's Reform Bill, which, though it admitted 500,000 new electors to the franchise, only redistributed fifteen seats; and quoted from the speeches of Mr. Walpole and Mr. Henley condemning that bill as a warning to the opposition that Mr. Disraeli and Lord Stanley were not safe guides in this matter. Turning to the bill he controverted the accuracy of the government statistics as to the proportion of the working-men now possessing the franchise, instancing the cases of Newark, Wakefield, and Stoke-upon-Trent. He calculated that the bill would only admit 116,000 working-men, and would give but one-fourth of the electoral power in the boroughs to the class which formed three-quarters of the people, and would leave 4,000,000 adult males entirely destitute of political power.

Mr. Lowe, in an elaborate speech, contended that the MR. GLAD-STONE'S BILL OF 1866. bill was not founded on calculated results, but on a broad sweeping principle, originating in the doctrine of the rights of man, which, if it meant anything, meant universal suffrage. He inferred, from the sweeping nature of the bill, from the manner in which it had been forced on the House, the treatment the House had received, and the arguments by which the bill had been supported, Mr. Lowe's speech. that it was founded upon the principle that the franchise was due to everyone whom they could show was fit for it, and that the House were bound to shut their eyes to all consequences, disregard all considerations of expediency, and leave the constituencies so appointed to take care of themselves. He pointed out the danger arising from the power of the working-classes to combine for the accomplishment of their objects, and the ease with which trades-unions might be converted into political organizations. Trades-unions were far more unions against the best, most skilful, industrious men themselves than against the masters. They made war upon all superiority and skilled industry, and made them the slaves of clumsiness, idleness, and ignorance. And see what a tremendous machinery they would have if they only allowed them to possess the one thing they wanted —the parliamentary vote. Adopt this bill and there was no saying where they would stop in the downward direction of democracy. Among the consequences which might be anticipated from it were the profession of politics as a last resource when every other had failed—a disposition to war, opposition to free-trade, and the concentration of power. Democratize the House of Commons and it would not rest until it had swept away the institutions which now stood between it and the throne, and supplied their

MR. GLAD-
STONE'S BILL
OF 1866.

places by other institutions deriving their origin directly from the people, and not having the *quasi* independence which those corporations and privileged classes now enjoyed. When that was done they would have face to face, with nothing to break the shock between them, the monarch for the time being, and a great democracy; and history had taught us little if we thought that those two powers would go on harmoniously.

Lord
Cranborne's
speech.

Lord Cranborne stated that in his opinion the House had heard a great deal too much about the working-men as if they were different from other Englishmen. In his view there were two classes of persons to whom the franchise had a money value—those who did not care about public affairs, and those who had an interest in promoting class or unjust legislation. If the franchise were intrusted to those who did not take an interest in public affairs they would be liable to the temptation of treating it as a saleable commodity, whilst the others would regard it as especially adapted to enable them to carry out their peculiar political theories. The question of fitness was not to be assumed without proof; and it required careful consideration before the proposition was accepted, that because certain persons lay between two strata of the population, therefore they were fit for the franchise. But the House, he complained, were kept in ignorance of what the new constituency was really to be; and, from what was known of the chancellor of the exchequer's opinions, they had little ground for confiding absolutely in him as to the supplementary measures he was likely to bring in to complete the entire scheme. It was said, however, that the House was pledged to reform. What, he asked, was that pledge? If it had been made, surely it would be found in some document. But what were

the grounds on which it was urged that the pledge had Mr. Glad-
been given? True, there were a certain number of queen's stone's Bill of 1866.
speeches in which the question was referred to, but the
House was not to be bound by them.

Mr. Disraeli did not deny that if this measure were Mr. Dis-
passed the country would have a great Parliament, con- raeli's speech.
taining the principal landed proprietors, manufacturers,
and some merchants; but they would soon discover that
they were losing their hold on the executive. In proportion as their command over the executive was diminished, the great proprietors and manufacturers would
cease to belong to the House. Then they would be told
that the House of Commons was no longer what it was.
The franchise would again be extended; all command
over the executive would cease, and when that was the
state of things they would have a hall of selfish and
obscure mediocrities, incapable of anything but mischief,
and that mischief devised and regulated by the raging
demagogue of the hour. The question before the House
was, not whether the working-men should be introduced
to the franchise, but whether the working of the English
constitution could be improved; and he was convinced
that, although it was the opinion of the thoughtful portion of the community that the choicest members of the
working-classes should form a part, and no unimportant
part, of the estate of the Commons, they recoiled from
attaining that result by an undistinguishing reduction of
the franchise. He did not say that the working-classes
had their full share of the franchise. But before proceeding to invest them with it, the House ought to obtain
accurate information; and, above all, they should legislate in the spirit of the English constitution, so that this
House should remain a House of Commons, and not the

MR. GLAD-
STONE'S BILL
OF 1866. House of the people or of an indiscriminate multitude. In voting for this bill they would act, not in the spirit of the British constitution, but in the spirit of the constitution of America. He denied the charges made by Mr. Bright against the Tory party, that they would plunge the country into war. On the contrary, theirs was a policy of peace, and he claimed for them the credit of having promoted measures for the amelioration of the condition of the working-classes in the mine, the colliery, and the factory, when they were opposed with all his

Mr. Dis-
raeli's
speech. energy by the member for Birmingham. That gentleman was entitled to admiration for his indomitable energy, plain outspokenness, and candour, and he had a confederate on the treasury bench in the chancellor of the exchequer, who did not display the like candour in that House, but went down to Liverpool and professed American principles in the widest acceptation of the term. It was because he wished to avert the calamities which must ensue from the establishment of our institutions upon such principles that he should vote for the amendment.

Mr. Glad-
stone's
reply. In his reply Mr. Gladstone said: "The wealth of the country is rapidly progressing, and its vast increase has been almost entirely in the upper and middle classes, and yet the number of electors does not keep pace with the population. I hope, therefore, I shall hear no more of this absorption of the working-classes into the franchise. I am justified, then, in stating the working-classes are not represented in this House either according to their numbers or their wealth. I think they are not represented in proportion to their intelligence, their virtue, or their loyalty. They are less represented now than they were thirty-six years ago, when they were less

coinpetent to exercise the franchise. A greater amount MR. GLAL-
of representation with a less amount of fitness was not STONE'S BILL
found to be injurious but wholesome for the state; and OF 1866.
now, when, as you admit, there is a greater amount of
fitness, and, as you must grant, a less amount of representation, you are not disposed to accede to a measure of
enfranchisement. May I say to honourable gentlemen
opposite, as some of them have addressed advice to gentlemen on this side of the House, Will you not consider,
before you embark in this new crusade, whether the results of the others in which you have engaged have been
so satisfactory? Great battles you have fought, and
fought them manfully. The battle of maintaining civil Mr. Glad-
disabilities on account of religious belief, the battle of stone's
reply.
resisting the first Reform Act, the battle of Protection—
all these battles have been fought by the great party that
I see opposite; and, as to some of them, I admit my own
share of the responsibility. But have their results been
such as that you should be disposed to renew these con-
flicts again? Certainly those who sit on this side have
no reason or title to find fault. The effect of your course
has been to give them for five out of six, or for six out
of seven years, the conduct and management of public
affairs. The effect has been to lower, to reduce, and
contract your just influence in the country, and to abridge
your share in the administration of the government. It
is good for the public interest that you should be strong;
but if you are to be strong you can only be so by showing, as well as the kindness and the personal generosity
which I am sure you feel towards the people, a public
trust and confidence in them. What I now say can
hardly be said with an evil motive. But, sir, we are
assailed; this bill is in a state of crisis and of peril, and

MR. GLAD-
STONE'S BILL
OF 1866.

the government along with it. We stand or fall with it, as has been declared by my noble friend. We stand with it now, we may fall with it in a short time hence, but if we do we shall rise with it hereafter. I shall not attempt to measure with precision the forces that are to be arrayed in the coming struggle. Perhaps the great division of to-night is not the last that must take place in the struggle."

Division.

The division took place with the following result:—

For the second reading, ... 318
Against it, ... 313
Majority for government, . . 5

On April 30 Mr. Gladstone stated that the course which the government intended to pursue in the circum-

Redistribu-
tion Bill.

stances was to introduce at once the Redistribution Bill and the bills for Scotland and Ireland; and on May 7 this was done. In explaining the measure for a redistribution of seats Mr. Gladstone remarked that the two aspects of the case were that large communities were inadequately represented, while there were others stationary, and consequently over-represented. These last were the small boroughs. And the government had come to the conclusion that no borough should be absolutely extinguished, but that, in lieu thereof, recourse should be had to the system which answered so well in Scotland, that of grouping such boroughs. Thirty years'

Mr. Glad-
stone's
speech.

experience of the Reform Act went to show that if any one class of boroughs was entitled to be selected for the praise of comparative purity it was the grouped boroughs. Consequently this would be a measure of reform in the sense of its tending to purify elections from what was beyond all doubt a grievous national evil. The number

of seats which it was proposed to obtain for redistribution MR. GLAD-
by the bill was forty-nine. And this would be done by STONE'S BILL OF 1866.
a double operation. He proposed, first, to withdraw one
member from every borough having a population under
8000, by which thirty seats would be placed at the disposal of Parliament, and these boroughs be still left in
possession of one member each. The second part of the
proposal was to group as many of these boroughs as
could be joined together with geographical convenience.
The population of the groups would differ, and with
respect to that difference he proposed to assign one or
two representatives, as the case might be. Where the
population of a group was less than 15,000 there would
be one member, and where it was above 15,000 there Mr. Glad-
would be two members for the group. The lowest in stone's speech.
population of the groups would be a little under 10,000,
and the highest of them 20,000 or 21,000. The right
honourable gentleman then read a list of the proposed
groups, as follows:—

1. Woodstock, Wallingford, and Abingdon, Two members.
2. Liskeard, Bodmin, and Launceston, . Two members.
3. Totnes, Dartmouth, and Ashburton, . One member.
4. Bridport, Honiton, and Lyme, . . . One member.
5. Dorchester and Wareham, ... One member.
6. Maldon and Harwich, ... One member.
7. Tewkesbury, Cirencester, and Evesham, Two members.
8. Andover and Leamington, ... One member.
9. Ludlow and Leominster, ... One member.
10. Eye and Thetford, ... One member.
11. Horsham, Petersfield, Midhurst, and
    Arundel, ... Two members.
12. Chippenham, Malmesbury, and Calne, Two members.
13. Westbury and Wells, ... One member.
14. Devizes and Marlborough, , ... One member.
15. Ripon, Knaresborough, and Thirsk, . Two members.
16. Richmond and Northallerton, . . . One member.

Besides these, there were eight towns with a population under 8000, which, owing to local circumstances and geographical convenience, could not be brought within the limits of any group. These were Bridgenorth, Buckingham, Cockermouth, Lichfield, Stamford, Stafford, Wenlock, and Newport. A considerable portion of the seats liberated by disfranchisement had in all former cases been assigned to divisions of counties, and there had been a just tendency to increase the number of seats so assigned. Here, besides counties, there were the claims of towns to be considered, and these under two heads—those of the large communities which had either reached such a point as to make it expedient to divide them or which had a claim for some addition to the actual number of their representatives, and those new and growing towns whose progress was so rapid as to be continually assuming an increased magnitude. He proposed to give twenty-six seats to counties in England; first, by dividing the southern division of Lancashire and giving to each division three members. Then, taking every county or division of a county, with one exception only, not now having a population above 150,000, and not having three members already, he proposed to give each of them an additional member so as to raise the number of their representatives to three. This arrangement would absorb twenty-three seats. He excepted Middlesex from the scheme, because, upon the whole, that county ought to be regarded as having an affinity to the metropolis rather than to the rest of the country. Further, he proposed to give a third member to four boroughs having a population exceeding 200,000 each. These were Liverpool, Manchester, Birmingham, and Leeds, and a second member to Salford, which had a population of 100,000.

He would next divide the borough of the Tower Hamlets into two sections, each to return two members, and unite Chelsea and Kensington into one borough with two members. He proposed, likewise, to give one member to each of all unrepresented municipal boroughs having a population exceeding 18,000. These were Burnley, Staleybridge, Gravesend, Hartlepool, Middlesborough, and Dewsbury. By these arrangements forty-one seats out of the forty-nine were disposed of. The forty-second seat he proposed to confer upon the University of London. Forty-two seats being thus distributed, he turned now to consider the important and irrefutable claims of Scotland. The government had to consider whether the demand of Scotland should be met by a transfer of seats from Eng- land or an addition to the number of members of this House; and, believing that the House would be disinclined to increase its numbers, they had resolved that the remaining seven seats should be transferred to Scotland. An additional member would, therefore, be given to each of three counties—Ayr, Lanark, and Aberdeen—a third member to the city of Glasgow, a third to the city of Edinburgh, a second to Dundee, and one member to the Scottish universities. So far as the Welsh constituencies were concerned he did not propose to interfere with the existing arrangements, the boroughs there being grouped and the system working satisfactorily. With regard to the question of the boundaries of boroughs the bill proposed that the parliamentary boundary should be co-equal with the municipal, and that the Enclosure Commissioners should consider the proper boundaries for the newly-enfranchised towns and the limits which should divide the two sections of the Tower Hamlets. As to the course of proceeding on these bills, when the two

P

MR. GLAD-
STONE'S BILL
OF 1866.
measures relating to Scotland and Ireland had been introduced there would be four bills upon the table affecting the representation of the people. Thus the whole
scheme of the government would be before the House.
The noble lord the member for King's Lynn had suggested that there should be some guarantee that the two
questions of an extension of the franchise and the redistribution of seats should be dealt with by the same Parliament. This he was willing to concede; but he was
not prepared to agree to the loss of a whole year by postponing the subject. His intention, therefore, was to persevere with the proposals he had made; and the government would not advise a prorogation of Parliament until
the whole subject—meaning by that the questions of the
franchise and redistribution—had been disposed of. The
bill was read a first time.

Scotch Bill.
The lord-advocate asked leave to bring in a bill to
amend the representation in Scotland, which was based
upon the same principle as the English Franchise Bill,
viz. a qualification of £7 in boroughs and £14 in counties.
It would increase the borough constituencies by 26,000
electors, of whom 17,000 would be of the working-classes.
The bill would also reduce the property franchise in
counties from £10 to £5, with the condition, however, of
personal residence. Amongst the new seats an additional
seat would be given to Edinburgh, and a member would
be given to the Scotch universities.

Irish Bill.
Mr. Fortescue asked leave to bring in this bill. He
said it was not of an extensive nature, as the question
had been dealt with in 1850 by Sir W. Sommerville.
The borough constituencies had greatly diminished in
numbers since that date. He proposed to reduce the
rating occupation franchise from £8 to £6, the effect of

which would be to add about 5500 persons to the borough MR. GLAD-
register. The bill also contained a clause creating a lodger STONE'S BILL OF 1866.
franchise, also a clause creating a savings-bank franchise
on the model of that in the English bill. There were
only three cases so peculiar as to justify a transfer of seats,
and an additional member would be given to Dublin city
and Cork county; and the Queen's University would be
placed on the same footing as the London University,
and have a right to return one member to the House.
To provide these three seats six smaller boroughs would
be thus grouped: Bandon with Kinsale, Portarlington
with Athlone, and Dungannon with Enniskillen. There
were also seven boroughs with a population less than
8000 each, which would be united to other places, and
so raise a number of grouped boroughs with large populations, and more respectable and numerous constituencies.
Leave was given to bring in both bills.

The second reading of the Redistribution Bill was
moved on May 14. In the meantime two notices Notices of
were given, one by Mr. Bouverie, to the effect that the motion.
Franchise and Redistribution Bills should both be referred
to the same committee; and the other by Captain Hayter
to the effect that the system of grouping proposed in the
Redistribution Bill was neither convenient nor equitable,
and that the scheme is not sufficiently matured to form
the basis of a satisfactory measure. Mr. Disraeli also
expressed his views on the subject; stated his opinion
that it would be expedient for the government to collect
statistics of the franchise for a bill next year, and meantime to drop the present measure. This counsel was not
adopted. The government, however, were prepared to
consult the House with regard to the amalgamation of
the bills.

MR. GLAD-
STONE'S BILL
OF 1866.

Fusion of
the Bills.

Debate.

On May 28, when the House met after the Whit-suntide holidays, Mr. Gladstone stated that he would not oppose Mr. Bouverie's motion for a fusion of the two bills into one, and this accordingly was done. Sir R. Knightley then moved that it be an instruction to the committee to make provision for the better prevention of bribery and corruption at elections, and this gave rise to a smart discussion. Mr. Gladstone opposed this on the ground that it ought to be made the subject of a separate measure, but the government were outvoted by a majority of 10. Captain Hayter then made his motion condemning the government scheme of redistribution, and a debate took place which went on for four nights. It was characterized by much ability on both sides, but the issue was not doubtful. The Liberal party was divided, and the country was not in earnest. Mr. Goschen contended for the measure. He was followed by Sir John Pakington, who professed his anxiety to have the question settled this session, but the government had rendered that impossible by having precipitately produced a vague and immature measure. They had called for electoral statistics, for which they did not wait before they produced their bill. They should have carefully considered the whole question, and then presented a mature measure to Parliament next year. The statistics produced showed that a large proportion of the working-classes already possessed the franchise; that the reduction of the franchise to £7 would add 200,000 of that class to the registry; this would render that class half the electors in boroughs, and would give them a preponderance over the other half, which represented property, and to this he objected. It had been laid down in the works of Mr. J. S. Mill, that according to the law of necessity the Conservative party were the

stupidest in the state; but what did that honourable
member think now?

He was immediately succeeded by Mr. Mill, who explained his views on the subject of the franchise; and in reference to the allegation that he had called the Conser- vatives the stupidest of parties, he said: "I never meant to say that the Conservatives are generally stupid. I meant to say that stupid persons are generally conservative. I believe that is so obviously and universally admitted a principle that I hardly think any gentleman will deny it. Suppose any party, in addition to whatever share it may possess of the ability of the community, has nearly the whole of its stupidity, that party must, by the law of its constitution, be the stupidest party; and I don't see why honourable gentlemen should see that position at all offensive to them, for it insures their being always an extremely powerful party. I know I am liable to a retort, and an obvious one enough, and as I do not wish to allow any honourable gentleman the credit of making it, I make it myself. It may be said that if stupidity has a tendency to conservatism, sciolism, or half knowledge, has a tendency to liberalism. Something might be said for that, but it is not at all so clear as the other. There is an uncertainty about sciolists; we cannot count upon them, and therefore they are a less dangerous class. But there is so much dense solid force in sheer stupidity that any body of able men with that force pressing behind them may insure victory in many a struggle, and many a victory the Conservative party has gained through that power."

Captain Hayter announced that as there was little doubt that the bill would now be withdrawn he would not persevere with his amendment. It was then nega- tived. Mr. Walpole proposed an amendment to the effect

MR. GLAD-
STONE'S BILL
OF 1866.
that the county occupation franchise should be fixed at £20 instead of £14; but this was negatived by a majority of 14. Mr. Hunt proposed an amendment to the effect that, in defining the county franchise, rating should be substituted for rental, but it was rejected by a majority of 280 against 273.

Lord Dun-
kellin's
amendment.
The amendment now to be proposed by Lord Dunkellin was to be fatal to the bill. It was the substitution of a £6 rating clause instead of a £7 rental clause for the borough franchise. Mr. Gladstone vigorously opposed this amendment, and declared that the government would not depart one jot from the very moderate amount of enfranchisement they had proposed. The bill as it stood would enfranchise 200,000 men in the boroughs—140,000 by the £7 franchise and 60,000 by the provisions as to payment of rates and compound householders; and a £7 or £6, or even £5 rating franchise, he showed, would not admit so many. He was supported by Mr. Bright, who asserted that the real object of the amendment and the real reason for its unanimous support by the opposition

Debate.
was to substitute £9 for £7, and that there was nothing in the old constitution to show that rateable value had ever been employed to determine the number and quality of the electors. If the amendment were carried, and if £5 were not substituted for £7, the great aim and object of this bill would be defeated, and the practical effect would be to limit the reduction of the franchise to £9 householders; and he illustrated this by showing how a reduction of the franchise to £7, £6, and £5, rating and rental respectively, would effect the managers of the Rochdale Co-operative Society. It was on this clause he urged that the attention of the working-classes was chiefly fixed; and passing to the general question of re-

duction of the franchise, after deploring the persistent
efforts of the opposition to dig an impassable gulf between the working and the middle classes, he warned them
that the war which had been referred to as a reason for
not proceeding with the bill, might end in a fever of
revolution in Germany, and that every interest in this
country would be safer and happier for the introduction
of some 200,000 of the working-classes to the electoral
franchise. If the amendment were carried, and the
government ejected from office, the question would not
be disposed of; it would rise up again and break up every
government until it was settled; and he put it to the
opposition whether it would not be wiser to accept this
moderate measure frankly and show a confidence in the
people, which would be repaid by increased loyalty and
obedience to the law.

MR. GLAD-
STONE'S BILL
OF 1866.

The vote being taken with the following result:—

For the amendment, ...	315
Against it, ...	304
	—
Majority against government, . , . .	11

Government
defeated.

The Russell administration then resigned office, and
Lord Derby became prime-minister, with Mr. Disraeli as
leader in the House of Commons. In the course of the
electioneering campaign Mr. Disraeli referred to the subject of parliamentary reform, and said, "I frankly tell .
you that I am not going to give any pledge on the part
of her majesty's government that when Parliament meets
next year we are going to deal with the question of Parliamentary Reform. We hold ourselves perfectly free to
do that which is best for the country. I see no downcast
or disconsolate faces in consequence of this announcement. At the same time it is my duty to assure you

Resignation
of ministers.

Mr. Dis-
raeli's ef-
forts at
Reform,
1867.
that if we do deal with the subject at any time we shall
deal with it in the spirit of the English constitution.
We shall not attempt to remodel the institutions of the
country upon any foreign type whatever, whether it be
American or whether it be French." A little later,
July 9, Lord Derby in the House of Lords said with
respect to the question of Parliamentary reform that he
held himself and his colleagues entirely free and un-
pledged, and should carefully consider the wise maxim
which had been laid down by Earl Russell himself, that
no government would be justified in bringing in a reform
bill without a fair prospect of being able to carry it, and
without an understanding between the two great political
parties in the state. He did not deny, however, that
there were practical anomalies in our representative system which it was desirable to redress, and that there
were persons now excluded from the franchise who had
a fair claim to be admitted to it. Nothing would give
him greater pleasure than to see a large increase in the
number of electors, and a considerable infusion of persons
who were now excluded from the representation; but he
feared that that portion of the community who were most
clamorous for a reform bill were not those who would be
satisfied with any measure that was likely to be concurred
in by the two great political parties. He should rejoice,
however, at any prospect of passing a safe and moderate
measure.

Lord
Derby's
speech.

Accomplish-
ment of Sec-
ond Reform.
The session of 1867 brings us down to the accomplishment of the second reform of the House of Commons.
The epoch from the date of the first reform was thirty-
five years. The struggle during that period was com-
paratively mild and peaceful, and was not conducted by
the populace. Its mode of action was moral rather than

physical. It was a movement rather than an agitation, and never once descended to coercion. There were two occasions, however, on which breaches of the peace were imminent, if not actually committed, although it could not be said exactly that this took place in promoting the cause of reform. The first was on the occasion of the great Chartist demonstration in 1848; but this was not so much a call for a reform of the House of Commons as for the overthrow of the constitution. The second was the riot in Hyde Park in 1866; but this was not a proceeding so much for the immediate reform as for asserting the right of public meeting in the London parks. With these modifications it may be said that the progress of the movement for parliamentary reform from the period from 1832 to 1867 was most orderly, so far as the people were concerned, and most constitutional so far as regards the mode of procedure.

MR. DIS-
RAELI'S EF-
FORTS AT
REFORM,
1867.

The year 1867 opened with the Conservatives in office, but not in power, for as a party they did not command a majority of the House of Commons. They were there on sufferance, it is true, but they were there especially because the Liberals had failed to carry a reform bill. It was therefore questionable whether the Conservatives would attempt a measure of reform. If they did, it would be a very moderate one, and be of course only a compromise of different interests. In the Queen's speech it was announced that the attention of Parliament would be called to the subject, in the hope that a measure might be passed, which, without unduly disturbing the balance of political power, should freely extend the elective franchise. The meaning of this was, that the right of voting would be largely given, but that the distribution of political *power* would remain very much as it was.

A Conserva-
tive govern-
ment.

Mr. Dis-
raeli's ef-
forts at
Reform,
1867.

Mr. Dis-
raeli's
speech on
reform.

The first step was soon taken. On February 11 Mr. Disraeli announced what the government intended to do. They asked the members of the House to divest themselves of all party feeling in dealing with the subject of Parliamentary reform. They conceived that it ought no longer to be a question which should determine the fate of cabinets (a statement that was received with some laughter), for the reason that all parties had attempted to deal with it in 1852, 1854, 1859, and 1860, and had failed. As it was the House of Commons—not a political party or any political leader—which had disturbed the settlement of 1832, so it was the House of Commons, and not any party, which had baffled every effort to pass a new reform bill. When that attempt at disturbance was commenced, the Conservatives determined not to make opposition to Parliamentary reform a principle of action, and they have never opposed the second reading of any of the bills introduced since 1850; nor did the question, he asserted, assume a party character until the vote of 1859 on Lord Russell's resolution. The House of Commons therefore had incurred a peculiar responsibility in this matter; and was it not wise to consider whether it could not pursue a course which, while not relieving the government from its due share of responsibility, would insure them against a repetition of former mishaps? This advantage might be attained if the House would give the government some intimation of its views on the main points of the controversy by resolution, before a bill was introduced—a course, as he showed, which was constitutional, justified by successful precedents, would not lead to delay, and which, though to require too much precision would be unreasonable, need not entail vagueness and uncertainty. The government

would that day lay on the table the resolutions they proposed for this purpose, and in shadowing out the chief
of them he intimated that rating, not rental, would be
the basis of the franchise; that there would be a reduction both of the county and borough franchises, though
the precise limit, depending as it did on so many other
points to be subsequently settled, could not be stated in
the resolutions. The government would proceed in their
task of reconstructing the House of Commons on the
principles of the British constitution. They would
sanction no course which would alter the characteristics
by which it had risen to its present pitch of power (not
enjoyed, as he showed, by any of the democratic assemblies of foreign countries), and would strenuously contend
that the electoral franchise must be considered a popular
privilege, not a democratic right. Notwithstanding the
violent and pernicious doctrines recently circulated, he
hoped the House would agree to resolutions in unison
with these views. On the important question of redistribution of seats, resolutions would be produced in harmony with the principles by which the vast and varied
interests of the empire secured a representation in the
House; the government being fully conscious that by
any attempt to obtain artificial symmetry the character
of the House might be changed, and its authority destroyed. The resolutions would lay down that no
borough should be wholly disenfranchised, except in
cases where systematic corruption was proved; that
representation should be extended to boroughs now
unrepresented, whose circumstances demanded it, and
would provide for the extension of boundaries. On this
last point Mr. Disraeli dwelt at some length, arguing
that as the 11,500,000 county population was repre-

sented by 162 members, while the borough population of
9,500,000, had 324 members, the county population had
a right to complain if their representation was interfered
with by the borough population—an injustice now existing, and which would be increased by the proposed
reduction of the county franchise, from the overflow of
many boroughs beyond the boundaries fixed in 1832.
Halifax, for instance, if its boundaries were not widened
would contribute to the constituency of the West Riding
a large band of voters, whose sympathies and interests
were borough, not county.   At the same time, he repudiated any desire to prevent the blending of country and
urban populations, which was inevitable and desirable.
The government only intended to remedy an injustice,
and he defended himself from the imputation of endeavouring to eliminate all independence from the county
representation, and to hand it over to the landlords and
farmers; showing that while these classes, including farm
labourers, only amounted to 2,000,000, there remained
in the counties over and above them a scattered village
population, as it was statistically called, of 7,000,000—
the backbone of the country, including the most valuable
of all classes, the county freeholders.   The course the
government had chosen was not flattering to themselves,
but they deemed it more honourable to take a part,
however humble, in the settlement of this controversy,
than to bring in a mock measure, which party spirit
would not have allowed to pass.   They were not angling
for a policy, they had a policy of their own, and though
they were prepared not to shrink from the main points
of it, they would receive any suggestion or any assistance
in a candid spirit.   He concluded by saying that he
would bring up the resolutions on the 25th.

He accordingly did so. They were in the following terms:—" This House having, in the last session of Parlia- ment, assented to the second reading of a bill entitled 'A Bill to extend the right of Voting at Elections of Members of Parliament in England and Wales,' is of opinion—

" 1. That the number of electors for counties and bor- oughs in England and Wales ought to be increased.

" 2. That such increase may best be effected by both reducing the value of the qualifying tenement in counties and boroughs, and by adding other franchises not dependent on such value.

" 3. That while it is desirable that a more direct representation should be given to the labouring classes, it is contrary to the constitution of this realm to give to any one class or interest a predominating power over the rest of the community.

" 4. That the occupation franchise in counties and boroughs shall be based upon the principle of rating.

" 5. That the principle of plurality of votes, if adopted by Parliament, would facilitate the settlement of the borough franchise on an extensive basis.

" 6. That it is expedient to revise the existing distribution of seats.

" 7. That in such revision it is not expedient that any boroughs now represented in Parliament shall be wholly disfranchised.

" 8. That in revising the existing distribution of seats this House will acknowledge as its main consideration the expediency of supplying representation to places not at present represented, and which may be considered entitled to that privilege.

" 9. That it is expedient that provision should be made

for the better prevention of bribery and corruption at elections.

"10. That it is expedient that the system of registration of voters in counties should be assimilated, as far as possible, to that which prevails in boroughs.

"11. That it shall be open to every parliamentary elector, if he thinks fit, to record his vote by means of a polling paper duly signed and authenticated.

"12. That provision be made for diminishing the distance which voters have to travel for the purpose of recording their votes, so that no expenditure for such purpose shall hereafter be legal.

"13. That a humble address be presented to her majesty praying her majesty to issue a Royal Commission to form and submit to the consideration of Parliament a scheme for new and enlarged boundaries of the existing parliamentary boroughs, where the population extends beyond the limits now assigned to such boroughs, and to fix, subject to the decision of Parliament, the boundaries of such other boroughs as Parliament may deem fit to be represented in this House."

Mr. Disraeli then proceeded to explain the resolutions. He began by observing that the Reform Act of 1832 threw the government of this country into the hands of the middle-classes. The country had never been better governed than during the period that it had been in operation. But that act abolished the political rights of the working-classes, and it was now his duty to propose to restore those rights, and to bring back the former balance of power and the old constitution of the country. He proposed four new franchises: first, educational, which included persons who had taken a degree, ministers of religion, and others; second, savings-banks. Under the latter franchise a deposit of £30, and a retention of it for one year, would give a qualification. The third new franchise would be the possession of £50 in the public Funds; and the fourth the payment of 20s. in direct taxation. The addition of voters in boroughs, under the first head, would be 10,000, under the second 35,000, under the third 7000, and under the fourth 30,000. The fifth resolution affirmed that the principle of plurality of votes would facilitate the settlement of the borough franchise; but objections had been made to this, and it seemed desirable that they should not make a proposition on this question which they had not a fair prospect of carrying, and therefore he should not recommend it to the House. Parliament having committed itself to the principle that rating should be the basis of the occupation franchise, government had adopted that principle. He proposed a £6 rating franchise for boroughs, which he calculated would give an addition of 130,000 voters. Then he proposed to extend the four new franchises also to the counties, and to reduce the occupation franchise in counties from £50 to £20. These different franchises would add 82,500 to the county electors. In round numbers 400,000 additional votes would be added to the constituencies by this measure. He proposed to dis- franchise the following boroughs, which had been con- victed of extensive corruption:—Great Yarmouth, return- ing two members; Lancaster, two members; Totnes, two members; and Reigate, one member; and to transfer the seven seats thus placed at their disposal to towns that had risen into importance since 1832. The towns which it was. proposed to enfranchise were Hartlepool, Darling- ton, Burnley, Staleybridge, St. Helen's, Dewsbury, Barns- ley, Middlesborough, one town which he could not yet

name in what was called the Black Country, and Croydon, Gravesend, and Torquay.   Then he proposed to
divide the Tower Hamlets, and to give two members to
each division.   Then he proposed to take the following
counties and divide them so that in every case there
would be a population of 100,000 persons, irrespective of
the borough population: North Lancashire, North Lincolnshire, West Kent, East Surrey, Middlesex, South
Staffordshire, and South Devon.   There would thus be
fourteen new members for counties, and fourteen for
boroughs.   The number of seats it was proposed to deal
with was thirty, and he had explained how twenty-eight
of them were to be appropriated.   Then it was proposed
to divide South Lancashire and give it one more member,
and to give one member to London University.   These
made up the thirty seats.   So far, however, he had only
seven seats at his disposal, and he should have to appeal
to the patriotism of the smaller boroughs for the remainder.   It was proposed to take away one member
from twenty-three of these.   He would not then give
the names, but they had each a population under 7000.

Mr. Lowe—"This day fortnight the right honourable
gentleman made a speech of two hours and a quarter, in
which, unlike his speech of to night of one hour and a
quarter, which tells us everything, he told us nothing,
except that, come what may, it was obsolete to think
that government would go out of office on a Reform Bill.
Why is it an irresistible reason, because Whigs and
Tories have alike failed on this question, that the right
honourable gentleman and his colleagues should enjoy
absolute impunity?   Why are they to have the mark of
Cain set upon them, that nobody may kill them?   I
should have thought just the contrary, that where per-

sons had tried on both sides and failed in an adventure
of this kind, it was a very good reason why you should
not relax the penalties attendant upon such an attempt.
The true principle is that the executive government must
be responsible; but what does the right honourable
gentleman propose? With a deal of candid courtesy he
beseeches us—in language which I was ashamed to hear
addressed to me as a 658th part of the House, and that
he should have thought it necessary to address to the
House—he says: 'If the House will deign to take us
into its counsel, if it will co-operate with us in this
matter, we will receive with cordiality, with deference,
nay, even with gratitude, any suggestions it may like to
offer. Say what you like to us, only for God's sake leave
us our places.' Let us bid a long adieu to sham pretences; let us deal more frankly, and call upon the government to withdraw their Resolutions, and to introduce
a bill and bring the matter to an issue in the old English
fashion. There is no danger in such a course, but there
will be enormous danger if every member during the discussion on these propositions is to be pressed by his constituency, while the press is hounding all on, so as to
bring the institutions of the country down to the level of
democracy."

A long and variegated debate now took place, in which
it was soon made evident that the ordinary forms of parliamentary practice were to be set aside. The government gave up the leadership of the House. Defeat was
not to be followed by the ordinary consequences. It was
assigned to them to make up a measure by compromising
the differences of the Liberals, consistently, of course, with
holding their own opinions. This being all adjusted, the
various sections of Liberals directed the government to

MR. DIS-
RAELI'S BILL
OF 1867.

give up the Resolutions, which they ultimately agreed to do, and bring in a bill. This entailed on them a loss to begin with—namely, the secession of Mr. Walpole, Lord Cranborne, and General Peel. This was only an "incident" in the drama, however, and did not disconcert Mr. Disraeli at all.

He brought in the promised bill on March 19. He stated that the object was to strengthen the character and functions of that House and to establish them on a broad and popular basis. Popular privileges and democratic rights were not identical. More than that, they were contradictory. He hoped that it would never be the fate of this country to live under a democracy, and this bill had no tendency in that direction. Every reform bill proposed since 1832 had proceeded on diminishing the amount of the franchise qualification, and the majority in this House on Lord Dunkellin's motion last year

His speech. decided, with unerring instinct, that rating ought to be the basis of valuation. The government had accepted the principle that the franchise should be associated with the payment of rates, and they proposed that every householder paying rates and having resided two years should be admitted to vote. This would admit 237,000 men who live in houses under £10 and pay rates, leaving unenfranchised 486,000 householders not paying their own rates. But every facility would be given to compound householders to take upon themselves the payment of their own rates and to obtain in consequence the right of voting. After an elaborate argument upon the £5 franchise, which he strongly condemned, characterizing it as a Serbonian bog, and asserting that its logical result in many places would be manhood suffrage, Mr. Disraeli next announced that the bill would confer the franchise on payers

of £1 direct taxes (not including licenses of any kind); and
householders (in towns only) paying £1 direct taxes would be allowed to exercise the franchise in respect of both suffrages. The bill would also contain an education franchise, and would give votes to the holders of savings-bank deposits and funded property to the amount of £50. The direct-tax franchise would add a number greatly exceeding 200,000 (though this was only an estimate), the education franchise 35,000, the funded property franchise 25,000, and the savings-bank franchise 45,000— in all, more than 1,000,000 would be added to the borough constituency. In the counties the franchise would be fixed at £15 rating, which would add 171,000, and the lateral franchises would bring the total additions to the county constituencies to some 330,000. The government, Mr. Disraeli said, had carefully considered the plan of cumulative voting and three-cornered constituencies, and had tried it at every point, but had come to the conclusion that it was erroneous in principle and would be pernicious in practice; and passing to the redistribution scheme, he announced that it was substantially the same as that described by him on February 25 —viz. that thirty seats should be redistributed: fourteen to new boroughs, fifteen to counties, and one to the London University.

After some observations from Mr. Gladstone, Mr. Lowe, and others, the bill was read a first time, and the second reading was moved on March 25. Mr. Gladstone began the debate. He said that the bill as then framed, he was confident, would be rejected by a large majority of the House. There was a general agreement, Mr. Gladstone said, that a measure should be passed this year, that it should embrace a liberal enfranchisement of the labour-

ing classes, and that it should carry with it some promise
of fixedness; and this last, he added, must be attended
by two conditions, that there should be no arbitrary or
unintelligible exclusions, and that within the pale of the

franchise there should be no needless or vexatious distinctions between individuals. But while the £6 rating
scheme, the untimely disappearance of which he regretted,
did seem to afford a basis for a settlement, the prospect
offered by this bill was very discouraging, and he summed
up thus the alteration it would require:—A lodger franchise must be inserted; means must be provided to prevent
traffic in the votes of the lowest classes of householders,
the distinction between the different classes of ratepaying householders must be abolished; the tax-paying
franchise and the dual vote must be abandoned; the
redistribution part of the scheme must be enlarged,
the county franchise reduced, and voting-papers must
be dropped.

Mr. Roebuck stated his intention to support the second
reading of the bill, and explained that his motive was not
to improve the character of the House, which he did not
think necessary, nor to carry out any theory of the
"rights of man," which he did not believe in, but to admit to the franchise the sober, the industrious, and saga-
cious portion of the working-classes, and to keep out the
rest, in whose hands he confessed himself afraid to trust
it. As a test of this industry and sobriety he could conceive nothing more satisfactory than residence and personal payment of rates.

Mr. Bright made a speech of great power. He said:
"The bill as a whole I regard as very unsatisfactory. It
has marks upon it of being the product, not of the friends,
but of the enemies of reform. It is wonderful what

clever men will do when a dozen of them are shut up in
a room. Now look at the chancellor of the exchequer.
Why, he is a marvel of cleverness, or else he would not
have been for twenty years at the head of honourable
gentlemen opposite to lead them into this—what shall I
call it?—great difficulty at last. Take the right honourable member who sits next him, representing a very
learned university—Cambridge. Take the president of
the Poor Law Board, who represents the wisdom, and it
may be to some extent the prejudices of Oxford. Take
the right honourable member for Droitwich; I fear to
speak of so potent a personage. Why, at this moment he
directs the whole of the armies of the empire. There is
not a soldier who shivers amid the snows of Canada, or
who sweats under the sun of India, but shivers and
sweats under the influence of the right honourable gentleman. Why, it was only the other day he was Lord High
Admiral of England. His march was 'on the mountain
wave, his home was on the deep.' But all these gentlemen retire into a mysterious apartment in Downing
Street, and they set to work and concoct a Reform Bill,
and with all their capacity it seems to me to come out a
bill marvellously like that which would have been made
by the honourable member for North Lincolnshire (Mr.
Banks Stanhope), who last night gave us an account of
his conversion. Anything more affecting could hardly be
heard in any class-meeting. But he spoke of 'we' all
the time—what 'we' did, what determination 'we' had
come to. In thinking over it to-day I have come to
the conclusion that he is the author of the bill. Now I
complain of this bill, that in regard to the working-
classes there is in it nothing clear, there is nothing generous, there is nothing statesmanlike. I believe that if

MR. DIS-
RAELI'S BILL
OF 1867. the House were to pass it there would be universal dissatisfaction throughout the country. It would leave the greatest question of our time absolutely unsolved. I tell the House frankly, and the chancellor of the exchequer will believe me when I say there is not a man in this House who would be more glad than I to give the warmest support, whatever it be worth, to a fair and honest measure on this question. I regret what honourable gentlemen opposite did, led by the chancellor of the exchequer and his friends last year. I shall never cease to regret it, and never cease to blame them; but still I would help any government to bring this question to a just conclusion.

Mr. Bright's
speech. But, sir, it seems to me impossible to assist a government which will not tell us frankly what it intends, what it stands by, what it will get rid of; which asks us to go into its confidence, and yet is probably the most reticent government that ever sat on those benches. If any gentleman on this side were to treat you as you treated us last year, I should denounce them with the strongest language I could use. I hate the ways, I scorn the purposes of factions; and if I am driven now or at any stage of this bill to oppose the government, it is because the measure they have offered to us bears upon its face marks of deception and disappointment, and because I will be no party to any bill which would cheat the great body of my countrymen of the possession of that power in this House on which they have set their hearts, and which, as I believe, by the constitution of this country they may most justly claim."

Mr. Dis-
raeli's reply.   Mr. Disraeli replied, and let be known the readiness of the government to consent to some important modifications of their scheme and to abandon some of the securities which had been the objects of special animadversion

in the House. The bill was then read a second time with- out opposition.

The reconstruction of the bill in committee now began. The government gave up the dual vote, and the energies of all parties were next directed towards the question of a rating franchise as compared with one of rental. Mr. Gladstone urged that the bill opposed great barriers to enfranchisement. The rates of two-thirds of the houses under the value of £10 in boroughs were compounded for, and as the occupiers of these houses would practically remain disfranchised the bill would do little towards enfranchising the working-class in towns. It was no answer to say that by paying the rates the occupier might get the vote, for besides the expenditure of money, there would be the expenditure of time to take the necessary steps. Besides, the effect would be different in different towns, and in some cases in different parts of the same town, and it was absurd to suppose that by such a bill they would settle the question. If they passed the bill in the form in which it stood an agitation would commence as soon as its true character was seen, which would never cease till the last vestige of such legislation was swept away. His proposal, therefore, was that the franchise should be granted whether the tenant paid the rates directly or through his landlord.

Mr. Bright supported Mr. Gladstone's amendment, that every person who had the borough franchise should be put on the same footing. At the present moment the law required the occupier to be on the rate-book, and the landlord's payment was, for the purpose of enfranchise- ment, the tenant's payment. Why for the purposes of disfranchisement alter the law? In Birmingham the bill would enfranchise 2300 persons and exclude 36,000. The chancellor of the exchequer in 1859 said he knew there were tricks by which it was easy to appear to extend the suffrage and yet not give it, and that he had them all in his pigeon - holes. After examining them the right honourable gentleman had found and produced this as the cleverest scheme, and by it he had caught many professed Liberals. The amendment was lost by a majority of 21.

Mr. Ayrton then proposed an amendment to the effect that the residential part of the qualification should be reduced from two years to twelve months, and on a vote this was carried by a majority of 81.

A number of amendments were now made and divisions taken; a number of demands were made and concessions granted, and the startling result to the members on both sides was, that they were now face to face with household suffrage. This became so obvious and so alarming that Mr. Sanford had to ask Mr. Disraeli whether he had the consent of the cabinet to the steps he had taken; and on the next meeting of the committee he announced that he had. The question being put, Mr. Lowe said that they all now knew that the real principle of the bill was, that all householders were to have votes, except persons excused on the ground of their poverty from the payment of rates. Heretofore the franchise appeared with restrictions, but now the restrictions were swept away. The chancellor of the exchequer had not shown his supporters his whole plan at once, for they would have been frightened at it; but he told them it was not a democratic measure, and he dandled before them dual voting, and personal payment of rates, and other restrictions. But now these were all removed. The right honourable gentleman had also conceded the lodger franchise, which

might be defined to be a franchise to give everybody a
vote who liked to have one, provided he is not a householder. They were going to transfer power to the most
dependent and the most ignorant. He warned the House
of the dangers they would incur in doing this. The
transfer, once made, would be irrevocable. He asked if
the new electors would not elect members pledged to
substitute direct for indirect taxation, and when they
learned that £26,000,000 a year were paid for the interest on the debt, whether they would not say that it
was incurred when they were not represented, and for
purposes with which they had no sympathy, and whether
they would not refuse to pay it. In passing this bill they
were going to embark in a sea of corruption, and could
anyone doubt that this was the beginning of that downward course which would place the House of Commons
in the position in which so many legislatures had been
placed? Did they think that the House of Peers could
co-exist with this state of things? and were they prepared
for its abolition? How was the House to face the country?
and how was it to face history, when it was recorded of
them that the same Parliament that had rejected a bill
for a £7 franchise had passed a bill for household suffrage? He had before predicted that honourable gentleman opposite, by passing this bill, would ruin either their
party or their country. He was wrong—they would ruin
both.

The definition of the borough franchise being now disposed of, Mr. Mill proposed the enfranchisement of
women. He said he did not claim the vote for women
as an abstract right, but his argument was entirely one
of expediency and justice. It was a doctrine of the
British constitution that taxation and representation

Mr. Dis-
raeli's Bill
of 1867.

should co-exist, and many women paid taxes, and there-fore should be allowed to vote. There was evidence in our records that women in a distant period of our history had voted for counties and some boroughs, and there was no reason why they should not vote now. Women, he submitted, ought no longer to be classed with children, and idiots, and lunatics, who needed to have everything done for them, but they ought to be treated as being equal in intelligence to, and having rights equally with man, and the disadvantages under which they now laboured with respect to the laws affect-ing property, and the admission into professions ought to be removed. The motion was negatived by a majority of 196 against 73.

Minority
representa-
tion.

The occupation franchise in counties was then reduced to £13; a number of "fancy franchises" were disposed of, and thereafter a series of amendments were moved by Mr. Mill, so as to enable minorities to elect repre-sentatives. This he proposed to do by enacting that those who declined to vote for the candidates of the locality should have the power of bestowing their votes on one who was a candidate for Parliament generally, and if there were found in the whole country a sufficient number who had fixed their choice on the same person he would be elected. The plan, he said, was known as Mr. Hare's plan, and there was not really any difficulty in it. At present the representation was imperfect and insufficient, inasmuch as there was a great minority who were not represented at all. They were as completely blotted out as if they were expressly disfranchised. The apprehended evil of democracy was, that particular classes would swamp the others; but under this plan that could not happen, for no considerable minority would remain unrepresented. In that way it would have a conservative effect. It would also have a democratic effect, because every man would be represented, which at present was not the case—for how could an elector be said to be represented by a man against whom he had voted? Without some plan of the kind it was impossible to have a representative system applicable to the exigencies of modern society. Lord Cranborne and other members spoke in complimentary terms of Mr. Mill's efforts in the cause of reform, but urged the withdrawal of the amendments as impracticable. Mr. Mill consented.

The redistribution department of the bill, if it could be called so, was now taken up. Three delinquent boroughs were disfranchised, when Mr. Laing made an important motion which had the effect of modifying to a considerable extent the original scheme of the latter portion of the bill. Certain boroughs named in the schedule were designed by the government to be deprived of one of their members. This proposition Mr. Laing sought to extend further by a series of amendments embracing an entire new plan for the distribution of seats. In his opinion the scheme of the government did not go far enough to give a reasonable hope of a permanent settlement. It proposed to go no further than to take the second member from boroughs having a population of less than 7000, and it left uncorrected great anomalies. Take, for instance, Cockermouth—it had a population of 7075, and it was to continue to return two members, being the same share in the national representation as Liverpool with a population of 442,000. The present bill made a much smaller proposal than the bill of last year or the bill of 1854. The first proposal which he made was that every borough with a population of 10,000 persons, which now returns two members, shall in future return only one. There were thirty-eight boroughs in that condition, and therefore by this means he should obtain thirty - eight seats. He further proposed the grouping of the smaller boroughs, by which he would gain seven seats, and seven seats more by the disfranchisement of the corrupt boroughs already agreed upon, making an entire gain of fifty-two seats. In distributing these seats he assumed that the demand of Scotland for an addition to its representation, to which it was fairly entitled, was to be met, not by taking away from the representation of England or of Ireland, but by the only other possible alternative, namely, a small addition to the number of members. He further proposed that six towns, with a population of more than 150,000 each, should have their representatives increased from two to three. Next he proposed that large towns, with a population exceeding 50,000, and which had now one member, should have two. Of these towns there were four. Then, as to new boroughs, he proposed to adopt the proposal of the government, giving twelve members to those boroughs; and he also adopted the proposal to give two additional members to the Tower Hamlets; that made a total of twenty-four seats assigned to cities and boroughs, and one to the London University, making twenty-five. Then he applied the same principle to counties that he applied to boroughs, by giving to counties with a population of 150,000 a third member. That would require twenty-six seats, which, added to the twenty-five given to boroughs, made fifty-one, leaving a small margin to be dealt with hereafter.

Mr. Disraeli said he should not argue the case upon anomalies. It was very likely that by sudden changes they might produce anomalies as flagrant as those which now existed. Besides, anomalies would still remain; there would still be towns with a population of a little more than 10,000 returning as many members as another town with a population of half a million. In a question of this kind they must go on some principle, and the principle that had guided the government was to supply representation to those communities that had sprung up or greatly increased since the bill of 1832, and which were not represented. But he thought they should not have a mere knot of towns enfranchised in one portion of the kingdom. With the exception of giving one seat to the London University, that was the principle on which the government had proceeded. It was a practical principle which met the exigencies of the moment, and he advised the committee to pause before they passed that line. It was easy to disfranchise, but when they came to apply the seats at their disposal they would find themselves in a great difficulty. They were perfectly safe as long as they confined themselves to giving representation to places that were not represented. If they departed from that they would have all kinds of proposals. On a former occasion a distinguished member of the House had brought forward a scheme for the representation of minorities. Another plan was, when a place returned three members, to enable a voter to give three votes to one candidate. He thought that the House, before it sanctioned any of these schemes, should consider whether the business of that House was not to represent the majority, and that all those schemes for the representation of minorities would only tend to form a feeble executive. It was said that agitation would follow unless there was a more extensive scheme of redistribution, but

MR. DIS-
RAELI'S BILL
OF 1867.

where was it to come from? The dissatisfaction now was in the communities that were not represented; but by this bill their claims would be satisfied.

Mr. Glad-
stone's re-
marks.

Mr. Gladstone said the argument of the chancellor of the exchequer was based on an assumption which was not well founded, namely, that if they were to have a large system of redistribution there was no method of assigning the seats but by having what was called the "unicorn" system of representation. But that was not the general desire. He had that morning been told by a deputation from Birmingham that if that town had three members they would wish that the town should be divided—one portion returning two members and the other returning one. The chancellor of the exchequer said the government plan was based on the principle of meeting existing wants and necessities; but was that altogether true? He thought that in the redistribution but very few members were given to satisfy the claims of a large population. He did not deny the claims of the county constituencies. On the contrary, one of the objects he had in view in voting for this amendment was that they might be able to increase the number of mem bers given to counties. In conclusion, he suggested to the Scotch members that it was a more easy way to obtain the increased representation for Scotland which they desired, by supporting this motion, than by depending on the House resolving to increase the existing number of 658 members.

New scheme
of redistri-
bution.

A division having taken place, Mr. Laing's amendment was carried by 179 against 127, when Mr. Disraeli intimated that the effect would be that the whole scheme of redistribution would have to be reconsidered. Accordingly on June 13 he stated the propositions which the

government had to make in consequence of the vote
which the committee came to on Mr. Laing's resolution.
By that resolution they took away one member from
every borough now returning two which has a population
not amounting to 10,000, and fifteen members were
thereby added to the thirty originally contemplated for
reappropriation, and as they had to deal with forty-five
seats they had thought it better to consider the whole
question *de novo.* They proposed that the representation
of the metropolis should be increased by four members—
two of the additional members to be given to the Tower
Hamlets, which would be divided into two boroughs, one
of them to be called the borough of Hackney, which
would return two members, making four altogether. The
other two members would be given to a new metropolitan
borough comprising Chelsea and the parts adjacent.
Then they recommended the House to confer one member on each of the following towns:—Hartlepool, Darlington, Middlesborough, Burnley, St. Helen's, Barnsley,
Dewsbury, Staleybridge, Wednesbury, and Gravesend.
These were the towns that were comprised in the former
plan. He now proposed to add the towns of Stockton,
Keighley, and Luton (with the parts adjacent). He proposed also an additional member for the two boroughs of
Salford and Merthyr-Tydvil. These made nineteen additional borough seats. The government were still of
opinion that the London University should be represented
in Parliament, but they recommended the committee to
consider whether it would not be expedient to connect
with it the representation of the University of Durham.
There remained twenty-five seats, which he proposed
should be allotted to counties. He proposed that West
Kent, North Lancashire, East Surrey, and South Lanca-

MR. DIS-
RAELI'S BILL
OF 1867.

shire should be divided, and have seven additional members amongst them. He then took nine of the most
considerable counties in England—Lincolnshire, Derby-
shire, Devonshire, Somersetshire, West Riding of Yorkshire, Cheshire, Norfolk, Staffordshire, and Essex—and
he proposed that these counties should each be divided
into three parts, and that each part should be represented
by two members, and the eighteen seats thus allotted
would make up the forty-five seats which were placed at
their disposal. He believed that these counties contained
a population, irrespective of that of the parliamentary
boroughs in them, of something like four millions, and
they represented agricultural, manufacturing, and mineral
industries to an enormous extent.

Mr. Laing's
amend-
ment.

On the next meeting of committee Mr. Laing moved
an amendment giving an additional member, making
three members each, to the following towns:—Birmingham, Bristol, Leeds, Liverpool, Manchester, and Sheffield.
He said there were three other large cities with a population of more than 150,000, Edinburgh, Glasgow, and
Dublin. The government had already proposed to give
a third member to Glasgow, and Dublin not being in
England could not be dealt with by this bill; but if this
amendment were carried Dublin would no doubt be dealt
with in the same manner, and the proposition therefore
involved eight seats. These six cities comprised a population altogether of 1,644,000 persons, while six boroughs
which the House had refused to disfranchise contained
a population of only 20,728 persons. He had already
stated that the precise number of twenty-five seats which
the government had taken to increase the county representation was not more than the counties were fairly
entitled to, and he therefore did not propose to take

these seats from the counties, but he proposed to obtain
them by grouping the smaller boroughs.

Mr. Baines seconded the amendment, which was also
supported by Mr. Gladstone. The chancellor of the
exchequer opposed it, stating the reason why the government proposed to give additional representatives to
counties and not to large boroughs, namely, that the
population of the counties exceeded the population of
the boroughs, and they had proposed to give the counties
additional members in order to create a counterbalance.
The amendment was rejected by 247 to 239.

A number of minor amendments were then made upon
the bill, when the question as to the use of voting-papers
instead of personal voting at the poll was raised. Mr.
M'Cullagh Torrens moved to have the clause expunged,
which he thought was open to great objection. In the
first place, voting-papers might be mislaid, tampered
with, not properly collected, or if collected, not brought
forward. Such papers had failed in the election of
guardians, and a number of frauds and forgeries had been
committed. The system was liable to every species of
fraud, whenever the motive was strong enough, and in
support of his argument he quoted passages from a speech
of Lord Stanley in 1857, in which that noble lord said
he objected to voting-papers because they would greatly
increase the practice of personation, would aggravate the
practice of intimidation, and still more increase bribery
by making it safe, because, instead of the briber getting
a mere promise, he would get the thing itself.

Viscount Cranborne said the system under this clause
was different from that of voting-papers for guardians.
All that this clause did was to carry the poll into the
magistrate's room. By the precaution taken every abuse

R

would be prevented, for the paper must be signed in the
presence of a magistrate, and it must be attested by a
person personally acquainted with the voter, and the
paper so attested must be presented at the poll by another
elector. He supported the clause also because it would
save expense. In counties the great burden of the expense of a contested election was the conveyance of voters
to the poll; and as the House had increased the number
of voters, the expense would be proportionally increased.
At present a great proportion of the voters in large constituencies did not vote, because they objected to mixing
in the turmoil of elections; but if they could vote by
voting-papers this objection would be obviated. On the
vote being taken the clause authorizing the use of voting-
papers was struck out by a majority of 38.

Mr. Lowe then moved an amendment in favour of
cumulative voting, but it was lost by a majority of 141.

The third reading was moved on July 15. Lord
Cranborne spoke severely on the way the bill had been
conducted through the House. When it passed the
second reading it bristled with securities and precautions, but these had now wholly disappeared. He was
astonished to hear the passing of this bill described as
a Conservative triumph, and it was right that its real
parentage should be established. This bill had been
modified at the dictation of Mr. Gladstone, who demanded first the lodger franchise—that had been given;
secondly, the abolition of distinctions between com-
pounders and noncompounders had been conceded; as
likewise had been, thirdly, a provision to prevent traffic
in votes; fourthly, the omission of the taxing franchise;
fifthly, the omission of the dual vote; sixthly, the enlargement of the distribution of seats, which had been

enlarged by fifty per cent; seventhly, the reduction of the county franchise; eightly, the omission of voting-papers; ninthly and tenthly, the omission of the educational and savings-bank franchises. If the omission of these clauses and the adoption of the principles of Mr. Bright be a triumph, then the Conservative party, in the whole history of its previous annals, had won no triumph so signal as this.

Mr. Lowe said the bill was founded on the principle of equality, and on the presumption that all men were equally entitled to the franchise. He protested against this dangerous innovation. Now, however, that the House had declared in its favour, all he could do was to express a hope that the people would be educated up to the standard to which they were to be raised. For his own part he would have endeavoured to prevail upon his master to learn his letters before giving him so much power. But as matters now stood, all he could do was to urge upon the House the necessity of turning its early attention to the education of the people in order to avert the consequences of a measure which every honest and educated Englishman regarded with shame, scorn, and indignation.

Mr. Osborne held that the real author of the bill was not the chancellor of the exchequer, but the honourable member for Birmingham. In 1858 the latter brought in a bill the principle of which was rating and household suffrage. This principle had been seized by the chancellor of the exchequer, who played the part of a gipsy in the matter. He had stolen the child and disfigured it in order to make it pass for his own. But immense credit attached to him for the tact and temper he had shown in the conduct of the measure. The conversion wrought by

MR. DIS-
RAELI'S BILL
OF 1867. him in the obtuse and obstinate party which sat behind him was without a precedent since the days of St. Augustine, for he had effected a perfect change in the opinions of the most aristocratic cabinet which had ever governed since that of Pelham, which contained eight dukes, five earls, and only one commoner.

Bill in the
Lords. The bill was then finally carried through the House of Commons, and on July 22 the discussion of it commenced in the House of Lords. The debate has not much interest. It was a foregone conclusion. Earl Grey moved as an amendment that the second reading be passed in order to the bill being improved in committee, but he declined to press it. The bill was committed on July 29, when Lord Halifax moved an amendment to the effect that the proposed scheme for the redistribution of seats was inadequate; but after a debate the amendment was negatived by a majority of 48. Lord Cairns proposed that the lodger franchise be raised from £10 to £15, and this amendment was carried by 121 to 89. So also was an amendment by the Earl of Harrowby to raise the copyhold franchise from £5 to £10. The clauses anent the compound householders were affirmed. The decision of the House of Commons regarding minority representation, and the disfranchising clauses were also affirmed. But an amendment was carried in favour of the use of voting-papers. Some other amendments having been
Bill passed. adopted, the bill passed through committee. The bill being read a third time, and a motion made that the bill do pass, Lord Derby on the part of the government expressed his thanks to their lordships for the spirit of impartiality and consideration in which they had dealt with the measure. During an experience of forty-five years, he said, he never knew a bill of so much importance dis-

SECOND REFORM. 261

cussed with so little acerbity and party spirit. He then MR. DIS-
spoke of the experimental character of the bill, and in so RAELI'S BILL
doing let fall an expression which was afterwards much
commented on, and formed the theme of many criticisms
in the public press. "No doubt we are making a great
experiment *and taking a leap in the dark*, but I have the
greatest confidence in the sound sense of my fellow-
countrymen, and I entertain a strong hope that the extended franchise which we are now conferring upon them
will be the means of placing the institutions of this
country on a firmer basis, and that the passing of this
measure will tend to increase the loyalty and contentment of a great portion of her majesty's subjects."

The differences between the two Houses having been
settled, the bill received the royal assent on August 15,
1867. The Scotch and Irish bills were passed in the
following session on similar lines.

So passed into law the bill of 1867. It is of little use Remarks.
discussing the question why it took so long as thirty-five
years to bring about a second reform of the House of
Commons, or why it was that nineteen years elapsed
from the time when, in 1848, Mr. Hume brought forward the first of many bills before one was successful. It
is more open to inquiry why a bill was passed at all. The
country as a whole was indifferent. The leaders of the
Liberal party were much divided. Many of them had
become quite as conservative as the Tories, and in these
circumstances there was an excellent opening for a man
with the peculiar genius of Mr. Disraeli. He had an opportunity of "dishing the Whigs"—he and his party
could pose as Reformers—he could compete with the
Liberals for the favour of the working-classes. He could
confer the franchise on a great many people without

MR. DIS-
RAELI'S BILL
OF 1867.

producing much effect on the House of Commons—he could settle the question for a length of time, and he could perhaps remain in office. He laid the question of reform at rest for only seventeen years, and in the interval he disappeared from the scene.

Extent of
the reform.

The *extent* generally of the changes produced by the Reform Acts of 1867 and 1868 for the three kingdoms was as follows. The electorate was 1,352,970 in 1867 and rose to 2,243,259 in 1870. The membership of the House was not altered. It remained at 658. It was, however, distributed differently. England, instead of 500 seats, was reduced to 493. Scotland was raised to 60, while Ireland remained at 105. The changes otherwise were not so great as in 1832. There was the disfranchisement of four English boroughs for corrupt practices, and all boroughs with a population under 10,000, being 38 in all, were reduced to one member each. The four English towns of Manchester, Liverpool, Birmingham, and Leeds were assigned three members each, and the London University one. Counties were likewise divided. It was similarly arranged for Scotland. Counties got nine members, and Glasgow got three. The universities were grouped and got representation. The three-cornered constituencies were introduced—that is, although there were three members to be elected, each elector had only two votes. The *effect* of these reforms will be seen further on.

THIRD REFORM.

The reform of the House of Commons was now about to take place for the third time, and it was to be effected in a way somewhat different from any of the previous reforms. In 1832 it was accomplished by pressure from without, pressure that was disorganized and tumultuous, pressure that was accompanied with threats, and violence, and rioting, and even bloodshed. In 1867 there was some pressure from without, but the movement was like that of an army under the control of its leaders. It was quite different from the times of 1832, when the country rose up and created a reform party for the express purpose of carrying through a Reform Bill. In 1867 there was no such party called into existence. The leaders of the movement were the Liberals;—the party who actually did the work, as the condition of their being permitted to remain in office and carry on for a time the government of the country, being the Conservatives. The reform of 1884 was different from both of the preceding reforms. There was nothing tumultuous from without, and no leadership from within. There was a mandate to the government from an orderly assemblage of delegates appointed by the Liberal associations of the country sitting at Leeds in the autumn of 1883. The movement may be said to originate directly from that meeting, and nothing else than that was required to bring it to a successful termination except an orderly demonstration in the autumn of 1884, for the enlightenment of the House of Lords. Those differences are very suggestive of the progress of the people. The short period that had elapsed from the time of the previous bill is likewise suggestive. It shows the

Constitu-
tion of 1867

Differences
in the three
Reforms.

CONSTITU-
TION OF 1867. great activity of political life, and the rapidity of its processes compared with what once was. There was no reform
of the House of Commons from 1688 to 1832, a period
of 144 years. The next reform was in 1867, after a lapse
of 35 years. The last reform was in 1884, at an interval
of only 17 years.

Effects of
second
reform.

After the bill of 1867 was passed into law, the elections
took place, and the result was that the Liberal party had
a considerable majority in the House of Commons. Mr.
Gladstone therefore became premier, and his government
forthwith proceeded to execute the commission given
them by the country. They disestablished the Irish
Church. They passed an Irish Land Act. They enacted
the Ballot. They passed the Education Acts, and opened
all civil service appointments to competition. They likewise abolished purchase in the army, and furthermore,
placed the commander-in-chief under the secretary for
war. But they could go no further. It was felt that
the mandate ended at this point. Then in 1874 there
was a change of ministry, the Tories came into office, and
there was a spirited foreign policy pursued at once. The
country by and by got tired of this, recalled Mr. Gladstone, and gave him a considerable majority in 1880. He
carried through a second Land Act, but further than this
he could not go.

Further
progress
stopped.

Indeed under the constitution as amended by the Act
1867, any further progress was impossible. Irish University education could not be touched. Neither could self-
government in any form be successfully dealt with,
whether it was national self-government or county self-
government, or even the self-government of the metropolis.
The question of land, as well as of imperial and local
taxation, remained over. These were subjects for an

extended constitution. After 1872 it was felt that it was
only by a broadening of the electorate and by a better distribution of political power that questions of that magnitude could be grappled with.

The state of the electoral roll was greatly improved by
the act of 1867. Immediately before that act was passed the roll for the United Kingdom contained 1,352,970 names. Three years after that act was passed, that is in 1870, the same roll had 2,423,259. This was a considerable addition to the gross numbers of the constituencies, and if they had been properly distributed the power of the new electorate would have been more widely felt. But this was not done. Lord Beaconsfield, while the bill was under discussion, admitted that the distribution would be anomalous. He did not profess to make it as perfect as it could be. And as time passed things did not improve. No doubt the gross electorate increased, but so did the population, until the figures stood as follows:—

Constituencies in 1870.

England and Wales,	...	...	...	1,944,022
Scotland, ...	...	...	...	256,841
Ireland, ...	...	...	...	222,396
United Kingdom,		...	...	2,423,259

Constituencies in 1884.

England and Wales,	...	...	...	2,632,223
Scotland, ...	...	...	...	331,676
Ireland, ...	...	...	...	226,511
United Kingdom,		...	...	3,190,410

This was the state of the roll *after* passing the Act of 1867, and immediately *before* the passing of the last Franchise Bill in 1884. In the meantime the population of

the United Kingdom rose from 29,321,288 in 1861 to
31,845,379 in 1871, and from that to 35,262,762 in 1881.
The electorate was growing, therefore, with the population in a ratio that was roughly equal. But the distribution was getting worse; it was bound to do so as the
population was growing unequally, and besides, was shifting very much. The system was consequently ceasing
to be representative. It was well known, for example,
that at the election of 1874 the Conservative party polled
a smaller number of voters than the Liberals, and yet
they had a majority in the House of Commons. It was
well known that in large boroughs like Birmingham and
Glasgow it took over 20,000 votes to elect a member,
while in certain small boroughs less than a couple of hundred would do it. It was also evident from an examination
of the electoral return of April 7, 1881, that a number of
constituencies could be selected, whose numerical strength
is only 578,828, and yet they really sent to Parliament
330 members; in other words, a majority of the House
of Commons; so that this minority of 578,828 electors
could outvote the large majority of 2,498,661. Of course
all these anomalies arise from the fact that there was a bad
distribution of what voting power the country possessed,
and from that voting power being based on the principle
of giving the working-class in the boroughs a vote, which
was denied to the same class in the counties. Of late years,
therefore, it became evident that there must be an effort
made to get those two millions of non-voters imported
into the electoral system, and have the constituencies
properly arranged. This was the work of the Liberal
party for 1884 and 1885, assigned to them by the Liberal
associations of the country.

Before going into the subject of the Franchise Bill of

1884 let us refer back to certain preliminary efforts made in previous years to bring the Reform question to the front. We need not take into account two attempts made in 1876 to have the Irish borough franchise assimilated to the English, but which were unsuccessful. Nor shall we do more than mention that a resolution was moved by Mr. Courtenay in 1879 in favour of removing the electoral disabilities of women, which was also unsuccessful. We will refer only to the general question, and that, we may mention, was kept alive for many years by the efforts of Mr. Trevelyan. He made successive motions to have the subject taken up by Parliament, no- tably in 1877, 1878, and 1879—all during the administration of Lord Beaconsfield, and all unsuccessful. In 1877 he brought his motion before a full House in the form of two resolutions:—"1. That in the opinion of this House it would be desirable to adopt a uniform parliamentary franchise for borough and county constituencies. 2. That it would be desirable to so redistribute political power as to obtain a more complete representation of the opinion of the electoral body." He contended that on such questions as the Burials Bill, flogging in the navy, and recruiting for the army the voice of the county householders ought to be heard. They were not merely not represented; they were misrepresented, especially by the creation of faggot-votes. The representative system was so anomalous that two-fifths of the membership of the House only represented two-fifths of the population of the counties. Sir Charles Dilke seconded the motion, and it was supported by Mr. Stansfeld, Lord Edward Fitzmaurice, and Mr. Sergeant Spinks. It was opposed by Mr. Smollett, Mr. Goldney, Viscount Emlyn, and Mr. Gregory. Mr. Knatchbull-Huggessen held that the payment of taxes gave every man a *prima facie* right to a voice in the government of the country. Mr. E. Stanhope from the treasury bench objected to the resolutions as there was no finality in them. He held that if they were adopted there would be no variety in the representation, and that sufficient time had not been allowed to test the last experiment on reform. Mr. Goschen objected to the scheme as inopportune. He pointed out that the rural classes had not had any training from municipal institutions, and that our experience of the voters enfranchised by the last Reform Act had not been such as to warrant a further extension at present. He feared the reign of numbers. Sir Stafford Northcote repudiated the doctrine that every citizen had a right to the vote. The Marquis of Hartington held that he had. On a division the motion was rejected by a majority of 276 against 220.

On the occasion of this debate a great meeting of agricultural labourers' delegates was held in Exeter Hall to support the motion—Mr. Bright in the chair. There were 1200 delegates from the associations over the country, and they passed resolutions in favour of household suffrage in the counties and a redistribution of seats. Mr. Bright made an effective and vigorous speech, in which he told them that he looked to them in particular for a total change in the land laws.

In the following year (1878) the motion was renewed by Mr. Trevelyan. He referred to a charge made by Mr. Lowe in a paper in the *Fortnightly*, that great corruption had resulted from the wide suffrage in the United States, by pointing out that similar corruption was common enough in our own country under a very narrow suffrage. Sir Charles Dilke seconded the motion, and showed that the 222 Liberal members (including tellers) who voted for the motion last year represented 1,215,151 electors, while the 278 (also including tellers) who voted the other way, represented only 1,083,758. The popular vote therefore showed a majority of 132,000 electors for the motion. Mr. Lowe made a speech against the resolution on the old ground of the new electors outvoting all the other classes. The debate was otherwise much the same as last year's. On a vote the motion was rejected by a majority of 271 against 219.

The motion was repeated in 1879. On this occasion Mr. Trevelyan referred to the practice of "faggot" votes in Scotland as a practice carried on to a great extent, and as very reprehensible. It enabled non-residents by the acquisition and subdivision of a property in a county to swamp the resident electors. Lord Claud Hamilton defended it. The only speech that imported any freshness into the discussion was from Mr. Courtney. He did not object to the assimilation of the franchises, but objected that no clear principle had been stated upon which re-distribution was to proceed. He wanted the electoral so arranged as to secure a fair representation of opinion in Parliament. He instanced Lancashire. Its voting strength was 104,000 Liberals and 102,000 Conservatives, and yet at last election it returned 22 Conservatives and 11 Liberals. This showed the necessity for providing for the representation of the minority as well as the majority. On a vote the motion was rejected by a majority of 291 against 226.

The Tory government ceased to exist in 1880, and the Liberals came into power. For a period of three years there was little said about reform, as various other questions arose that required immediate settlement. It was

MR. GLAD-
STONE'S
FIRST BILL
OF 1884. in the autumn of 1883 that the question was raised in a letter from Mr. Chamberlain to the Battersea Radical Association. Then followed a meeting at Newcastle-on-Tyne, at which it is said there were 50,000 present, and which passed resolutions in favour of reform. This was succeeded by a conference at Leeds, at which were assem· bled 2500 delegates, representing no less than 500 Liberal associations; Mr. Morley, M.P., in the chair; and this conference also passed resolutions in favour of immediate action in the cause of reform. At a subsequent meeting there Mr. Bright endorsed these resolutions, and advocated a reform of the House of Lords also, especially to the effect that it should not possess the power of rejecting a bill *twice* that has been sent up by the House of Commons. A series of public meetings then took place all over the country, and the result was that Mr. Gladstone's government felt constrained to attempt legislation.

In pursuance of notice given on February 5 Mr. Gladstone on the 28th moved for leave to introduce the "Representation of the People Amendment Bill" into the House of Commons. He said that in doing so he was fulfilling a pledge to the country made by the Liberal party; that he was satisfying a desire for the extension of the franchise generally entertained by the classes who His speech. were to be affected by the extension; that he was also making a proposal which would add to the strength of the state. He held that the strength of the modern state lay in the representative system, and no better proof of that could be found than in the case of the great war of the American Republic between the years 1861 and 1865, a war that could never have been carried on except by a country where every capable citizen was enfranchised. The capable citizens of our own country, whom it was

now proposed to enfranchise, were the inhabitants of the
counties, the minor tradesman, the skilled labourers and
artisans in all the common arts of life, and especially in
connection with our great mining industry; and last of
all, the peasantry. He then proceeded to explain the
borough system of the country, as that was the hinge of
the whole bill. He would take England to begin with,
and would put entirely out of sight what are called the
"ancient right" franchises, the case of freemen, the case
of liverymen, the case of burgess-tenure, and other mis-
cellaneous franchises surviving under the old system.
These were not to be touched by the bill. Setting them
all aside there were three well-known borough franchises—
1. The enfranchised occupiers of buildings, with or without land, of £10 annual value, established by the Act
of 1832. 2. The inhabiting occupiers of rated dwelling-
houses enfranchised by the Act of 1867. 3. The lodger
franchise. That was the present English borough franchise system. He would not touch the "ancient right"
franchises, nor the household franchise of 1867, nor the
lodger franchise. He would extend the £10 franchise of
1832 to the case of land without buildings. He would
also introduce a service franchise to meet the case of
officers, servants, or the like who occupy houses but do
not pay rent. There would thus for the future be a
fourfold borough franchise—the yearly-value franchise of
the Act of 1832, the lodger franchise of 1867, the service
franchise of this bill, and the household franchise of
1867. Passing to the counties of England, the right
honourable gentleman proposed to abolish the £50 franchise, reduce the £12 rating franchise to £10 of yearly
value, and lastly, dispense with residence as a qualification. Then he proposed to import into the counties the

four franchises of the boroughs, the £10 yearly value, the
household, the lodger, and the service franchises. That
proposal was the main object of the bill. In the case of
Scotland and Ireland the changes would be similar.
Scotland would also retain her peculiar franchises. The
service franchise would be introduced, the Scotch boroughs
being already possessed of the other three franchises, the
lodger, the household, and the £10 clear yearly value.
There would thus be an identity of the Scotch with the
English borough system, with the exception of the small
peculiarities found in each country. He then proposed
the same changes with Scotch county franchises as he
did in the case of the English ones, and imported into
these counties the same borough franchises that he proposed to introduce into English counties. Thus there
would be an identity of suffrage in Scotch and English
counties, excepting always the little peculiarities above
referred to. In regard to Ireland there were in existence
two borough franchises, a £4 rating franchise which applied to buildings, or land, or both, and a lodger franchise. The lodger franchise he proposed to leave alone
and to abolish the rating franchise. The £10 clear yearly
value franchise of the English and Scotch boroughs would
be introduced, as also the service and household franchises.
There are to be the same changes in the Irish counties as
in the case of the counties of England and Scotland, so
as to produce as nearly as possible an assimilation of the
franchise generally over the whole of the three kingdoms.
Mr. Gladstone then referred to the act passed in the
reign of George III. by the spontaneous action of the
House of Commons, whereby residence was dissociated
from the franchise in respect of property, and announced
that that law would be maintained, but that safeguards

would be introduced to prevent the creation of fictitious or faggot votes. He then went at great length into the question of the redistribution of seats, and stated his reasons for declining to mix that department of the subject with the subject of the franchise. He said: "The question of the franchise is a large and national one, and ought to be determined upon imperial considerations. I take it there is no doubt about that. Is redistribution a question that is only determined upon imperial and national considerations? Of course the question of re-distribution raises up local feeling, and what may be de-scribed without offence as a selfish feeling. The effect of that is this, that where the two measures are mixed together those who think their local interests are touched by the measures oppose the extension of the franchise for fear of the redistribution which is to follow. The conse-quence is that they decide the great imperial question of the franchise on grounds which are sectional and local, if not selfish.

"The only substitute I can offer is a very humble one. I have not the least objection to make a little sketch of my own views upon redistribution; and although I can-not commit my colleagues absolutely to them, yet I cer-tainly would say this, that I would not submit them if I believed them to be vitally in conflict with any of the opinions they entertain. I need not detain the House long with them, but I will just run through the main features. In the first place I think when a measure of redistribution comes, as it may come, I hope, next year, in order that it may have that sort of relative finality to which we ought always to look forward especially when organic changes are in question, it must be a large mea-sure of redistribution. I do not know whether it need

S   ·

be so large as the measure of 1831, which of course
effected a wholesale slaughter of nominally existing
boroughs and constituencies in this country; but at any-
rate it must be nearer the measure of 1831 than the one
of 1867 in order to attain its object. At the same time
I am not personally at all favourable to what is called
the system of electoral districts, or to the adoption of
any pure population scale. I cannot pretend to have the
fear and horror which some people have with regard to
the consequences of electoral districts. My objection is
a very simple and practical one. In the first place,
electoral districts would involve a great deal of unnecessary displacement and disturbance of traditions, which, I
think, you ought to respect. But my second objection
is, and I regard it as a very important one, that I do not
believe that public opinion at all requires it, and I doubt
whether it would warrant it. Next I should say that in
a sound measure of redistribution the distinction between
town and country, known to the electoral law as borough
and shire, ought to be maintained. Although our franchise is nearly identical, that is not the question. The
question is, whether there is not in pursuits and associations, and in social circumstances, a difference between
town and country, between borough and shire, which it
is expedient, becoming, and useful to maintain? Now,
sir, I do not think we ought to have any absolute population scale. I would respect within moderate limits the
individuality of constituencies, and I would not attempt
to place towns which have had representation for many
generations precisely and mathematically upon the footing of towns that have not.

"There is another principle to which I would call
attention. I am certainly disposed to admit that very

large and closely-concentrated populations need not have,
and perhaps ought not to have, quite so high a proportional share in the representation of the country as rural
and dispersed populations, because the actual political
power in these concentrated masses is sharper, quicker,
and more vehement. That consideration, of course,
would apply most of all to the metropolis. Another
proposition I would lay down is this—I would not
reduce the proportional share of representation, according to the present law, to Ireland. In the case of Ireland, as in the case of some other parts of the country,
in my opinion some regard ought to be had to relative
nearness and distance. Take Scotland, for example.
The nearest part of it is 350 miles off, and some parts
of it are between 600 and 700 miles off. It is impossible to say that numerical representation meets the case,
though I grant it is pretty well made up for, by the
shrewdness of the men whom Scotland sends; but it is
her virtue and good fortune which cause her to make so
excellent a choice. Undoubtedly, however, the representation is exercised under greater difficulties, and it is
fair that those parts of the country which, like Scotland and Ireland, are separated by great distances, not
omitting the element of the sea, should be more liberally
dealt with in proportion to the representatives they
ought to send. Well, sir, that is pretty nearly all I have
to say, excepting one other proposition which I am disposed to lay down with considerable hesitation, and not
as giving a final opinion. Speaking roughly, what will
happen will be this. Smaller boroughs, so many of
which are in the south of England, must yield seats for
London and other great towns, for the counties, and
thirdly for Scotland and the north of England, which

MR. GLAD-STONE'S FIRST BILL OF 1884.

have, perhaps, the largest and most salient of all these claims. The prospect of that operation certainly suggests a proposition, if, under the altered circumstances of Parliament and its increasing business, Parliament was disposed to entertain it, but which it has not yet favourably entertained, and I think ought not to entertain unless for grave cause, for a limited addition to the number of its members. I ask no assent of the House to that proposition. All I say is, I do not exclude it from the view of the whole circumstances of the case; and it may be found materially to ease the operation, which is one, taken altogether, of no slight magnitude and difficulty. Finally, when redistribution has come forward, then will be the proper time for considering all His speech. the propositions with regard to minority representation, and with regard to modes of voting. These very important subjects will have to be fully considered, but I myself see no cause to change the opinion I have always entertained with regard to them. I admit they have claims which ought to receive the full and impartial consideration of Parliament.

" Before sitting down, I wish to make two appeals. One is an appeal to honourable gentlemen, whom I am afraid I cannot class as friends, and more particularly to the right honourable and gallant gentleman opposite (Sir John Hay), who has given notice of the first amendment. He knows my sentiment on that subject. It is impossible to entertain the question of redistribution at all without including in a measure a liberal enlargement of the number of members accorded to Scotland. If we are called upon to set aside this bill, to make that assertion which is totally unnecessary, we may equally well be called upon to make any other assertion. We

then come to the amendment of the honourable member
for Knaresborough (Mr. T. Collins); it is one of those
motions which might be multiplied by the score, and of
which it is too obvious the object is to say 'We will not
entertain your bill, we will not consider it.' Then comes
the motion of the honourable member for Stafford (Mr.
Salt). That is a distinct refusal. He proposes to the
House distinctly to refuse to entertain the subject recommended by the initiative of the government and the
crown. The House has never taken such a course.
The House has, upon very rare occasions indeed, entertained motions analogous to that of the honourable
gentleman—that is to say touching the subject-matter
even of measures recommended in the Queen's speech;
but that has been extremely rare, and I submit to the
House that it is rather hard, that after more than 100
persons have been allowed upon their own authority and
recommendation to bring bills into the House of Commons without resistance, that the speech from the throne
on the responsibility of the government recommended
in the most prominent manner the subject of parliamentary reform to the consideration of Parliament, is
to be met for the first time in our history by an absolute refusal to entertain the subject at all, and by setting up another reason which in the opinion of the
honourable member are reasons why the recommenda-
tions from the throne should be contemptuously trodden
down. That is my appeal to the opponents of the
measure.

"But I have the strongest appeal to make to its friends.
I entreat them not to endanger the bill by additions.
This bill is in no danger from direct opposition. It has
some danger to encounter from indirect opposition, but

of these dangers from indirect opposition I for one am
not afraid unless they be aggravated by the addition of
dangers which it may have to encounter from friendship,
for I do not hesitate to say that it is just as possible for
friends to destroy the measure by additions which it will
not bear as it is from enemies. If I may presume to
tender advice it is this, Ask yourselves whether the measure is worth having. What does it do, and what does it
do in comparison to what has been done before? In 1832
there was passed what was considered a *Magna Charta* of
British liberties; but that *Magna Charta* of British liberties added, according to the previous estimate of Lord
John Russell, 500,000, while, according to the results,
considerably less than 500,000 were added to the entire
constituency of the three countries. After 1832 we come
to 1866. At that time the total constituency of the
United Kingdom reached 1,364,000. By the bills which
were passed between 1867 and 1869 the number was
raised to 2,448,000. And now, sir, under the action of
the present law the constituency has reached in round
numbers what I would call 3,000,000. I will not enter
into details; but what is the increase we are going to
make? There is a basis of computation, but it is a basis
which affords, I admit, ground for conjecture and opinion.
That basis of computation is the present ratio in towns
between inhabited houses and the number of town electors.
Of course we have availed ourselves of that basis for the
purpose of computation. I have gone into the matter as
carefully as I can, and the best results I can attain are
these. The bill, if it passes as presented, will add to the
English constituency over 1,300,000 persons. It will
add to the Scotch constituency—Scotland being at present rather better provided for in this respect than either

of the other countries—over 200,000, and to the Irish
constituency over 400,000, or, in the main, to the present
aggregate constituency of the United Kingdom, taken at
3,000,000, it will add 2,000,000 more, nearly twice as
much as was added since 1867 and more than four times
as much as was added in 1832. Surely, I say, that is
worth doing—that is worth not endangering. Surely
that is worth some sacrifice.

" This is a measure with results such as I have ventured
to sketch them that they ought to bring home to the mind
of every man favourable to the extension of popular liberty
the solemn question what course he is to pursue in regard
to it. I hope the House will look at it as the Liberal party
in 1831 looked at the Reform Bill of that date, and determined that they would waive criticism of minute details,
that they would waive particular preferences and predi-
lections, and would look at the broad scope and general
effect of the measure. Do that upon this occasion. It is
a bill worth having; and if it is worth having, again I
say it is a bill worth your not endangering. Let us enter
into no by-ways which would lead us off the path marked
out straight before us; let us not wander on the hill-tops
of speculation, let us not wander into the morasses and
fogs of doubt. We are firm in the faith that enfranchisement is a good—that the people may be trusted—that the
voters under the constitution are the strength of the constitution. What we want in order to carry this bill—considering, as I fully believe, that the very large majority of
this country are favourable to its principle—what we want
in order to carry it is union and union only. What will
endanger it is disunion and disunion only. Let us hold
firmly together and success will crown our effort. You
will as much as any former Parliament that has con-

ferred great legislative benefits on the nation have your
reward, and

         'Read your history in a nation's eye,'

for you will have deserved it by the benefits you will
have conferred. You will have made this strong nation
stronger still—stronger by its closer union without;
stronger against its foes, if and when it has any foes
without; stronger within by union between class and
class, and by arraying all classes and all portions of the
community in one solid compacted mass round the ancient
throne which it has loved so well, and round a constitution now to be more than ever powerful and more than
ever free."

Sir John Hay, member for the Wigtown Burghs, moved
an amendment to the effect that no Reform Bill would
be satisfactory which did not provide for an adequate
increase to the number of representatives for Scotland.
He said that, after the appeal made to him by the prime
minister, he felt a little diffidence in speaking on his
motion. He approved of the bill, but considered what
was said as to the representation of Scotland to be extremely unsatisfactory. He was glad the three kingdoms
were to be treated with uniformity; but he thought if
the number of Scottish members was to be increased the
method of effecting this by an absolute increase of the
membership of the House would not meet with the
approbation either of the House or the country. He
said it would be expected that the Redistribution Bill
would be in the hands of members before the second
reading of the Franchise Bill. He then quoted statistics
to show the additional number of members that Scotland
was entitled to. Mr. Cochrane Patrick seconded the
amendment.

Mr. Salt, member for Stafford, then moved an amend- ment to the effect that it was undesirable to introduce great changes in our representative system, looking at the position of affairs in Egypt and in Ireland. He made a long speech—went fully into Egyptian and Irish difficulties, and quoted the cases of postponement of reform by Mr. Pitt in 1785 and Lord John Russell in 1854 as precedents for his amendment.

Mr. Anderson, of Glasgow, replied to Sir John Hay, and said he was glad to hear that he was prepared to support the present bill. Mr. Anderson had also some little objections to offer to the redistribution scheme, but he would do so at the proper time. He held that both England and Ireland were over-represented, and that Scotland was entitled to more representation than she had at present. He congratulated the prime minister in having offered to the House a really great measure. A bill to enfranchise 2,000,000 could not be described otherwise than as a great measure. That was only an estimate, and an uncertain one, but it was a good reason for putting off the matter of redistribution in the meantime.

Mr. Gibson, member for the University of Dublin, op- posed the bill on various grounds. He remarked that it had been the lot of the prime minister, eighteen years ago, to introduce a Reform Bill of considerable importance, and which met with a fate that, he thought, would to a certain extent determine the fate of the ministry on the present occasion. The topics that were at the present time most prominent in the public mind were the fate of the forces near Suakim and the prospect of the bill for the protection of our flocks and herds from imported disease. The ministry were not enthusiastic on the sub-

ject. He denied that Parliament was elected to deal
with the subject of electoral reform. The House, besides,
was asked to deal with the subject without statistics.
It was not suggested that the bill would improve the
House of Commons or make the legislative machine work
more smoothly. He did not dispute the fitness for the
franchise of those who would be admitted. They would
be as fit as thousands of those who had the franchise, and
just as fit as thousands of those who would be left out.
The bill would exaggerate and develop inequalities and
anomalies, and what the public wanted to know was
what was to be done with minority representation and
redistribution. The bill ought to contain a clause to the
effect that it was not to come into operation until a redistribution bill is passed. As to redistribution, the information they had got was most unsatisfactory, and that
portion of the subject was of immense importance.

Mr. H. H. Fowler, member for Wolverhampton, said,
in reference to Mr. Gibson's great anxiety for statistics,
that he would trouble the House with two statistical
statements that would form a sufficient basis for the
bill, namely, that there were in the United Kingdom
6,500,000 householders who earned their bread, paid
taxes, and discharged all the responsibilities of householders in a civilized community, and that of those
6,500,000 there were only 3,000,000, or less than one-half,
who had a right to vote in the election of a member of
Parliament. These were all capable citizens. He believed the House of Commons would be improved by
admitting them, as the House would be more in touch
with the people and would better represent them. The
distribution of political power at present was exceedingly
bad. While the total number of electors was about

3,000,000, it was a fact that *two-thirds* of the members of the House were returned by 1,000,000, while the remaining 2,000,000 only returned *one-third*. The redistribution ought to be thorough. He approved of the scheme which the prime minister had foreshadowed. He also thought that Ireland should be put on the same footing as England and Scotland. It had a right to be properly represented, and that would be an element of strength. The bill was a great measure, and what the Liberal party and the Liberal government meant was that the majority of the electors of the country was to choose the majority of the members of the House of Commons.

Lord Randolph Churchill, member for Woodstock, made some critical observations upon the Radical party, the prime minister, and the bill. He did not dispute the intelligence of the Radicals of the day, but he noticed their want of independence. He thought they were guilty of a slavish servility to the government and their party. He considered the prime minister had given the House a great speech; but the attendance of the Liberal party was scanty, and the Radicals were mute. As to the bill, it was plain that the only effect of the service franchise would be the enfranchisement of the whole of the Scotch agricultural population. He, of course, did not mean to oppose it on that ground, although he could say without fear of contradiction that the agricultural labourer, as a general rule, was absolutely unfitted for the exercise of the franchise. He knew this from experience. He would recommend the government to confine the bill to the mining population. He also noticed that the bill made no provision for female suffrage, nor for proportional representation, nor for dealing with plurality of votes or the representation of minorities. There was

Mr. Glad-stone's first Bill of 1884.

Lord R. Churchill's speech.

MR. GLAD-
STONE'S
FIRST BILL
OF 1884. no care taken that classes and interests should be represented, but merely numbers. He thought the government would be better employed in dealing with questions
of taxation or the depression of trade or local government. He believed there was a popular demand for the
bill. The debate was then adjourned.

Mr. Blennerhasset's
speech. It was resumed on March 3 by Mr. Blennerhasset,
member for the county of Kerry. He said that the
country was not indifferent about the bill. It was not excited, but the reason was that it had perfect faith that
the bill was safe in the hands of the government. He
heard with great satisfaction that the bill was to be extended to Ireland, and he rejoiced to think that the great
bulk of the Irish householders were to be told that there
was a place ready for them in the constitution. He
thought that it would be unjust to reduce the number of
representatives for Ireland merely because the present
population was low. He then went on at considerable
length to show that there ought to be a representation of
minorities.

Mr. E.
Clarke's
speech. Mr. Edward Clarke, member for Plymouth, agreed
with the previous speaker on the subject of proportional
representation, and urged that the franchise and distribution should be dealt with in the same act. He
thought that the shipbuilders on the Clyde ought to
have votes, but this was to be attained by including
them within the borough of Glasgow, and not by extending the franchise into the counties. He believed
the bill would be mischievous.

Mr. Walter's
speech. Mr. Walter, member for Berks, seemed to think that
in principle the householder in a county was as much
entitled to the franchise as a householder in a borough.
There were some boroughs in England larger than

counties, *e.g.* East Retford covered an area of 212,100
acres, while Rutland county had only 51,000.   He held
that redistribution should be inseparable from an extension of the franchise, but he was willing to accept the
assurance of the prime minister that redistribution would
follow immediately afterwards.   He had observed that
the agricultural labourer was oftentimes a man of good
sense, moderation, and good conduct.   He also thought
the large artisan class in large towns were very intelligent.
He thought, however, that the rising generation should
be taught the duties of citizenship, and that elementary
books should be introduced into schools for that purpose.
In regard to the "service" franchise clause, he thought
it unnecessary to import a new name into the act, as
occupation was all that was necessary.   In regard to the
number of representatives for each of the three kingdoms,
he held that the rule laid down by Pitt with reference to
Ireland should hold good, that the proportion should be
fixed on a combined basis of population and taxation.
He likewise thought the prime minister right in so far as
regards the elements of distance.   He expressed his hearty
concurrence in the scheme of the Franchise Bill.

Mr. W. H. Smith, member for Westminister, introduced his remarks with the statement that no greater
change had ever been proposed to Parliament, for it
amounted to a complete transfer of political power from
those who had it now to those who had it not.   In the
case of Ireland it meant that there would be an addition
of 400,000 or 500,000 new electors to the roll.   The
farming population lived with great difficulty.   Was it
statesmanlike to add these to the electoral roll?   They
were also very ignorant and very subject to corrupt
influences, and the result would be that a compact body

of 90 members would be returned, whose object was th disintegration of the empire and the confiscation of th property of the landlords of Ireland. The minority, wh possessed the property, paid the taxes, and bore th burdens of government would practically be trample out. He was surprised to hear that the number of Iris members was not to be reduced. He was also surprise that the membership of the House was to be increase(He thought that a reduction ought rather to have bee aimed at. It was clear that Ireland was not entitled t retain her present number of seats. Their membei would be able to hold the scale between the two gre: parties. The prime minister would have the satisfactio of knowing that he had been the means of making parli: mentary government impossible. He saw nothing bi evil in the bill.

Mr. Goschen, member for Ripon, did not hold that th agricultural labourers were quite fitted for the franchis(and he would have liked that they should be prepare for political life by a previous admission to the discharg of civic duties. The artisan class had inspired him wit confidence as to what attitude they will take in the futur(In times of severe trade depression they had not hesitate to reject obsolete and exploded doctrines, and their pr(ceedings at the Trades-union Congress had shown gre: moderation. They have likewise shown no dispositio to combine on any special question where their pecuniar interests were concerned, and in this respect were quit in contrast with the traders. They may make mistake: but so far as can be judged their desire is to do righ(On the other-hand, it is obvious that the power of resi: tance to any popular demand has notably decreased, bot outside and inside the House. He held that the polic of Lord Beaconsfield had borne its fruit by discovering the Conservative working-man, and that the attitude of the Conservative party was entirely changed since 1867. Since that date democracy has been making tremendous strides, and the Conservatives compete with the other side in carrying out its wishes. By the present bill those classes who are to be enfranchised will be a clear majority of the country, and care must be taken to guard the rights of minorities. The system must be truly a representative system, and if that is of importance in England, then it is of still more importance in Ireland that the loyal minority shall have a chance of making itself heard. This has evidently not entered into the prime minister's mind. To put Ireland on the same footing of an extended franchise is an act of tremendous courage, and to give her a membership that she is not entitled to is what it is impossible to explain. He did not wish the Franchise and Redistribution Bills tied together. He did not wish the Franchise Bill lost. "I think it is well that the question of the franchise should be settled, and if possible that both the franchise and distribution should be settled by the present Parliament. My right honourable friend spoke of the deck cargo which might lead to the foundering of the ship. Another right honourable member took up the simile, and spoke of the stowing of the cargo. Let me continue the simile. When I was in the admiralty, one of the first lessons I learned was that when there was a fresh distribution of weights in a ship which was being rebuilt, it was the paramount duty of those who were responsible for her safety when sent to sea to calculate afresh the centre of gravity and the angle of vanishing stability. Gigantic new engines are being put into the old hull of the British constitution. I believe the hull

is strong enough to bear them, for of stouter or more
seasoned stuff has never craft been built; but those who
will be responsible for the seaworthiness of the recon-
structed ship would, it appears to me, be reckless to a
crime if before they sent her to face the perils of the sea
they had not made themselves absolutely sure that no
change in the weights had shifted dangerously the centre
of gravity, and that she would still preserve a sufficient
reserve of stability to prevent her heeling over to the
angle of danger under the pressure of wind or waves."

Mr. Parnell, member for Cork, thought that Mr. Smith
and his party would take up a consistent position if they
asked Parliament to exclude Ireland altogether from representation, and to govern her as a crown colony.   But
he could not understand the position of Mr. Goschen, who
has repeatedly asked the House to look upon Ireland as
if it were Yorkshire, and yet declines to include it in the
same measure that he is inclined to give to England and
Scotland.   He (Mr. Goschen) seemed to fear that if Ireland got her present quota of members, both life and
property there would be at the mercy of the majority of
the Irish people.   He forgot that the Irish members
would not have the making of the laws, even after the
bill passed.   Under any circumstances, and whether
population or the number added to the constituencies be
taken, the total number that could be taken from the
Irish membership would not exceed 6 or 7, and that was
surely a very paltry result to justify the violation of the
Act of Union.   At present the Irish boroughs are very
inadequately represented as compared with English
boroughs.   In the latter the electors number 1 in $7\frac{1}{2}$ of
the population, while in Ireland it is 1 in $15\frac{1}{2}$.   He contended that you cannot with any show of consistency, or

the slightest scrap of self-respect, deny to Ireland the MR. GLAD-
same franchise as is claimed for England. Those who STONE'S FIRST BILL
oppose it are doing so for the real purpose of opposing OF 1884.
the bill for England. It is a mere appeal to passion and
prejudice.

Mr. Trevelyan, member for the Hawick Burghs, re- Mr. Trevel-
marked with regard to Mr. Salt's amendment, that there yan's speech.
would hardly ever be a time when we had no foreign
business in hand, and that in 1867 the Abyssinian expedition was engaged in battle at the very time when
Lord Beaconsfield was passing his Reform Bill. That
was no argument acceptable by an English statesman.
In the course of the debate the government had been
asked why they had not been occupying themselves in
bringing Ireland into a state of peace and freedom such
as it had had under the late government, instead of proposing to extend the franchise there. This question, he
said, showed pretty clearly that honourable members did
not often carefully study facts and figures, when those
facts and figures did not serve their purpose. If honourable members would carefully study the statistics of Irish
crime, and they made great use of them when the story
was a great deal blacker, they would find results that
would make them stare. During the last six months of
the late government there were 688 outrages; during the
six months terminating at the end of February last there
were only 354. Exclusive of threatening letters during
the last six months of the late government there were
375 very serious outrages; during the last six months
there have been only 183, or about one-half. That preliminary condition has therefore been fulfilled. In regard to extending the franchise to Ireland, it seemed to
him of importance that the members they return should

T

MR. GLAD-
STONE'S
FIRST BILL
OF 1884.
be representatives of the nation and not of a class, and
that amidst all the difficulties and dangers of Ireland
there was only one course by which success could even
, be remotely gained, and that was, while steadily preserving the public peace of the country to import into Ireland
all the privileges and rights which were enjoyed in the
rest of the United Kingdom. The member for Plymouth
(Mr. Clarke) complained that redistribution was not provided for in the bill, and he thought that was a course
most inconvenient, but it was not at all inconvenient for
those who wished to have the bill passed. It might be
so to those who did *not* wish to have it passed. The
government would be bound to bring in a measure of redistribution. It was stated by the member for the Dublin
University (Mr. Gibson) that this bill would be a settlement for perhaps five years. He (Mr. Trevelyan) believed
that no man living would be troubled with the franchise
again. It has been said that the country is indifferent
upon the subject. That was said also in 1866, and the
House of Commons threw out the bill of that year. But
what was the consequence? It was the old story of the
Sybilline Books: the Conservatives had to buy very dear
next year what they might have bought very cheap the
year before. There is no indifference in the country, but
a deep interest which is increasing and strengthening.

Sir J. Lub-
bock's
speech.
Sir John Lubbock, member for London University,
considered the bill just and right, and calculated to
strengthen and improve the government of the country;
but at same time he had so much faith in her majesty's
government, in the House, and in the justice of the principle, that he hoped to see secured some system of proportional representation. In the course of a powerful
speech he contended that the introduction of the bill did

justify, "nay necessitate, the careful consideration of the subject. It is, of course, clear that additional members will be given to our large cities. Liverpool, for instance, would be entitled to, say, eight members. Now, I under-stand the prime minister to condemn electoral districts. But if Liverpool is to remain an undivided constituency returning eight members, it is of great importance that we should know how the votes are to be given. If every elector is to have a number of votes equal to the number of members, with no form of proportional representation, then it is obvious that the slightest majority on either side would return the whole eight members. We know that in Liverpool the two great parties are very evenly balanced; and the result would be that a majority of a few hundreds, perhaps of only a few units, would return the whole eight members, counting sixteen votes on a division in this House. And, sir, the journal published by the Electoral Reform Association of Belgium gives a striking illustration of such a case. In 1882 elections the Liberals carried their election in the city of Ghent by a majority of forty only. Now Ghent returns eight members to the chamber out of 138. If therefore twenty-one electors had gone over to the other side, Ghent would have returned eight Roman Catholics, counting sixteen on a division; and there would have been a Roman Catholic instead of a Liberal majority in the chamber, which would have led to a complete change of govern-ment. Even under the franchise as it stands the system is very unsatisfactory and imperfect. In my own county of Kent we polled in the three divisions 13,000 votes against 16,000 given to our opponents, and yet they have all the six seats. Taking the county as a whole, we polled 32,000 votes against 36,000, yet they have carried

16 members and we 2. If we draw a line down England
from Lincolnshire to Devonshire there are on the south
side 99 county seats. In many of these the Conservatives had no contest, but the majority of the seats were
fought, and the Liberals polled 96,000 votes, against
116,000 given to the Tories. On this basis, therefore,
we ought to have had, say, 40 seats, and honourable gentlemen opposite 59. As a matter of fact, however, we
only secured 15 against 84. Moreover, of our 15, 5 were
minority seats, so that but for the introduction of the
principle of minority representation, limited though it
was, we should have only had 10 seats out of 99 in the
whole district, while we were fairly entitled to 40. The
Roman Catholics are a very large and respectable portion

of the nation, yet in the whole of England and Scotland
they have never, I believe, for years past secured more
than a single seat at any one time. The case of Ireland
is the most serious of all. Certainly one-third of its
population is moderate, loyal, and desirous of maintaining
the integrity of the empire; but we are told on high
authority that under this bill, unless some system of
proportional representation be adopted, the honourable
member for the city of Cork (Mr. Parnell) will secure
95 seats out of 100, leaving only 5 to the Liberals and
Conservatives together, whereas it is clear that under
any just system of representation they ought to have
over 30; and the result of such a system would be that
Ireland would be entirely misrepresented, and that we
shall gratuitously create terrible difficulties for ourselves.
Sir, it is often said that inequalities in one district are
neutralized by compensating inequalities in another. We
are told that the Liberals of Kent and Surrey are represented by the Liberal members for Scotch and Welsh

counties; but this is just the old and exploded argument
which used to maintain that the people of Birmingham
and Manchester were really represented by the Liberal
members of some other boroughs. We are glad, no doubt,
that Scotland and Wales send us such admirable colleagues; it is a consolation, but it is not the same thing.
Perhaps the one question about which our farmers in
Kent care most is the subject of extraordinary tithes.
My right honourable friend the prime minister will sym-
pathize with us, because he has so powerfully advocated
the cultivation of vegetables and the growth of fruit; he
has raised the question of jam to a dignity which it never
before attained. But while the extraordinary tithe question remains in its present position I fear it will still be
with us a case of jam every other day. Jam yesterday
and jam to-morrow, but not jam to-day. But, sir, the
farmers of West Kent cannot expect the Liberal members
from Scotland to help them as regards extraordinary
tithes. It is conceivable that they do not even know
what extraordinary tithes are. It would not then be
satisfactory, even if it were true, that inequalities in one
district are made up for them by another. But it is not
true. Let us look, for instance, at the elections of 1874
and 1880. In the former the Conservatives had a majority of 60 over the Liberals and Home Rulers put
together, while in 1880 the Liberals had a majority over
the Conservatives and Home Rulers of more than 50.
Of course if this change were due to a corresponding
alteration in public opinion, then, however much each
side of the House might regret its defeat in the one case,
and rejoice over its victory in the other, there would be
nothing to be said as regards the system. But what are
the facts? In 1874, against 1,436,000 votes given to the

MR. GLAD-
STONE'S
FIRST BILL
OF 1884.

Liberals and Home Rulers, the Conservatives polled
1,222,000 votes, so that, although they were in a majority
of 50 in this House, they actually polled 200,000 votes
in the country less than their opponents. Perhaps I
shall be told that this was due to the small boroughs.
But the experience of 1880 proves that this was not so,
or only to a certain extent. In 1880 the Liberals and

Sir J. Lub-
bock's
speech.

Home Rulers together polled 1,880,000 votes, against
1,418,000 given to the Conservative candidates. The
proportions ought then to have been 370 Liberal and
Home Rule to 280 Conservative members, whereas they
really were 414 to 236. In 1874, therefore, the Liberals
and Home Rulers had 56 members too few in relation
to their total poll, while, on the contrary, in 1880 they
secured 43 too many. The difference between the two
elections was therefore enormous, namely, 99 out of a
total of 650. The present system, then, renders the
result of a general election uncertain, and to a large extent a matter of chance. It leads to violent fluctuations
in the balance of political power, and consequently in the
policy of the country. The present system then may be
good or may be bad, but it is not representation."

Sir S.
Northcote's
speech.

Sir Stafford Northcote, the leader of the opposition,
characterized the speech of the Chief-secretary for Ireland
(Mr. Trevelyan) as very sanguine when he used the
expression that if the bill were passed he thought nobody
in the House, nor anybody living, would be troubled
with the franchise question again. And no doubt, if the
matter were left with the prime minister, it might be so;
but the President of the Board of Trade (Mr. Chamberlain) unfortunately had a different opinion, and he had
given fair notice that he for his part looks on any measure of this kind as the merest instalment. He (Sir

Stafford) looked upon the question of redistribution of seats as most important, and that ought to be discussed at the same time. He hoped that Sir John Hay would not think it necessary to come to a division on the subject of his amendment. MR. GLAD-
STONE'S
FIRST BILL
OF 1884

Mr. W. E. Forster, member for Bradford, thought the government had done right in separating the redistribution question from the franchise question. He also thought that the electoral roll was not the best basis to go upon in assigning to each kingdom the membership that it ought to have. He rather thought it should be on the number of families; and if that was the case then England would gain five additional members, Scotland would gain eleven, and Ireland would lose sixteen. The question of proportional representation was likewise of great importance, and one as to which he would have liked to have some further information. Mr.Forster's
speech.

The bill was ordered to be brought in, and was then read the first time.

The second reading was moved on March 24 by the Marquis of Hartington. Second
reading.

Lord John Manners, member for Leicester (Western Division), then proposed the following amendment:— "That the House declines to proceed further with a measure having for its object the addition of two million voters to the electoral body of the United Kingdom until it has before it the entire scheme contemplated by the government for the amendment of the representation of the people." He set out with the remark that the proposed bill was more complicated and far-reaching than any measure of parliamentary reform ever submitted to the House. It provided for the enfranchisement of 2,000,000 electors without any hint as to how they were to be allocated. He Lord J.Man-
ners'amend-
ment.

MR. GLAD-
STONE'S
FIRST BILL
OF 1884.

then quoted from a speech of Lord Derby in 1866, when a similar proposal was made of enfranchisement without distribution, a passage to the effect that Parliament might be dissolved before a redistribution bill was carried through, and that the government might thus be unable to fulfil their engagement to have one passed. He said further that the measure proposed a gigantic and far-reaching change in Ireland, and that the effect would be to create Mr. Parnell the grand elector for four-fifths of Ireland. He then pointed out that our foreign relations were not so good as they were in 1866, when Mr. Gladstone's previous bill was introduced. In regard to the vote itself, he considered it was not a right, but a trust,

Lord John
Manners'
speech.

and the question was, How will it affect—not individuals —but the state? By this bill power is handed over from those who exercise it to those who do not, and the country constituencies will be absolutely unmanageable. Look at the size to which some of them will reach. How can a member canvas them? The bill, besides, will not remove the anomalies of the system. It does not enfranchise women, and yet there are 20,000 female farmers in England. The result will be that the work-people of the lady of the farm will have the vote while she will not. Ireland also is exceptionally favoured in the size of her membership; and as Scotland is to get additional members, this is to be done at the expense of England. The government have not expressed their views on minority or proportional representation. He did not believe that the country wanted the bill—if this was questionable, then appeal to it. Under the present franchise great things have been accomplished. Before the whole system is subverted, and a new one substituted, let the House know what the new scheme is in its details and in its entirety.

Mr. John Bright, member for Birmingham, never
thought much of the passage quoted from Lord Derby's
speech, and he had no doubt that his lordship has long
ago convinced himself that he was wrong. Mr. Bright
would like to ask the member for Leicester whether there
ever was a time when he would have thought the condition of our foreign affairs justified the introduction of a
measure of reform from the Liberal side of the House.
The noble lord had nothing to say against the bill itself.
He does not say whether he is in favour of the extension
of the county franchise or not. It is another bill he is
afraid of. He repeats all the old arguments of 1866. He
differs from Mr. Goschen, as that honourable member
now admits that the disasters that he feared from the
enfranchisement of 1867 have not followed. He is now
converted. Honourable members opposite need no conversion; they were converted in 1867. There was, therefore, no one against the bill. It is one for carrying out
the principle advocated by Mr. Disraeli; that is, the
principle of recognizing the identity of suffrage between
county and town. You have no right to deny that the
agricultural labourer is as competent to exercise the franchise as the artisan in towns. In regard to Ireland,
which has never been governed except by force, and
where the representation was a farce, he conceived that
we should begin on new lines—begin to rule on the principles of justice and equity—and then we shall bring about
tranquillity. He strongly advocated the extension of the
act to Ireland, and so far as its membership was concerned, he considered that we should adhere to the Act
of Union, which fixed the number. No doubt the population has been diminishing, but it does not follow that
this will continue. He concluded: "I trust and believe

MR. GLAD-
STONE'S
FIRST BILL
OF 1884.

Colonel
Dawnay's
speech.

Mr. H. S.
Northcote's
speech.

that the measure will prove hereafter to be a new charter
of freedom and union to the three nations, in whose name
we sit here, and for whose dignity and welfare it is our
duty and honour to labour."

Colonel Dawnay asked whether the honourable member for Birmingham meant to say that if the population
of Ireland dwindled down to 103, that country was still
to have the representation of 103 members ? He (Colonel
Dawnay) considered that none of the prime minister's
reasons for the bill would bear looking into. The pledge
given by the Liberal party need not be fulfilled when
there were so many unfulfilled pledges all around them.
Then as to meeting the desires of the unfranchised
classes, that was of no importance—it was the safety of
the state that fell to be considered. If it is the country
that wants this measure of reform, then the country, so
far as its representatives in Parliament are concerned,
means the existing constituencies. Lastly, as to strengthening the empire, every one knows that it will do the
exact opposite, and that instead of strengthening it will
swamp and destroy the loyal classes in Ireland. The
prime minister has made a tremendous bid for the Home
Rule vote. Ireland is to have an undue proportion of
members, and the representation of Scotland is to be increased, and all at the expense of England.

Mr. H. S. Northcote, member for Exeter, said that
there might be a practical difficulty in working the
three bills for extending the franchise, for redistribution,
and registration, if they were coming into force at different periods. The membership of Ireland would need
to be rearranged. He objected to the south of England
suffering a loss of members, especially as Ireland was
over-represented. So was Wales. And it was unfair that

constituencies should be disfranchised because they happened to be Conservative.   He considered that all the
legitimate purposes of the government could have been
secured by means of a **boundary commission.**

Mr. Baxter, member for Montrose Burghs, expressed
the great satisfaction which he had in voting for the bill,
which was in some respects the greatest and best of all
the measures of reform that had been introduced during
the last thirty years. He was always of opinion that each
householder should have only one vote, and should simply
vote for the house he occupies.   The bill was an emin-
ently Conservative measure and was sure to pass. There
are those who advocate manhood suffrage—and he would
not deny that it might be safe after a generation or two
have passed away.   At present that was not within the
range of practical politics. There were two points on
which he could not agree with the prime minister. He
objected to increase the number of the House. He also
considered that Ireland was over-represented. But these
were matters of discussion under the Redistribution Bill,
and perhaps both the prime minister and Mr. Bright
may find themselves in a minority on the latter point.
He considered the amendment as a simple obstruction.
He approved of the proposal to make registration self-
acting, so that candidates, political parties, and agents,
had nothing to do with it.   It would be all done by the
registrar, as it has been done in Scotland for over twenty
years.   No doubt there are many gentlemen among the
Conservatives who lament the democratic wave passing
over the country; but you cannot educate the masses
without giving them the vote.

Mr. C. Ross, member for St. Ives, considered that the
bill was not generally required by the country; that it

was inopportune, and offered no final solution of the difficulty; and that it was incomplete without redistribution.
He appealed to members who like himself represented
small constituencies to pause before they gave any support to the bill.

    Mr. E. A. Leatham, member for Huddersfield, held
that this measure would not only redress a great and
manifest injustice, but be a measure of arriving at better
government. It was true, as Mr. Disraeli said in 1860,
that you could not admit the working-classes in towns
and exclude them in counties. He (Mr. Leatham) admitted it would be better if redistribution could take
place in the same session, but it was impossible. The
insatiable thirst for information on the part of honourable gentlemen opposite was too great to admit of
that.

    Mr. Mulholland, member for Downpatrick, was of
opinion that the House ought to be made acquainted
with the whole of the government scheme before they
committed themselves to any part of it. He thought it
would be a great mistake to throw 500,000 voters of the
lowest and most ignorant class into the constituency of
Ireland. And to do so would not be to strengthen but
to weaken the state. Was it reasonable that the classes
which possessed the best interests in the state, the most
intelligence, property, and education, should be permanently deprived of political influence and divorced
from public life? Were the interests of Ireland to be
sacrificed to the interests of the Liberal party? Would
this bill make Ireland more loyal or more peaceable? He
thought not. The present electorate consisted of 220,000
votes. By this bill was to be added 400,000 or 500,000.
He considered that the passing of the bill would not be

"a leap in the dark," but a deliberate leap over a preci-
pice.

Mr. Jesse Collings, member for Ipswich, considered the
speech of the previous speaker to be one of vague alarm.
To his mind there was more danger in keeping the Irish
people out of the constitution than taking them within it.
The population of Ireland had diminished, but this was
the result of misgovernment. It was no ground for
lessening the number of their members. He would have
preferred to remove all property franchises, but the
enfranchisement of 2,000,000 people disarmed all criticism. Terrors as to results had been conjured up in 1832
and 1867, but had never been realized. Both of these
acts had been beneficial. The present measure was com
plete in itself, and had no absolute connection with the
redistribution of seats. They had only a consequential
reference. As to the fitness of the agricultural classes
for the vote, he held that although they did not know
how to use it that was no reason why they should not
have it. The way to teach a man to use a responsibility was to give him that responsibility. But really it
was not our part to judge whether a man was fit to exercise the right of citizenship. The extension of the franchise was necessary to the settlement of the land question. There was abundant evidence that the county
labourers wished the franchise.

Mr. James Lowther, member for Lincoln, professed to
approach the question entirely apart from the spirit of
party. He would, however, be guided by political principles. He denounced the Conservative surrender of 1867.
In the course of his remarks he said that the member for
Birmingham told the House that there were 2,000,000 of
persons outside the constitution who were demanding to

MR. GLAD-
STONE'S
FIRST BILL
OF 1884.

be admitted — that the prime minister called them capable citizens, but that on a previous occasion Mr. Bright had referred to them as a "residuum." Mr. Bright thereupon rose and denied this, and explained that what he did say was that there was a residuum in the poorest class of ignorant and abject persons to whom probably it would do no good to give them votes; that he had never applied this to the working-classes or any class; that there was a residuum in every class; that he had even known a residuum in the House of Commons. Mr. Lowther resumed, and said that the bill would practically annihilate the agricultural interest in Parliament, and that to give Ireland a greater amount of representation than she was entitled to was indefensible.

Lord Har-
tington.

The Marquis of Hartington, member for Lancaster, said that the right honourable gentleman who had just spoken was the only speaker who had entered a direct objection to the principle of the extension of the franchise to the counties. It may be admitted that this bill, if passed into law, will terminate the supremacy of tenant-farmers at elections, but it is a grave statement to make that it will annihilate the agricultural interest. It does not follow that a measure which will place a greater share of political power in the hands of agricultural labourers will annihilate the agricultural interest. In regard to the objection of the bill being incomplete, he admitted that it would have been desirable that all the branches of this great subject should have been dealt with by one Parliament, in one session, and it might be by one bill; but this would have required some general agreement on the part of the House. There has been no desire on the part of the opposition to co-operate in such a mode of settling the question. There is, on the contrary, great opposition. The opposition would be great against the one measure—it would be still greater against the two. It would be impossible to carry a bill for extending the franchise and one for redistribution through Parliament in one session. The noble marquis would ask the opposition to complete their own work by extending to the counties the franchise which they granted to the boroughs. He would ask them whether the anomalies in our electoral system can be permanently maintained. He would ask them what conceivable object can be attained by further delay in the settlement of the question. The general lines of the measure of redistribution were contained in the speech of the prime minister. He did not know that the statement of these will be satisfactory to the opposition, but he did expect that the declaration of the prime minister, made with the assent of his colleagues, would satisfy those who profess to feel confidence in their intentions. It appeared to him that an undue importance had been attached to the question of the Irish representation. It would be a grave evil to exclude Ireland from this measure of reform—it would perpetuate and intensify almost the only real grievance to which the Irish representatives can now point, an inequality of political rights as between the three kingdoms. It is said that if this franchise is conferred on the Irish people it will then be impossible to pass for Ireland a measure of redistribution of seats which will give a fair representation to the minority of that country. He denied that altogether, as he knew of no reason why any measure or any principle of redistribution or of the representation of minorities which might be applied to Scotland or England might not, and would not, be applied by Parliament also to the case of Ireland. But apart from that, he contended the

MR. GLAD-
STONE'S
FIRST BILL
OF 1884.

Mr. Raikes.

real protection and the real safety of the minority in Ireland would be found in the English and Scotch representatives in the House.

The debate was adjourned to March 27, and was then
continued by Mr. Raikes, member for Cambridge University, who criticised his opponents and the bill in a lengthy
speech. He supposed the advocates of the bill must
either base their arguments upon expediency or abstract
right; he would say it was rather a question of political
expediency than of philosophical theory. The case of
1867 was different from the present. The persons upon
whom the franchise was then conferred were accustomed
to political discussions and political combinations. They
had knowledge of trades-unions and of all the controversies that arose between capital and labour. They had
been in the habit of criticising the budget of their town-
councils and of voting for or against their municipal representatives according as they made good use of the
rates or otherwise. They had been concerned in the
management of benefit societies. In the main, therefore,
that measure was sound and had answered. But if the
proposed measure was carried, then a Parliament might
be returned in which the whole face of the country representation might be absolutely changed. It was in no
sense a bill supplementary to the bill of 1867. In
measures of reform hitherto passed the principle acted
on was that property should be represented in the
counties and population in the boroughs. It was said
that the Conservative party were hostile to the aspirations
of the labourers. That was not true. At same time he
did not believe that rural labourers were the persons best
qualified to administer the affairs of the country. The
class in Ireland that is to be enfranchised by the bill is

the lowest and most ignorant, and the vote of Protestant
Ulster is about to be silenced. The bill is not wanted,
and the whole policy of the government is a policy of
despair.

Mr. George Russell, member for Aylesbury, did not
think the previous speaker could speak of the last Reform
Bill as being followed by legislative sterility, when it was
considered that after it was passed there followed the
Irish Church Bill, the Irish Land Bill, the Education
Acts, and the Abolition of Purchase in the Army. But
after the advent of the Tories in 1874 legislative sterility
did commence. Not only so, but obstruction was elevated
into a fine art ever since the present government came
into power. It had been said that the time of 1866 was
different from the present. There was a difference. The
House of Commons of 1866 was rotten to the core on the
question of reform. The present is sound as a bell. It
had been said that there was little enthusiasm in favour
of the bill—no large meetings. The great representative
meeting at Leeds was forgotten; and besides it must be
kept in view that at every Liberal meeting since Mr.
Trevelyan carried his motion in 1877, resolutions had
been carried in favour of an extension of the franchise.
They were told by some that the agricultural labourer
was not fitted for the vote. This was untrue. The agricultural labourer yielded to none in his eagerness for
political knowledge, his zeal for the principles which he
had espoused, and his unfailing steadfastness to those
to whom he had once given his allegiance.

Mr. Cubitt, member for Surrey, opposed the bill. He
said that much had been expected from the lodger franchise, but it appeared from a parliamentary return that
in Scotland there were only 323 lodgers on the roll; in

MR. GLAD-
STONE'S
FIRST BILL
OF 1884. Ireland, 1213; in England, 21,918. The cause of this was the difficulty of getting them put on the roll. An agent required to be specially employed. The reason why this franchise was to be extended to counties was for the sake of uniformity. They were really preparing the way for electoral districts. He would support any amendment hostile to the bill.

Mr. Spencer. Mr. Spencer, member for North Northampton, thought that those who argued that there was no desire for the bill could not be conversant with the feeling of the country. If the country was not in favour of the bill, or if it was a bad bill, how was it that there was no motion to have it rejected? The Conservatives knew what that would mean at the next general election. In regard to the Cambridgeshire election, he had no doubt that it was influenced by the fact that the farmers had been told that they would be swamped if the labourers had the vote. He considered that to exclude Ireland from the bill would have been an injustice, and he also was of opinion that the agricultural labourer was as anxious for the welfare of the country and as able to exercise the vote as any other member of the community.

Mr. J. A.
Campbell. Mr. J. A. Campbell, member for the Glasgow and Aberdeen Universities, opposed the bill upon the ground that it was not associated with one for redistribution. He also contended that the demand for the bill came not from the agricultural population, but from people in towns. The grievances that had been heard of were quite capable of being remedied by a Redistribution Bill. The House had little or no information, at least of a binding character, as to what the scheme of redistribution was to be. He considered Ireland to be over-represented.

Mr. Anderson, member for Glasgow, did not think the franchise was a trust, but a right. He looked upon it as the inherent right of every one of full age and sound mind, and it was for those who denied any class their right in that respect to show good reason for it. The franchise was a great educator, and if once it were given to the agricultural labourer he would soon know what to do with it. He considered that Scotland ought to have eleven more members. He would abolish the university franchise, as it was a mere device to give certain classes a double vote. He disapproved entirely of proportional representation and of the attempt to represent minorities. The best and the only correct way of getting minorities represented was to abandon the system of having double or triple constituencies, and have moderate-sized constituencies with only one member for each.

Colonel Walrond, member for Devonshire, admitted that such a bill as the one proposed ought naturally to follow the bill of 1867, but he would not give a very willing assent to it unless it were accompanied by a redistribution which would ensure a due maintenance of the distinction between borough and shire. He was also convinced that this was not a proper time for a change in the franchise. He thought it unwise to extend the franchise to Ireland, as the Irish voters could not be called loyal or industrious citizens. The rural population did not desire this change; indeed, among farmers there was a feeling of alarm lest their interests should be annihilated by the bill. He thought that instead of such a bill as this the requirements of the case might be met by the appointment of a boundary commission to enlarge some of the present boroughs and to group certain of the small boroughs together. He then recapitulated a num-

Marginal notes: MR. GLADSTONE'S FIRST BILL OF 1884. Mr. Anderson. Col. Walrond.

MR. GLAD-
STONE'S
FIRST BILL
OF 1884.

ber of other well-known objections to the bill, and concluded by cordially supporting the amendment.

Mr. Mellor.

Mr. Mellor, member for Grantham, was of opinion that if the noble lord who moved the amendment anticipated all the mischief which he says will result from the bill, he ought to have moved its rejection. If it is a serious matter to take in two millions into the constitution it is equally serious to keep them out. He trusted that the measure would be extended to Ireland, as you cannot legislate for one part of the United Kingdom only.

Mr. Ritchie.

Mr. Ritchie, member for the Tower Hamlets, supported some of the provisions of the bill. He asked his honourable friends not to lose courage at the prospect of an extension of the suffrage. It would entail trouble on them, for great attention would require to be paid to the wants and wishes of the people; but the working-classes would be grateful for that. It was difficult to deal with Ireland. Perhaps it would have been better to have deferred doing so. In many respects this bill was a Conservative measure. It retained the property qualification for the county voters. He did not think that distance from the seat of government should make any difference in the distribution of seats. It was a monstrous injustice to give Ireland so many seats. It was plain that bribery and corruption were not yet at an end. He would vote for the amendment, as he did not think a franchise bill should be passed without redistribution.

Viscount
Ebrington.

Viscount Ebrington, member for Tiverton, gave a general support to the bill. At same time he was not quite satisfied with the way in which Ireland was to be dealt with.

Mr. J. W.
Lowther.

Mr. J. W. Lowther, member for Rutland, referred to what had been said by the honourable member for Aylesbury (Mr. Russell), to the effect that this Parliament had been expressly elected to deal with reform. If so, why had the question been kept in the background for four years? It was questioned whether there was any considerable feeling in the country in favour of reform. The great boroughs had given expression to their opinions, but in a matter more affecting rural than urban interests. He was of opinion that if a franchise bill was to pass at all, the bill now proposed was an extremely moderate one. He was glad to see that faggot-votes were to be abolished, the 40s. freeholder to be retained, and Ireland included in the measure. But it was possible that a dissolution might take place without any redistribution. That rested in the mind and will of the prime minister—a mind and will in which that House was not afraid at times to place implicit confidence. He then pointed out some anomalies that would result, and concluded by asserting that none of the virtues fitting a man for the exercise of the franchise—at least few of them—could be attributed to the class of Irishmen who would be enfranchised by the proposed bill.

Mr. Chamberlain, member for Birmingham, began his observations with the remark that there was a sense of unreality in the debate, at least on the side of the Conservatives. Whether this arose from the belief that the bill was never to return from the House of Lords, or that it was so urgently called for by the country that it was needless to oppose it, he would not venture to say. The reticences of the debate have been as remarkable as the utterances. The member for North Leicestershire (Lord John Manners) made a demand for more light on the intentions of the government. But surely there ought to be some reciprocity. The government have produced

a great measure of reform, and the opposition is called
on to say whether it is in their opinion a just, expedient,
and beneficial object to aim at? Were they prepared for
an extension of the franchise? Did the bill go too far,
or not far enough? These are fair questions, and the
country would like to have an answer. From the amendment proposed he drew the inference, and he thought it
a fair one, that the Conservative party did not admit
that the franchise was either a good or a bad thing.
That would depend upon something else that followed.
He would take issue with them on that point, for he held
that the extension of the franchise was a good thing in
itself—that it was desirable to include the largest number
of capable citizens within the limits of the constitution,
whether or not that is followed up by a scheme of redistribution. He held that no scheme of redistribution could
possibly make the extension of the suffrage bad, although
it was quite possible to have a scheme so made as to de-
tract materially from its value. The way the government
meant to deal with it was, without attempting logical
completeness, without any unnecessary disturbance of
old traditions, without obliterating the distinction between town and country, to bring in a bill which should
be a great and generous measure of reform, and which, if
it did not entirely remove the existing anomalies, should
do so to such an extent as would settle the question at
all events for our time and generation, and should leave
no room now for further agitation. The right honourable
gentleman assumed that the opposition were honestly
desirous to pass the measure. That was perhaps a large
assumption. There was, however, another assumption
which the House was bound to keep in view. If they
were hostile to the measure what course would they take?

It would be their business to minimize the importance of MR. GLAD-STONE'S FIRST BILL OF 1884. the measure, to deny the interest the country takes in it, to magnify its evils. They would take every opportunity to delay the discussion of the bill by interposing debates upon every conceivable subject and at all possible times. Above all, they would strive to stifle the consideration of the bill by endeavouring to import into it an elaborate scheme of distribution, full of details which might easily arouse and perhaps offend local susceptibilities and local interests—and that is the course the opposition have taken. The country would not be slow to draw the natural conclusion. Nearly fifty years ago one of our elder generation of statesmen (Lord Durham) saw that it was the duty of a wise statesman to examine the objects the people have in view, and have determined to Mr. Chamberlain. obtain, and when he is satisfied of their justice he should not wait to be forced to the adoption of such measures as would realize them. But this is in decided contrast to the latest development of Tory democracy, which is represented by the member for Woodstock (Lord Randolph Churchill), who said in Edinburgh that if he saw the agricultural classes in a state of excitement over this question; if he saw them holding vast meetings, collecting together from all parts, neglecting their work, contributing from their scanty funds, marching on London, tearing down the railings of Hyde Park, engaging the police and even the military, he would conclude that they wanted the vote, and would give it to them, but on these grounds and on these grounds only. This was a very remarkable utterance, and appeared to be a direct incitement to violence and outrage. Both parties during the recess held meetings—the Conservatives perhaps more than the Liberals. The Liberal meetings one and all passed re-

solutions in favour of extending the franchise—in not a
single instance did a Conservative meeting pass a resolution condemning it. With reference to the remark that
the people are not in earnest, the right honourable gentleman said, "I do not think we shall be able to gratify the
noble lord the member for Woodstock (Lord Randolph
Churchill). I do not think we can get up meetings to
order as the right honourable gentleman, the member for
the University of Cambridge (Mr. Raikes), amiably im-
putes to us. That is not in our line. That is not to our
interest, and it has never been our policy. In the time
of the late government, when public feeling was greatly
excited, I am not aware that any prominent member of
the Conservative party was molested, or even insulted by
his political opponents. It was not the prime minister
of that day whose windows were broken by the mob. It
was the windows of the right honourable gentleman now
the prime minister of the country, and I do not suppose
they were broken by any Liberal organization." It had
been said that there was not the least chance of the bill
passing in the present Parliament. That was a threat.
It had been said also that this bill is inopportune; but all
reform bills are inopportune to the Tory party. They
have used the same argument on almost every occasion
on which reform has been brought before the House since
May, 1874. It had further been said that the bill will
be destructive of the agricultural interests of the country.
The right honourable gentleman said that the question
of agricultural interests were the interests of the men
who till the soil, and the bill would benefit them. Their
interests had been too long forgotten. They had been
robbed of their land. Not a bit of public land was to be
found anywhere. It had been almost all inclosed by

landowners. Not only has this injurious operation been going on with land; it is also going on with reference to the endowments of the poor, the result of which is that funds originally intended for the poor are appropriated by the rich. He did not blame one party more than another; but if the agricultural classes had been represented in Parliament such things would not have happened. It had been said that the honourable member for Cork (Mr. Parnell) would be the grand elector over four-fifths of Ireland. If that is to be, then it is proper that the representation be a reality and not a sham. At present Ireland is not represented. In England and Scotland every one in 10 has a vote. In Ireland only one in 25. The system was bad before 1867; it has been worse since the bill of that year. It is inequalities of this kind which encourages agitation in Ireland, and sharpens the weapons of those who wish to attack the British connection. He had to notice another argument which he might call the " mud-cabin" argument, that the Irish labourers who are to be enfranchised by the bill are poor and ignorant, and that they live in mud-cabins. This was very unfortunate for them; but from all he could learn of the conditions of the poorer classes in large towns in this country, they were not much better. He observed that there was some little objection to the number of representatives which it was proposed to give to Ireland; but if this was to be insisted on, then he thought they could not refuse to Irish opinion in our large towns in this country the full value of the vote to which by numbers it is entitled.

Lord George Hamilton, member for Middlesex, characterized the speech of the right honourable member for Birmingham as a most ill-conditioned speech. He said

MR. GLADSTONE'S FIRST BILL OF 1884.

Mr. Chamberlain.

Lord G. Hamilton.

Mr. Glad-
stone's
first Bill
of 1884.

that what the right honourable gentleman wanted was manhood suffrage and the payment of members, and that it is contrary to all precedent to introduce a measure of reform at the close of the life of a Parliament. If the bill became law it would do three things, it would indefinitely postpone redistribution, it would lead to an audacious manipulation of the electoral system for the benefit of the party in power, it would render it difficult to maintain the integrity of the United Kingdom. He likewise held that it was against all precedent to pass a Franchise Bill without redistribution. It had never been done. The fact was that an election would take place first, and the effect would be an enormous advantage to the party in power. The effect would also be to betray the loyalists of Ireland. He concluded by advocating a dissolution of Parliament as a means of ascertaining the voice of the country.

Mr. Forster.

The debate was resumed on March 31 by Mr. Forster, member for Bradford, who said that the question before the House was not the principle of the bill, but whether it should be passed this session or not, and whether it should be passed with or without, or before or after a dissolution of the present Parliament. In his opinion it would not matter much so far as the bill was concerned whether there was a dissolution or not, or whether the Conservatives got into power or not. If they did get in the same course would be taken as before, and they would themselves bring in a household Franchise Bill for the agricultural labourers. It would be inconvenient if there was to be an election before a Redistribution Bill is carried through; but what is inconvenience compared with injustice? After all, it is better for the constituents to exercise the franchise in company with a large number

than not at all.   It is better that the 2,000,000 of voters MR. GLAD-
should have a share in the work of redistribution.   The STONE'S
FIRST BILL
opposition want to have the settlement of the two ques- OF 1884.
tions in their own hands, but they cannot expect the
Liberal party to join with them in their endeavour.   I
think Ireland should be included in the measure, though
it is a difficult question.   As to the fitness of the Irish
agricultural labourers, I think they are as fit as the
English artisans in 1867.   I think there is nothing in the
state of Ireland to deprive the people of their electoral
rights.   As to membership, however, the right honourable gentleman said that he must not be committed to
the doctrine either that the present number of members
of the House must be increased or that the present membership of Ireland should not be diminished.   An Act of Mr. Forster.
Union might be modified; it was so in the case of Scotland when it got an addition to its membership, it was
so in the case of Ireland when the Church was abolished.
Any Act of Parliament must be capable of modification,
if circumstances have so changed as to require modification.   Scotland has been increasing and must get more
members.   Ireland has been decreasing, but it is said that
her membership must remain the same.   In 1707 the number of members for England and Wales was 513.   There
was by the Act of Union 45 given to Scotland, making
558.   In 1800 there was 100 allowed to Ireland, making
in all 658.   Deducting vacant seats the exact number is
652.   In 1832 there were eight seats given to Scotland
and five to Ireland, and in 1867–8 there were seven more
given to Scotland, all taken from England.   He did not
say that all this was not fair at the time, but it is not
the condition necessary for all ages in the future, and so
far as he could judge Ireland ought to have 91 instead

of 105, Scotland 71 instead of 60, and England and Wales 496 instead of 493. If, instead of persons, the number of families were taken, then Ireland would lose 17 members, Scotland would gain 11, and England 6. He did not think that distance from London should in any way regulate the number of members a country ought to have; neither did he think that London should have less than its fair share. He concluded by stating that he would not be tempted by any argument about redistribution, nor by any objection to details, to endanger the passing of the measure.

Sir R. Peel. Sir Robert Peel, in a long speech, characterized the debate as languid, always excepting the speech of the president of the board of trade. He agreed with a previous speaker in thinking it an ill-conditioned speech, and as being, in so far as it related to the inclosure of public lands, a direct incentive to violence. The House plainly cannot reconcile itself to the measure, because it as well as the country are absorbed by the current events of the day. They are eager for some sound, useful, domestic legislation. He was of opinion that no one would be opposed to a fair and equitable measure of reform for the good of the country, if it was proved to be necessary. He was quite opposed to the bill.

Mr. Craig-
Sellar. Mr. Craig-Sellar, member for the Haddington burghs, held that there would have been no chance of passing both a Franchise and Redistribution Bill in the same session. He considered the proposed bill as being a most skilfully-drafted bill, of which the central idea was household suffrage. The people who were to be enfranchised were in many cases poor and ignorant, and not over-industrious, but they would be helped by the measure. The franchise had a great educating tendency.

The "service" franchise was perhaps the most valuable MR. GLAD
provision in the bill. It would have the effect of giving STONE'S
FIRST BILL
the vote to the best of the unenfranchised people of OF 1884.
Scotland. The provision for the extinction of faggot-
votes was most acceptable, as that system was the curse
of the representation of Scotland. In regard to representation he held that Scotland was entitled to more and
Ireland to less, no matter whether population or taxation
or the number of inhabited houses were taken into consideration. He held, however, that it was right to extend
the franchise to Ireland, and he had no intention of supporting the amendment.

Mr. Sydney Herbert, member for Wilton, supported
the amendment.

Mr. Charles Russell, member for Dundalk, held that MR. C.
Russell.
to exclude Ireland from the measure would be a grave
political mistake. He was surprised that honourable
members opposite did not see that such a course would
strengthen immeasurably the position of those who maintain that although the three kingdoms were a united
kingdom in name they were not so in reality. Instead
of the franchise being the same in Ireland as in England,
the borough franchise in Ireland was in respect of a
house over £4 of ratable value, which was equivalent to
£5 or £6 rental, and that rental was equivalent to an
£8 or £9 rental in England. Now, the borough franchise
in England was in respect of a rated house. The county
franchise in both countries was nominally the same, a
rated occupation of £12, but practically the valuation in
Ireland was equivalent to a rental value of £18 or £20.
He held that Ireland would not be exceptionally treated
if she retained her present membership. It was said that
the effect of the measure would be to swamp the loyal

party in Ireland. He would say little about the loyal
party, it was mostly composed of the landlord party.
They had been loyal indeed, but this loyalty had had a
close relation to their own status and their own interest.
He thought that any government should be slow to lessen
the number of Irish representatives. What was the
position of Ireland? Englishmen governed in England,
Scotchmen governed in Scotland, but Irishmen did not
govern in Ireland. An Englishman was lord-lieutenant,
an Englishman chief secretary, a Scotchman the under
secretary, and they governed by means of stipendiary
magistrates who were accountable to them and not to the
people. There was no country on the face of the earth
in which the people had so little to do with the government of their country as the Irish people. In these circumstances he considered that in dealing with Ireland
Parliament should deal with justice and with generosity
in these questions of franchise and the distribution of
seats.

Sir R. A. Cross, member for the south-western division
of Lancashire, said that the previous speaker had represented Ireland as governed by Englishmen, who were not
responsible to the Irish people but to the House of Commons. But the House of Commons represented the
United Kingdom, and therefore the governors of Ireland
were responsible in the House to the Irish people. The
House was entitled to have a distinct declaration from
the government as to the number of members which Ireland was to have. He held that Ireland was not entitled
to have the same number as she had at the time of the
Union. He supposed they were all agreed that the franchise was not to be looked on as an abstract right, and
yet the framework of the bill was against that idea. The

only abstract right which he knew that an Englishman possessed was that he was to be well governed and remain as free as possible. He had not an abstract right to govern, but an abstract right to be well governed. The bill was intended to establish a uniform household suffrage, but it would create greater anomalies than already existed. The question of the franchise and of redistribution should be dealt with in one session. The opposition were not against reform. He had never made a speech against it; but what they wanted to see was the scheme of reform in the full extent to which the country was to be committed.

Mr. Shaw Lefevre, member for Reading, remarked that in 1866 the opposition used the same arguments against reform which they do now. The Franchise Bill was declared to be inopportune—it was incomplete—it was not required—there was danger in conferring redistribution —the existing constituencies would be swamped. The Liberal measure was thrown out, but Lord Derby had to introduce a bill of his own. He, however, felt it impossible to carry a wide scheme of redistribution and a franchise bill at the same time. Their scheme of redistribution only increased the existing anomalies. He (Mr. Lefevre) therefore thought the government right to pass their franchise bill first and pass the redistribution scheme in the following session. If this did not take place, then, after all, a Parliament elected under an extended franchise must be ultimately the arbiter. No injury could result to the constitution. It had been said that the proposed bill would extinguish the loyal party in Ireland. He did not think so. He held that in Ulster the Protestants would carry all the elections, and thus the loyal party would maintain its representation even under an extended franchise in proportion to its real force in the country. If, however, a scheme of proportional representation were adopted, and the Catholic minority in Ulster is to be represented, then the same rule would apply to England and Scotland, where there is a large minority — perhaps 1,500,000 — of Roman Catholics. They would also be entitled to representation. The loyal party would lose more than they would gain by such a scheme as that. The member for North Lincolnshire (Mr. Lowther) ventured to say that if the bill passed, the agricultural interest in England would be entirely obliterated. This was very absurd. Has it ever been contended that the manufacturing interest in this country was extinguished by giving votes to the labouring class?

And if votes are given to the labourers in the rural districts the agricultural interests are to be extinguished. Why should an extension of the franchise extinguish the agricultural interests? The labourers will be as much interested in any question affecting the true interests of agriculture as any other class connected with agriculture. The honourable member had hoped that the settlement of 1867 might be final for a generation, but it soon became evident that the question must be reopened. There were two great classes left out—the miners of England and the agricultural labourers. They have now demanded the franchise, and he thought it impossible to regard the condition of the agricultural labourers without very great concern. As a class they are not progressing—they are rather going back. The younger and more active and intelligent among them are being drawn into the towns, leaving the refuse, as it were, behind. What are the inducements to the labouring man to remain in the purely agricultural districts? He can never hope to become an

owner of land—he can never hope even to become possessed of his home—he must always be in a state of de-
pendence. In many parts of the country the number of
large farms have increased and all the small holdings
have disappeared. All the steps by which an agricultural
labourer could hope to rise to a higher status have been
taken away. It seemed to the honourable member therefore of the utmost importance that the opportunity should
be given to the agricultural labourer to state his case to
the House of Commons.

Sir Michael Hicks Beach, member for Gloucester (Eastern Division), thought the country had a very languid interest in the bill, perhaps from a belief that it would not
pass into law. He was not going to say that the agricultural labourers were not fit for the vote, but he saw no
reason why they should become county voters. There
might have been the extension of the boundaries of existing boroughs, or the creation of new boroughs, so as to
admit them, and yet a separate county representation be
retained. A great deal can be said in favour of proportional or minority representation, although the prime
minister is not in favour of it. When political power
was vested in the aristocracy its abuse was restrained by
the fact that the ultimate physical power rested with the
mass of the people; but when political power is given to
them who possess physical power, the minority have no
appeal. And if some system for the representation of
minorities is important here, it is doubly so in Ireland.
There is great strength in the argument that Ireland
should have the same franchise that is to be conferred on
Great Britain, but unless some provision is made for the
representation of the loyal minority then it will be
swamped. This is a strong argument in favour of con-

X

sidering the Redistribution Bill along with the extension of the franchise. The reason why both bills are not introduced together is that the government cannot agree as to what the redistribution should be. The secretary for war would not be prepared to support a bill for electoral districts, but the president of the Board of Trade would do so.

Mr. Albert Grey, member for Northumberlandshire (Southern Division), observed that the right honourable baronet (Sir Michael Hicks Beach) admitted that the Act of 1867 was not final, and that it was impossible that the exclusion of the county householders could be long continued. What he really wanted, as his argument showed, was that the same electorate which passed the franchise bill should also pass the measure for redistribution. If this were so, then some provision could be put into the bill that would secure this. There was no reason why he should refuse to vote for a second reading. He (Mr. Grey) held that it was statesmanlike to anticipate a demand, and not to be obliged to legislate in a panic. He then in a long speech dealt with the question of a definition of household suffrage, and with the subject of proportional representation. He proposed to support a clause that extension should not take effect until a date to be mentioned in the Redistribution Bill which was to follow.

Mr. Guy Dawnay, member for Yorkshire (North Riding), contended that in its present condition the bill was not worth having; it was untimely in its introduction, it was not justified by any genuine or general desire on the part of the people, it was absolutely dangerous and unconstitutional in the power it would give to one class, and that the least intelligent and least educated.

Mr. Woodall, member for Stoke-upon-Trent, said that Mr. Gladstone's First Bill of 1884. he had carefully followed the course of the debate, and was satisfied that on the part of the opposition there was an ill-concealed aversion to enfranchisement in any form whatever. He thought there was nothing in the Mr. Woodall. objection that had been taken to the want of a demand, of a clamour, in short, for the vote. The present state of the public mind was a testimony to the growth of a legitimate confidence on the part of the people that there would be an orderly and constitutional remedy for the grievances of which they complained. The honourable member was of opinion that there must be a female franchise, and he intended to propose it in committee.

Mr. Beresford Hope, member for Cambridge Univer- Mr. Beresford Hope. sity, said he had voted against the bills of 1866 and 1867, and did not regret having done so. Under the enlarged constituency of 1867, supplemented as it has been by secret voting, the oscillations of public opinion are more sudden, more unexpected, more violent, more uncontrolled than in former times—1874 and 1880 equally prove this. He did not see the benefit of conferring the franchise on these agricultural labourers. He praised them for self-denial, family affections, industry, and love of their country. He granted them every virtue in the world, except the virtues of political forethought, and grasp of the relations of public questions. He protested against the recklessness of introducing 2,000,000 of inexperienced voters into the electorate and thus swamping and overwhelming all other interests in the country. The argument as to the vote being a "right" is unsound, otherwise there ought to be universal suffrage. He acknowledged that the agricultural labourers ought to have a proportionate share in the government of the country; but he asserted that they had it already, as large numbers of them are voters in the agricultural boroughs. He characterized this effort at reform as a gambling and scrambling attempt of the government to clutch at the power which was slipping out of their hands.

Mr. Stansfeld, member for Halifax, said he intended to support the amendment to enfranchise women householders. He observed that the government was charged with insincerity, and the opposition with half-heartedness. He also observed that the Conservative party did not traverse the wisdom or justice of the measure. He thought the franchise should be extended in the way proposed; that it should be extended to Ireland; that the postponement of redistribution was not an evil. As to the country being apathetic, he could easily understand it, as the extension of the franchise was an absolutely foregone conclusion. It was a mere question of time. The Conservative party would oppose it, but their opposition did nothing but good to the cause of reform. If that opposition increased, the apathy of the country would be turned into enthusiasm. It had been said that the House of Lords would throw the bill out. If he cared only for the bill, for the government, or for his party, he should not wish it any other fate. As to the postponement of redistribution, he thought, whether honourable members liked it or not, that the government had a right so to arrange their measures as to give themselves a chance of passing them. The honourable member was strongly of opinion that Ireland should be included in the measure. The policy of equality between Ireland and England was our only chance in the future of harmonizing the two countries. He concluded as follows:—

"By bringing Ireland upon the floor of that House, and MR. GLAD-STONE'S FIRST BILL OF 1884. by compelling almost the action of Irish parties to become less violent and more constitutional than it had been in the past, they would eventually be able to dispense with coercion acts and all the mischievous consequences which followed from their enactment. The two populations would agree in a broader patriotism in place of that narrow and antagonistic patriotism which we ourselves forced into the minds of the Irish population, and the result would be a real act of union which would unite the two peoples, respecting each other's individualities and each other's rights, into one imperial bond for our common safety and our common interest."

Mr. Marriott, member for Brighton, said that the Mr. Marriott. government were asking the confidence of the House with regard to the Franchise Bill and to redistribution; but the opposition had always found that when they put confidence in the government that confidence was misplaced. The whole question depended on redistribution, and what the House and the country wanted to know was how it was to be manipulated—for manipulated it would be in the interests of the party in power?

The debate was continued on April 3 by Mr. Broad- Mr. Broad-hurst. hurst, member for Stoke-upon-Trent, who contradicted the assertion that had been made that there was no feeling among the masses of the people in favour of the extension of the franchise. If the workmen who felt strongly on the question would only address their letters to honourable members who were opposed to that change, instead of those who were in favour of it, he would venture to say that any such opinion on the opposite side of the House would be materially modified. Speaking, as he had a right to do, for the organized trades of the

country, he could assure the House that a motion in favour of the extension of the franchise was a chief resolution before their annual congresses. Besides that, there was a deputation—240 or 250 in number—of delegates representing the trades organizations of the United Kingdom, sent on January 31, to wait on the prime minister and declare to him their anxiety for a speedy dealing with the subject of reform. The cost would be £700 or £800, a sum, he need hardly say, which the trades-unions of this country would not spend on any matter which they had not deeply at heart. With regard to the bill itself, the honourable member said it was too complicated—it had too many qualifications. It was shaped too much to suit the prejudices and privileges of
the rich. There was no reason why a man should have two votes merely because he was a freeholder of landed property. His view was that there should be one vote to one man. It had been repeatedly said that the labouring-classes were not quite fitted for the franchise; but in his opinion the Conservative party had a much greater fear of the labourer's knowledge and intelligence than they had of their ignorance and incapacity. The member for Middlesex (Lord George Hamilton) was greatly alarmed at the idea of payment of members. The noble lord himself belonged to a "ring" that was paid for its services when in office, and why should not members who worked as hard be paid, since ministers were? The honourable member said that the time will come when the people will insist on having not only a share in the representation, but also in the administration and executive work of the nation. He held that the representation of the universities was very objectionable. He also held that it would be wicked and unwise to curtail the poli-

tical privileges of Irishmen, and that the government by
their proposal had given expression to the unanimous
wish of the Liberal party. He had listened to some parts
of the speech of the right honourable gentleman the
member for Ripon (Mr. Goschen), in which he stated his
reasons for his conversion on the fitness of the working-
man for the franchise, with pain and surprise. It was
lamentable to hear the right honourable gentleman, who
had been twice a cabinet minister, confessing that he
never understood the people. The agricultural labourers
could have no sordid or selfish motive in claiming the
franchise. They had no places to seek, no pensions to
secure, no court honours to look for. Their leading object in life was to secure those home comforts so long
denied to them, and the honour of the country, which
they loved no less than any other class in the kingdom.
Had the House forgotten how, when the great and powerful were weak and hesitating on the question of freedom
or slavery in America, our poorer countrymen and women
faced the prospect of starvation and ruin rather than sacrifice one atom of their principle and love of freedom all
the world over to black and white?

Mr. Biddell, member for Suffolk (Western Division),
was desirous of information with reference to the scheme
of redistribution. He thought the labouring-class should
have some more direct representation; but he objected to
the arrangement whereby the labouring-classes could completely swamp all the others in the counties.

Mr. Redmond, member for New Ross, was in favour
of the measure in so far as it conferred the franchise on a
large and respectable class, but he was decidedly opposed
to any diminution in the number of members for Ireland.

MR. GLAD-
STONE'S
FIRST BILL
OF 1884.

Mr. Morley.

Mr. John Morley, member for Newcastle, characterized the speech of the member for West Suffolk (Mr.
Biddell) as honest in the sense that it let out the secret
of the attitude taken up by honourable members opposite.
They only did not object to the extension of the franchise, on condition that in redistribution they could take
back with one hand what they had given with the other.
He considered the working-classes as the friends of peace
and of order, and at their trades-union congresses their
proceedings might well furnish a model for more august
assemblies.   Besides agricultural labourers, there would
be miners enfranchised by the bill.   Among no class was
there a keener thirst for knowledge.   The member for
Huntingdon (Sir R. Peel) had said that the only meetings
in favour of the bill had been held by a few scientific
Radicals.   He (Mr. Morley) did not know what a "scientific" Radical meant; but if it meant the opposite of a
harum-scarum Tory, he would not himself be disposed
to disown the name.   He regretted that the question
of proportional representation had been raised; but the
time for such schemes would come when it was proposed
to adjust representation on a numerical basis.   The question of Irish representation he would not discuss either
on the basis of numbers or that of the Act of Union, but
on the broad ground of policy and expediency.   Ireland
was entitled to exceptional legislation; not so much on
the score of geographical distance as on that of moral
distance, and the disadvantage under which her members
laboured from the ignorance and prejudice of Englishmen, arising out of the differences in race and religion.
Ireland, too, was under a great disadvantage in the hereditary branch of the legislature.   Honourable gentlemen
opposite had stated that they were in favour of an appeal

to the people. The supporters of the bill wanted to enable them to appeal to the *real* people, and not to a privileged section, with a narrow franchise, and jockeyed by an artificial arrangement of seats.

Mr. Strutt characterized the measure as revolutionary, and stated his intention to support the amendment.

Mr. Plunket, member for Dublin University, was of opinion that the bill would commit practically the whole parliamentary representation of Ireland to one social class which must overwhelm in numbers all the others, and that a class, notwithstanding its many virtues, who are ignorant, excitable, prejudiced, and absolutely unused to the duties and responsibilities of public life. The result would be a total misrepresentation of the Irish people. No less than 40 per cent of the new voters could not read nor write. No doubt there are anomalies in the present system, but the bill would aggravate them. It would give the member for Cork (Mr. Parnell) a very large following, as some say not less than 90 or 95. He himself expects, without a new franchise, to increase his numbers to 65 or 70, but to get such a representation as would secure the creation of national self-government for Ireland it would require 80 or 90! The honourable member (Mr. Plunket) held that to extend the franchise to Ireland would mean a repeal of the union, and that separation would be demanded after the next general election.

Mr. H. H. Fowler, member for Wolverhampton, held that the working-classes were entitled to representation. The wage-earning class comprised the bulk of the population; they produced the largest amount of national wealth and gave the largest amount to the national exchequer. Their production was valued at £500,000,000, while they contributed 40 per cent of the national revenue. He claimed the privilege of citizenship for all those who discharged its duties. The possession of political power and its use constituted the best education of the people; and he believed that the artisans of 1884 were superior in political information to the £10 householders of 1832. The artisans and peasants did not belong to one political party only; they had ranked themselves, some with one party and some with another; and he believed that their accession to political life would not only strengthen the working of our institutions but would add great political force to the two great parties of the state, whose healthy rivalry and whose common patriotism had been the story of our political freedom.

The debate was resumed on April 7 by Mr. Stuart Wortley, member for Sheffield, who did not dispute the justice of some such bill as that before the House. He held that not to admit the agricultural labourer to balance the vote of the artisan and the miner would not only be inequitable but unsafe. But the government, although they came into power in 1880, were suspiciously late in bringing in their bill. Their motives in bringing it in were also suspicious. The House knew nothing of their intention as regards its effects or the effects of the redistribution which is to follow. He would therefore vote for the amendment. The bill was entirely a party measure. He condemned the proposals with reference to Ireland, and characterized them as a bid for the Irish vote.

Mr. Barran, member for Leeds, contended that working-men were perfectly qualified to exercise the franchise. They had shown it in many ways, especially in the management of co-operative and friendly societies. He held that the franchise, although a very responsible privilege, was not a trust. What right had any man to judge of any other whether he should have the franchise? Agricultural labourers and artisans were responsible to the laws of the country, and they had therefore a right to a voice in the making of those laws. He thought that honourable gentlemen opposite should make a clean breast of it, and say at once that they did not wish an extension of the franchise. They had appealed to the House on behalf of the loyal portion of Ireland, but the honourable member would appeal to the House to increase the numbers of that loyal party in Ireland.

Mr. Grantham, member for East Surrey, said it was as clear as could be that if the bill became law there must be dissolution without redistribution, and it would bring about that which the government stated ought not to be tolerated, a Franchise Bill being passed by one Parliament and a Redistribution Bill by another. Even the Liberal members were trusting that the House of Lords would throw out the bill, as they themselves had not the courage to do it. He did not object to the representation of numbers, but to numbers being made supreme.

Mr. Gladstone said that the government had been charged with having adduced no arguments in support of the bill, but he had thought this would be an abuse of time when he observed the care and caution of members opposite in avoiding any declarations against the principle of the bill. Still he did not think that argument had been neglected, even by himself, as had been supposed. Did anyone contest the principle that it was good for the state that the largest numbers of capable citizens should be invested with the franchise? If that was denied, let the denial be heard in plain terms. If not, then the whole argument is at an end. The same classes

that the government proposed to enfranchise were already
enfranchised in towns and in the smaller boroughs, and
their capability was no longer to be disputed. Has the
constitution of the House been improved or not by the
Reform Bills which have already been enacted? (Cries
of No, no.) Perhaps those who say "No" will bring in
a bill to repeal these acts. He was not meaning to insti-
tute a comparison, man for man, of those who sit here
and those who sat here sixty or seventy years ago. When
he spoke of the improvement of the House, he did not
mean the bringing here of a finer set of private gentlemen,
not even of a set of more ·highly-educated men. He
meant an assembly better qualified to comprehend the
wants of the country and more disposed to deal with

those wants in the whole of their extended circumference.
He did not think that any gentleman would say "No"
when he affirmed that the House of Commons had been
improved and had shown a capacity for dealing with the
legislative exigencies of the nation such as unquestionably
under its former composition it could not and would not
have shown. The member for Huntingdon (Sir R. Peel)
and other members made a complaint that there was no
audible knocking at the door of Parliament for admission.
Did he remember what happened in 1866? There was
no greater desire then than now. It was a staple argument that there was no demand for the franchise. The
Parliament then was not in earnest. Yet the disappearance of a few railings in Hyde Park was enough to dispose of these arguments. Did the right honourable
gentleman wish that game played over again? It is
better not to dwell too much on the absence of vehement
demands for reform. He saw plainly why it was that the
severance of redistribution from the extension of the

franchise was made a matter of complaint on the other
side. They have a difficulty in finding grounds for criticism and opposition. The combination of the two measures would have been fatal to both. The effect of
combining redistribution in the same measure with the
franchise would be to cause an imperial question to be
settled upon local, sectional, partial, and selfish considerations. Furthermore, it is necessary to know how the
new franchises will distribute themselves before the
details of the plan of redistribution can be prudently
determined. With regard to his own outline of redistribution, he never supposed that it would conciliate a single
opponent—opponents were not to be conciliated in that
way. What they looked for are grounds of objection,
not reasons for assent. But really all the objections have
concentrated themselves upon the subject of the membership for Ireland. Perhaps if the present population of
Ireland is taken into account, her number of representatives should be 93 instead of 103. But he was not
willing to assume that the decline of population in Ireland
was to continue. Perhaps the present decline is a necessary road to the national well-being. Further, he would
say this, that those who have been niggardly and unjust
in former times must be very cautious when they come
to plead on their own behalf for the strict application of
laws, of which they might indeed have claimed the
strictest application had they never deviated from them
themselves. Look back at 1832 and see how Ireland was
dealt with on that occasion. She had then three-tenths
of the population of the United Kingdom, and she got
considerably less than one-sixth of the representation. It
was not handsome treatment, and it was not a desirable
position for a great country to occupy, to claim the most

MR. GLAD-
STONE'S
FIRST BILL
OF 1884.

rigid application of numerical laws when they tell in her favour, and on the other hand to apply a very lax view of them indeed when they tell against her. If Ireland had been treated according to her numbers her members would have been nearer 200 than 100. He concluded by urging that the whole question was *res judicata*, that there was no direct issue raised against the bill, and that the division would show that the House is not behind the sense and intention of the country.

Mr. Dal-
rymple.

Mr. Dalrymple, member for Bute, acknowledged that he had voted with the chief secretary, Mr. Trevelyan, in favour of the extension of the franchise to the counties, and he could not have voted for a direct negative to the proposed bill. He had also made a declaration that he would support an extension of the franchise to the counties when it should be proposed by the government of the day, and he was quite prepared to give effect to that declaration when the proper time came. But he guarded himself against being absolutely bound to support the measure in the particular form in which it might be introduced if it should be separated from the question of redistribution. There was much in the measure of which he approved : there was no disfranchisement; there was no question of the one-man-one-vote principle; there was no condition of residence, and there was the service franchise. He also approved of the extension of the measure to Ireland, although the condition of Ireland was an argument for postponing the bill altogether. He wanted, however, to see the whole of the government scheme. Unless a redistribution scheme accompanied the extension of the franchise the anomalies of the system would be increased twenty-fold. He would vote for the amendment.

Mr. Williamson, member for St. Andrews' Burghs, said he intended to give his vote for the bill, and to deal with redistribution when it came up. As well might honourable members opposite refuse to pay their greengrocers because they were afraid they might not make a good use of the money, as to refuse to assimilate the borough and county franchise because they did not know how political power was to be cast when redistribution took place. He considered the class to be enfranchised as quite fitted for exercising the vote. He also conceived that there was wisdom in postponing redistribution until the franchise question was settled. The Redistribution Bill of the gallant admiral (Sir John Hay) was a scheme for so distributing political power as to secure a Tory preponderance. It was an essay on redistribution jugglery.

Viscount Folkestone, member for South Wilts, had no faith in a Redistribution Bill following next year. Many circumstances might prevent it. Besides, the honourable member was of opinion that the proposed bill was not wanted by the people generally. He was not disposed to leave the question in the hands of certain right honourable gentlemen in the government, who could easily alter their opinion on questions of vital importance. He would heartily support the amendment.

The O'Donoghue, member for Tralee, could understand the measure being opposed by those who preferred an absolute monarchy, or an oligarchy, to a constitutional government. Theoretically the British government deserved all the praises which have been bestowed on it, but in practice it was an oligarchy which worked extremely well for the interests of those who were the exclusive depositories of power. A Reform Bill was a

Marginal notes: Mr. Gladstone's first bill of 1884. Mr. Williamson. Viscount Folkestone. The O'Donoghue.

MR. GLAD-
STONE'S
FIRST BILL
OF 1884.
party measure, and the Liberals were the party that existed for the defence and extension of popular rights. They were united in the pursuit of that object. The bill they proposed was so simple that the modern tactics of the Tory party were useless. He did not believe in proportional representation, and he could not without dismay contemplate the possibility of the government receding from their determination to give Ireland all the representation she had at present. He hoped the government would not spoil the measure in that way as so many Irish measures had been spoiled before.

Viscount
Newport.
Viscount Newport, member for North Shropshire, did not believe there was any strong feeling in the country in favour of the reduction of the franchise. Prices were low, but wages had not fallen, and his belief was that the agricultural labourer was satisfied with things as they were. The extension of the franchise was not for the good of the country, and besides, this was a most inopportune time to introduce a measure for that purpose. His idea was that all classes should have their due share of political power. But this bill would practically disfranchise culture and property, and owners and occupiers of land would have no power except through the labourers. He thought that any change which might be made ought to take the direction of redistribution, and in that way what was called "the-one-side-of-the-street" argument would be met.

Mr. Burt.
Mr. Burt, member for Morpeth, believed that the bill would be received with great satisfaction by the country, and would be productive of much good. He was glad to notice that very little had been said in the course of the debate that was offensive to the labouring classes. The member for Huntingdon (Sir R. Peel) had made some

strong remarks, but he appeared very speedily to come
to a penitent frame of mind. He (Mr. Burt) was of
opinion that the agricultural labourers and miners were
quite fitted for the franchise and quite as anxious to have
it as the artisans. He had attended meetings in all parts
of the country, the numbers of those attending varying
from 5000 to 60,000, and at all of them resolutions had
been passed unanimously in favour of the franchise.
Last week there were no fewer than fifty meetings held
in the county of Northumberland alone, at which resolutions in favour of the bill were passed. How much excitement did honourable members opposite want to see
in order to be convinced of the desire for electoral reform? The member for Woodstock (Lord R. Churchill)
told them exactly what would satisfy him: was that the
new qualification which the Tory party wished to insist
upon? and did they think that the labouring-classes
would be satisfied to march to London simply to pull
down the park railings? It was possible that suggestions
such as this one of the noble lord might provoke a spirit
that could not be controlled. It was not desirable that
there should be excitement on this subject. The honourable member hoped the House would pass the bill by a
decisive majority. Lord Salisbury spoke of an appeal to
the people. However, what he meant was not an appeal
to the people, but to the present electors. They were
not the proper judges.

Sir Walter B. Barttelot, member for West Sussex, was
disposed to ask whether the proposed change was for the
benefit and interest of the country? He would like it
discussed whether the reforms of 1832 and 1867 had improved the House. He objected to the extension of the
bill to Ireland, and he had no confidence in the govern-

ment that, if the Redistribution Bill was not produced now, they would hereafter do what was right and just in the interest of the country. He gave his cordial support to the amendment.

Mr. Goschen.   Mr. Goschen, member for Ripon, said that a mistake had been committed by some members in supposing that he had pledged himself to support the bill. He did not know whether the government intended to support minority representation. If the proposed bill passed without the government having declared in favour of such representation there was not much chance of its being secured. He had certain misgivings. The democracy was clutching the arm of the executive power. Its influence was felt in India in our hold upon subject races, in the relation of members to their constituents. He would not like to see democratic members in a vast majority in the House. He would not like to see a preponderating power given to a particular class. He said that the challenge had been thrown out to him and others to show what securities they wanted; but he had to reply that that would depend to a great extent on the Redistribution Bill of the government. He contended that in making electoral changes, if you pass the old lines the protection of minorities becomes indispensable. With reference to the prime minister's argument about dealing with Ireland, he could quite understand it if it was a question of population merely, but it was also one of taxation. He (Mr. Goschen) should be perfectly prepared to say, "Let Ireland be treated precisely as she has been treated before, taking all circumstances into consideration." It would be tremendously difficult to pass a Redistribution Bill next session, but the Conservative party would be wrong if they opposed it. He said that he had endeavoured to persuade himself that he could vote for the bill, but he had not been able. He hoped he was wrong in his misgivings, but he was compelled to vote against the bill.

Mr. O'Connor Power, member for County Mayo, noticed that the right honourable gentleman (Mr. Go- schen) harped upon a few strings, one of which was the Irish Separatist party. He (Mr. Power) would, however, emphatically deny that what had been described as the Constitutional Home Rule party in Ireland, which numbered amongst its ranks some of the most loyal subjects of her majesty in that country, was one which advocated a policy of separation. He lamented that such tactics should be resorted to by, it seemed to him, every English politician who wished to make it appear that the aspirations of Ireland were inconsistent with the integrity of the empire. The separatist bogey had been brought before the House some half a dozen times, a few nights ago by the member for the Dublin University (Mr. Plunket). It could serve no good purpose to put forward this erroneous conception of Irish demands. No member of the party led by the member for Cork (Mr. Parnell) would make any proposal for a separation of Ireland from the empire. He did not think the loyal minority in Ireland was in any danger. Their time of ascendency, however, was past. The junior member for the University of Dublin (Mr. Gibson) had argued that before extending the franchise to Ireland we should have waited till Ireland had quieted down. The answer was plain. It was vain to expect it so long as any inequality between the two peoples remained. He held that Ireland should retain her present number of members, and that the measure should be extended to Ireland.

Sir Stafford Northcote thought there was reason for

the observation of the prime minister, that the debate
was languid, but this was because of doubt as to the issue
involved in it. There is doubt as to the principle of the
measure, but there is none as to the principle of the
amendment. It is to the effect that what is proposed
will destroy the balance of the constitution, and that it
is impossible to pronounce upon it without knowing
whether it is part of a larger scheme, and if so, what that
larger scheme may be. The prime minister calls upon us
to trust the people, but it is a question whether you can
trust the government. It is not an insignificant transaction; it is a question of altering the whole basis of your
constitution. Now he argues we are bound to admit
the largest number of capable citizens; but if this is accurate, then you ought to admit a great many more than
you propose to admit, and you ought also to admit female
householders. Then comes the amendment in all its force.
We want to know your whole scheme. We want to know
how you are to deal with minority representation. We
want to know how you intend dealing with Irish representation. There is no doubt that redistribution is a difficult
subject. The prime minister's statement is to the effect
that the length of time taken to debate redistribution is
ten times as great as the time taken to deal with a bill
on the franchise. But what could be more important?
He (Mr. Gladstone) likewise stated that the reform bills
hitherto passed had improved the character and constitution of the House. He (Sir Stafford) was not prepared
to discuss that question. It was not quite self-evident,
but there was a considerable amount of truth in it. The
question is, what will be the effect of introducing so large
a body as 2,000,000 if you have not arranged the manner
in which they are to fall into your system? There is

always this to fear—that the masses you import will
prove unmanageable unless a system of training and
manipulation is adopted, and the difficulty you will have
to face will not be altogether with the masses themselves,
who will be untrustworthy and wanting in experience,
but it will be the danger of their falling into the hands
of persons who will misdirect them.

Sir Henry James, the attorney-general, thought that
the cause of the enfranchisement of the masses had made
great progress during the debate. The Conservatives
had been making prophecies about the bill, such as, that
the bill would destroy the rights of property, and also
that it would deprive freemen of their ancient privileges,
neither of which had been true. The noble lord (Lord
J. Manners) had proposed his amendment in a form
which no political opponent could object to. Years ago
he belonged to a party which took great interest in the
prosperity of the peasant class; but what has that interest
done for the peasantry? Has it made their position any
better or given them any greater power or opportunity of
speaking for themselves? He characterized the speech
of the honourable member for Ripon (Mr. Goschen) as
timid and distrustful, and concluded as follows:—"Will
not my right honourable friend consider that in thus
acting as an opponent to the bill on it second reading he
is taking a course which will do harm to those who are
seeking to secure the representation of minorities, to
those who as matters stand want to see no undue preponderance given to any particular class? What are we to
do? We are to introduce, I suppose, by way of a bill,
some measure which will show what safeguards are to be
given to minorities, and which will be satisfactory to the
right honourable gentleman. The price is too high and

the return too small. We shall endanger the franchise
bill and gain one vote on this coming division. What
would be the fate of such a bill if we placed it on the table,
and we had my right honourable friend discussing it, and
the noble lord opposite discussing it, while the bill which
is now before us, and which presents the main principles,
would have to be put on one side until we had satisfied
all the most learned views and scruples of my right
honourable friend and of all those who would support
him? My right honourable friend admits that he does
not claim to be a friend to this bill. At least he accepts
it reluctantly. He has told us he is not one of those who
wish to swim with the stream. Well, sir, that may be
true enough; perhaps it is not always wise to attempt to
do it. But has he not learned that there are some streams
that you cannot breast, some onward streams that bear
men with them? The question which we are now discussing is like one of those powerful currents. We have
gone too far with it to enable us to recede; and the
extent to which it has been developed rests not with individual members, but with the whole House."

Division.   The House divided—For the bill, 340; against it, 210.
Majority, 130.

FOR THE BILL.

Acland, Sir T. D.	Ashley, Hon. E. M.
Acland, C. T. D.	Baldwin, E.
Agnew, W.	Balfour, Sir G.
Ainsworth, J.	Balfour, Right Hon. J. B.
Allen, W. S.	Balfour, J. S.
Anderson, G.	Barclay, J. W.
Armitage, B.	Baring, Viscount.
Armitstead, G.	Barnes, A.
Arnold, A.	Barran, J.
Asher, A.	Barry, J.

Bass, Sir A.
Bass, H.
Baxter, Right Hon. W. E.
Beaumont, W. B.
Biddulph, M.
Biggar, J. G.
Blake, J. A.
Blennerhasset, Sir R.
Blennerhasset, R. P.
Bolton, J. C.
Borlase, W. C.
Brand, Hon. H R.
Brassey, Sir T.
Brassey, H. A.
Brett, R. B.
Briggs, W. E.
Bright, J.
Brinton, J.
Broadhurst, H.
Brogden, A.
Brooks, M.
Brown, A. H.
Bruce, Right Hon. Lord C.
Bruce, Hon. R. P.
Bryce, J.
Buchanan, T. R.
Burt, T.
Buszard, M. C.
Buxton, F. W.
Buxton, S. C.
Cameron, C.
Campbell, Lord C.
Campbell, Sir G.
Campbell, R. F. F.
Campbell-Bannerman, H.
Carbutt, E. H.
Carington, Hon. R.
Causton, R. K.
Cavendish, Lord E.

Chamberlain, Right Hon. J.
Chambers, Sir T.
Cheetham, J. F.
Childers, Right Hon. H. C. E.
Clark, S.
Clarke, J. C.
Clifford, C. C.
Cohen, A.
Colebrooke, Sir T. E.
Collings, J.
Collins, E.
Colman, J. J.
Colthurst, Colonel.
Corbet, W. J.
Corbett, J.
Cotes, C. C.
Courtauld, G.
Courtney, L. H.
Cowen, J.
Cowper, Hon. H. F.
Craig, W. Y.
Creyke, R.
Cropper, J.
Cross, J. K.
Crum, A.
Cummins, A.
Cunliffe, Sir R. A.
Currie, Sir D.
Davey, H.
Davies, D.
Davies, R.
Davies, W.
Dawson, C.
Deasy, J.
De Ferrières, Baron.
Dickson, T. A.
Dilke, Right Hon. Sir C. W.
Dilwyn, L. L.
Dodds, J.

MR. GLAD-
STONE'S
FIRST BILL
OF 1884.

Dodson, Right Hon. J. G.
Duckham, T.
Duff, R. W.
Earp, T.
Ebrington, Viscount.
Edwards, H.
Edwards, P.
Egerton, Admiral Hon. F.
Elliot, Hon. A. R. D.
Fairbairn, Sir A.
Farquharson, Dr. R.
Fawcett, Right Hon. H.
Ferguson, R.
Ffolkes, Sir W. H. B.
Findlater, W.
Firth, J. F. B.
Fitzmaurice, Lord E.
Fitzwilliam, Hon. H. W.
Fitzwilliam, Hon. W. J.
Flower, C.
Foljambe, C. G. S.
Foljambe, F. J. S.
Forster, Sir C.
Forster, Right Hon. W. E.
Fort, R.
Fowler, H. H.
Fowler, W.
Fry, L.
Fry, T.
Gabbett, D. F.
Gladstone, Right Hon. W. E.
Gladstone, H. J.
Gladstone, W. H.
Gordon, Sir A.
Gordon, Lord D.
Gourley, E. T.
Gower, Hon. E. F. L.
Grafton, F. W.
Grant, A.

Grant, D.
Gray, E. D.
Grey, A. H. G.
Guest, M. J.
Gurdon, R. T.
Hamilton, J. G. C.
Harcourt, Right Hon. Sir W. G.
  V. V.
Hardcastle, J. A.
Harrington, T.
Hartington, Marquis of.
Hayter, Sir A. D.
Healy, T. M.
Henderson, F.
Heneage, E.
Herschell, Sir F.
Hibbert, J. T.
Hill, T. R.
Holden, I.
Holland, S.
Hollond, J. R.
Holms, J.
Hopwood, C. H.
Howard, E. S.
Howard, G. J.
Howard, J.
Illingworth, A.
Ince, H. B.
Inderwick, F. A.
James, Sir H.
James, C.
James, W. H.
Jardine, R.
Jenkins, D. J.
Jerningham, H. E.
Johnson, E.
Jones-Parry, L.
Kenny, M. J.
Kingscote, Colonel R. N. F.

Kinnear, J.
Labouchere, H.
Lambton, Hon. F. W.
Lawrence, W.
Lawson, Sir W.
Lea, T.
Leahy, J.
Leake, R.
Leamy, E.
Leatham, E. A.
Lee, H.
Lefevre, Right Hon. G. J. S.
Lloyd, M.
Lubbock, Sir J.
Lusk, Sir A.
Lymington, Viscount.
Lynch, N.
Lyons, R. D.
Macfarlane, D. II.
Mackie, R. B.
Mackintosh, C. F.
Macliver, P. S.
M'Arthur, Sir W.
M'Arthur, A.
M'Carthy, J.
M'Coan, J. C.
M'Intyre, Æneas J.
M'Kenna, Sir J. W.
M'Lagan, P.
M'Laren, C. B. B.
M'Mahon, E.
Maitland, W. F.
Mappin, F. T.
Marjoribanks, E.
Martin, R. B.
Marum, E. M.
Maskelyne, M. H. N. Story.
Mason, H.
Maxwell-Heron, J.

Mayne, T.
Meagher, W.
Meldon, C. H.
Mellor, J. W.
Milbank, Sir F. A.
Molloy, B. C.
Monk, C. J.
Moore, A.
Moreton, Lord.
Morgan, Right Hon. G. O.
Morley, A.
Morley, J.
Morley, S.
Mundella, Right Hon. A. J.
Nicholson, W.
Noel, E.
Nolan, Colonel J. P.
Norwood, C. M.
O'Brien, Sir P.
O'Brien, W.
O'Connor, A.
O'Connor, T. P.
O'Donnell, F. H.
O'Donoghue, The.
O'Gorman Mahon, Col. The.
O'Shea, W. H.
Otway, Right Hon. Sir A. J.
Paget, T. T.
Palmer, C. M.
Palmer, G.
Palmer, J. H.
Parker, C. S.
Parnell, C. S.
Pease, A.
Peddie, J. D.
Pender, J.
Pennington, F.
Philips, R. N.
Playfair, Right Hon. Sir L.

MR. GLAD-
STONE'S
FIRST BILL
OF 1884.

Potter, T. B.
Powell, W. R. H.
Power, J. O'C.
Power, R.
Price, Sir R. G.
Pulley, J.
Ralli, P.
Ramsay, J.
Ramsden, Sir J.
Rathbone, W.
Redmond, J. E.
Redmond, W. R.
Reid, R. T.
Rendel, S.
Richard, H.
Roberts, J.
Robertson, H.
Roe, T.
Rogers, J. E. T.
Rothschild, Sir N. M. de.
Roundel, C. S.
Russell, Lord A.
Russell, C.
Russell, G. W. E.
Rylands, P.
Samuelson, B.
Samuelson, H.
Seely, C. (Lincoln).
Seely, C. (Nottingham).
Sellar, A. C.
Sexton, T.
Shaw, T.
Shaw, W.
Sheil, E.
Sheridan, H. B.
Shield, H.
Simon, Sergeant J.
Sinclair, Sir J. G. T.
Slagg, J.

Small, J. F.
Smillie, Lieut.-Col. P.
Smith, S.
Smithwick, J. F.
Smyth, P. J.
Spencer, The Hon. C. R.
Stafford, Marquis of.
Stanley, Hon. E. F.
Stansfeld, J.
Stanton, W. J.
Stevenson, J. C.
Storey, S.
Sullivan, T. D.
Summers, W.
Talbot, C. R. M
Tavistock, Marquis of.
Tennant, C.
Thomasson, J. P.
Thompson, T. C.
Tillet, J. H.
Torrens, W. J. M.
Tracey, Hon. J. S. A.
Trevelyan, G. O.
Villiers, C. P.
Vivian, Sir H. H.
Vivian, A. P.
Waddy, S. D.
Walker, S.
Walter, J.
Waterlow, Sir S.
Watkin, Sir E.
Waugh, E.
Webster, Dr. J.
West, W. H.
Whitbread, S.
Whitworth, B.
Wiggin, H.
Williams, S. C. E.
Williamson, S.

Willis, W.
Wills, W. H.
Willyams, E. W. B.
Wilson, Sir M.
Wilson, C. H.
Wilson, J.
Wodehouse E. R.

Woodall, W.
Wolff, F.

TELLERS.

Grosvenor, Lord R.
Kensington, Lord.

MR. GLAD-
STONE'S
FIRST BILL
OF 1884.

AGAINST THE BILL.

Alexander, Major-General.
Allsopp, C.
Amherst, W. A. T.
Archdale, W. H.
Ashmead-Bartlett, E.
Balfour, A. J.
Baring, J. C.
Barne, F. St. J. N.
Barttelot, Sir W. B.
Bateson, Sir T.
Beach, Sir Michael H.
Beach, W. W. B.
Bective, Earl of.
Bentinck, G. C.
Beresford, G. D. la P.
Biddell, W.
Birkbeck, B.
Blackburne, Col. J. J.
Boord, T. W.
Bourke, R.
Broadley, W. H. H.
Brodrick, W. St. J. F.
Brooke, Lord.
Brookes, W. C.
Bruce, Sir H. H.
Brymer, W. C.
Bulwer, J. R.
Burghley, Lord.
Buxton, Sir R. J.

Cameron, D.
Campbell, J. A.
Carden, Sir R. W.
Castlereagh, Viscount.
Cecil, Lord.
Chaplin, H.
Christie, W. L.
Churchill, R., Lord.
Clarke, E.
Clive, Colonel.
Coddington, W.
Cole, Viscount.
Collins, T.
Compton, F.
Coope, O. E.
Corry, J. P.
Cross, Sir R. A.
Cubitt, G.
Curzon, M.
Dalrymple, C.
Davenport, W. B.
Dawnay, L. P.
Dawnay, G. C.
De Worms, Baron.
Dickson, A. G.
Digby, E.
Dixon Hartland, P. D.
Donaldson, Hudson C.
Douglas, A. Akers.

Dyke, Sir W. H.
Eaton, W. H.
Ecroyd, W. F.
Egerton, A. de T.
Egerton, A. F.
Elcho, Lord.
Elliot, G. W.
Elton, C. J.
Emlyn, Viscount.
Ennis, Sir J.
Escourt, G. S.
Ewart, W.
Ewing, A. O.
Fielden, General.
Fellowes, W. H.
Finch, G. H.
Finch Hatton, M. F. G.
Fletcher, Sir H.
Folkeston, Viscount.
Forester, C. T. W.
Forster, W. H.
Fowler, R. N.
Freemantle, T. F.
French Brewster, R. A. B.
Galway, Viscount.
Garmer, J. C.
Gilson, E.
Giffard, Sir H. S.
Giles, A.
Goldney, Sir G.
Gore-Langton, W. S.
Gorst, J. E.
Goschen, G. J.
Grantham, W.
Greene, E.
Greer, T.
Gregory, G. B.
Halsey, T. F.
Hamilton, Lord G.

Hamilton, Lord Claud.
Hamilton, J. T
Harvey, Sir R. B.
Hay, Sir J. C. D.
Herbert, S.
Hicks, E.
Hildyard, T. B. T.
Hill, Lord A. W.
Hill, A. S.
Home, D. M.
Hope, A. J. B. B.
Houldsworth, W. H.
Hubbard, J. G.
Kennard, C. J.
Kennaway, Sir J. H.
King Harman, E. R.
Knight, F. W.
Knightley, Sir R.
Lawrence, J. C.
Lawrence, Sir T.
Lechmere, Sir E. A. H.
Legh, W. J.
Leighton, Sir B.
Leighton, S.
Lennox, Lord H. G. C. G.
Levett, T. D.
Lewis, C. E.
Lewisham, Viscount.
Loder, R.
Long, W. H.
Lopes, Sir M.
Lowther, J.
Lowther, W.
Lowther, T. W.
Macartney, T. W. E.
MacIver, D.
Macnaghton, E.
M'Garel-Hogg, Sir Jas.
Makins, Colonel.

Manners, Lord John.
Marriott, W. T.
Master, T. W. C.
Maxwell, Sir H. E.
Miles, Sir P. J. W.
Miles, C. W.
Mills, Sir C. H.
Milner, Sir F.
Monkton, T.
Morgan, F.
Moss, R.
Mowbray, Sir J. R.
Mulholland, T.
Newdegate, C. N.
Newport, Viscount.
Nicholson, W. N.
Northcote, Sir S.
Northcote, H. S.
Onslow, D. R.
Peeke, Sir H. W.
Peel, Sir R.
Pell, A.
Pemberton, E. L.
Percy, Earl.
Percy, Lord A.
Phipps, C. N. P.
Phipps, P.
Plunkett, D. R.
Price, Cap. G. E.
Puleston, J. H.
Raikes, H. C.
Rankin, J.
Read, C. S.
Rendlesham, Lord.
Repton, G. W.
Ritchie, C. T.
Rolls, J. A.
Ross, A. H.
Ross, C. C.

Round, James.
Salt, T.
Sclater Booth, G.
Scott, M. D.
Selwin Ibbetson, Sir H. J.
Severne, J. E.
Smith, W. H.
Smith, A.
Stanhope, E.
Stanley, Col. F.
Stanley, E. J.
Storer, J.
Strutt, C. H.
Sykes, C.
Talbot, J. G.
Thomson, H.
Thornhill, A. J.
Thornhill, T.
Thynne, Lord H. F.
Tollemache, H. J.
Tollemache, W. F.
Tomlinson, W. E. M.
Tottenham, A. L.
Tyler, Sir H. W.
Wallace, Sir R.
Walrond, Col. W. H.
Warburton, P. E.
Warton, C. N.
Watney, J.
Whitley, E.
Wilmott, Sir H.
Wolff, Sir H. D.
Wroughton, P.
Wyndham, P.
Yorke, J. R.

TELLERS.

Crichton, Viscount.
Winn, R.

MR. GLADSTONE'S FIRST BILL OF 1884.

MR. GLAD-
STONE'S
FIRST BILL
OF 1884.

The House of Commons then went into committee on the Franchise Bill on May 6, and it was under discussion for a period of eleven nights, terminating on June 19. As was to be expected there were many amendments, and some of them were amendments of importance. (1) The

Amend-
ments in
Committee.

question of the exclusion of Ireland from the measure was raised by an amendment proposed by Mr. Brodrick, member for West Surrey, and was debated at great length. It was supported by Mr. Lewis, Mr. Plunket, Sir Stafford Northcote, Lord Claud Hamilton, Mr. Tottenham, Mr. Chaplin, Mr. Ewart, Mr. Macartney, and Lord George Hamilton; and was opposed by Mr. Trevelyan, Dr. Lyons, the prime minister, Lord Randolph Churchill, Lord Edward Cavendish, Mr. Stavely Hill, and Sir Joseph M'Kenna. Upon a division it was lost upon a majority of 195. (2) Another important amendment was proposed by Colonel Stanley, to the effect that the bill should not come into force until a Redistribution Bill was passed, and this amendment was supported by Mr. E. Stanhope, Mr. A. J. Balfour, Mr. Sclater Booth, Lord John Manners, Mr. Lewis, and Sir Stafford Northcote; while it was opposed by the prime minister, Mr. W. E. Forster, Mr. Bryce, and others. Upon a division it was lost by a majority of 94. (3) An amendment to the effect that each voter should be capable of writing the name of the candidate for whom he recorded his vote was proposed by Mr. Stanley Leighton, but after a short debate it was withdrawn. (4) An important amendment on the subject of what are called "three-cornered constituencies" was proposed by Dr. Cameron, and was debated at some length. In the course of his remarks Mr. Gladstone said: "As far as I am concerned I do not think I require to do more than refer to the former speeches I have made on this subject, and to add that what I have said on my own part I now venture to say on behalf of the government, namely, that unquestionably in the view of my colleagues, as well as of myself, a most thorough consideration and examination of all the questions of minority voting must be an essential part of any new settlement of the representation of the people. With regard to the hope and desire that my honourable friend has expressed, that that may take place in the present Parliament, we reciprocate that hope and desire, and the pledge he has asked for that the question may be thoroughly inquired into and examined I think may be given; but if I am now asked to say what may be the result of that examination; if we were to give our opinions upon a matter of this kind, which I think would find its proper place in a Redistribution Bill, we shall open a field of debate which we would wish to avoid. Therefore I think there can be no doubt, and I think my honourable friend will admit it, that the argument is extremely strong for an adjournment of this question, and I believe he will not object to an adjournment after what I now say." The amendment was withdrawn. (5) An amendment was proposed by Sir Walter B. Barttelot to the effect, that to enable any one to vote it should be incumbent upon him that he personally pay his taxes. This was opposed by the prime minister and was negatived. (6) An amendment was next proposed to the effect that the franchise be only given to those who possess a dwelling-house of not less than two habitable apartments. It was proposed by Sir Edward Watkin, and in the course of his remarks he urged that the man who, from poverty, or intemperance, or low habits, was content to live with wife and children of both sexes, some adolescent, in one apart-

MR. GLAD-
STONE'S
FIRST BILL
OF 1884.

ment, was not in the sense in which the prime minister used the words a "capable citizen." Mr. Gladstone opposed the amendment upon the ground that it would disfranchise a vast number both in Ireland and in Scotland. In Glasgow there were 30,000 families out of 110,000 who live in single apartments. There are many in Edinburgh. There are a large number in Aberdeen, and it would be found very difficult to find any person there who is incapable of exercising the franchise. After

Franchise
Bill in Com-
mittee.

a debate the amendment was withdrawn. (7) An important amendment was proposed by Mr. M'Laren, the effect of which was to limit one man to one vote. He held that if the bill was passed in its present form there could be no possible objection to a man having a vote in every county in England. Mr. Gladstone's reply was as follows: —"Sir, the course which we take with regard to this amendment has no exclusive reference to the merits of the amendment itself. We announced at the time of the introduction of this bill, that in making so grave a proposal as the enfranchisement of a number of our fellow-citizens, estimated at 2,000,000, we deemed it a capital part of our duty so to adjust all the conditions of our proposition as to give it the best possible chance of passing into law. Now among those conditions we had to consider, first and foremost, the crowded state of the business of the House, and the enormous facilities which that state of business gives for opposition. We then, of course, had to consider that we should have to contend with the susceptibilities on the one hand of those who are jealous of all the privileges which property enjoys in this country, and who are anxious to extend them; and on the other hand, with the desires of those who, like my honourable friend the member for Stafford (Mr. M'Laren), are anxious to push popular privileges and equality to the furthest point that can be reached. We came to the conclusion that under this state of facts, if we were in earnest in our desire to pass the bill we had but one course to take, to set ourselves steadily against all changes in the bill, in whatever direction they might be aimed, to alter the basis of the measure. We do not pretend, sir, to offer a perfect system of franchise; we find that to be entirely out of the reach of possibility. We might have laid an elaborate bill upon the table, dealing with each and all of these subjects in a multitude of divisions, and we might have been able to boast of a very scientific measure; but if we had done so we should have been betraying the interests intrusted to our charge. A simple, and even a rough method of dealing with the subject, was a matter of absolute necessity under the conditions of the case if we were to have a practical end and aim in view. I am quite sure my honourable friend will understand the spirit in which I make these observations. I do not wish in the least degree to limit the field of discussion for such propositions, and I do not find it necessary to intimate any opinion upon them myself. But my belief is that the security of property and the privileges of classes in this country do not really rest upon certain artificial advantages which they possess under the present structure of our laws, but upon the general goodwill of the community. I have no bigoted or extreme sentiments on a proposition like this, but I put it to my honourable friend with all respect that we who are very anxious to pass this bill cannot afford to discuss these propositions. Perfection is not within our reach. If we go to work in that spirit we shall infallibly fail in it altogether. We have in view a great practical object, the

z

MR. GLAD-
STONE'S
FIRST BILL
OF 1884. meeting of the desires and necessities, and providing for
the interests, of vast numbers of men who desire the
franchise, and who are qualified to enjoy it. We must
go straight to our point, and decline to deviate either to
the right or to the left for the purpose of introducing
theoretical perfection. We do not want to prejudice discussion in any way whatever; but we earnestly beg the
committee, and especially those members who, like my
honourable friend, are anxious for the bill to pass, to
waive their efforts for the present, and to reserve them
for another opportunity, resting upon this, that all these
are questions which anybody can raise when they like.
I cannot undertake to shut the door against them for ever,
Franchise
Bill in Com-
mittee. and relying on it that if they are just and needful, the enlargement of the franchise which we are now making will
not tend to delay their adoption." The amendment was
withdrawn. (8) The next amendment was proposed by Mr.
Cavendish-Bentinck, the object of which was to delete a
clause directed against the creation of "faggot" votes.
The clause was to the effect that a man should not be
entitled to be registered as a voter in respect of the
ownership of any rent charge. It was explained on behalf of the government that while there was no disposition to disfranchise property in any way, it must really be
property and not merely money. The proposal was negatived. (9.) An amendment was proposed by Mr. Warton
to the effect that the qualification be given where the
rent charge amounts to a sum not less than £100, but
this was negatived. (10.) A proposal was made by Mr.
Ecroyd to the effect that the franchise should be extended to owners of copyhold estate, or of leases created
for a term not less than forty years, of a clear annual
value of £4; but Mr. Gladstone objected to this upon the

ground that while he would preserve existing electoral
rights of property he did not propose to extend them,
and that most of those who would be enfranchised by
the proposed amendment will come in under the occupation franchise. It was lost by a majority of 92. (11.)
An amendment was next proposed by Mr. Ecroyd to the
effect that a man may be qualified in respect of property
to exercise the franchise in a county or borough, although
he be also entitled to vote in respect of a householder
or lodger qualification. Mr. Gladstone objected to dual
voting. The effect of the proposal would be to give a
man a borough vote and a county vote, the one in respect of property and the other in respect of occupancy.
Furthermore, it would give a man a double vote, first
in respect of the occupancy and next in respect of the
ownership of the same property. He could not consent
to the amendment, and on a division there was a majority of 114 against it. (12.) There was an amendment to
be proposed by Mr. Anderson to the effect that a constituency shall have a claim on the services of the member elected, and that such member, if absent for three
months, may be summoned to attend, and, on failure for
one month more, a new writ may be issued; but as it
appeared to the chairman that that amendment had no
reference whatever to the question of the franchise, it was
out of order. (13.) Mr. Bryce proposed to limit the
period of occupation for the household and lodger franchise from twelve to six months, but the prime minister
having stated that this would be taken up under the
Registration Bill the amendment was withdrawn. (14.)
A highly important amendment in favour of the enfranchisement of women was proposed by Mr. Woodall, and
gave rise to a long debate. It was opposed by Mr. Glad-

stone on the ground that it would imperil the bill. The amendment was supported by Lord John Manners, Mr. Stansfeld, Baron Henry de Worms, Colonel King-Harman, Mr. Warton, Major-General Alexander, Mr. Joseph Cowan, Sir Wilfrid Lawson, Sir Stafford Northcote, and Mr. Storey; while it was opposed by Mr. E. A. Leatham, Mr. Newdegate, Sir Joseph Pease, Mr. Beresford Hope, Mr. Thorold Rodgers, Mr. Agnew, Mr. Inderwick, Mr. Bryce, Mr. Henry Labouchere, Mr. Goschen, Mr. John Morley, Mr. Raikes, and Mr. Illingworth. Upon a division the numbers were: for the amendment, 135; against, 271. Majority against the amendment, 136. (15.) An amendment was next proposed by Mr. Albert

Grey the object of which was to secure the passing of the Redistribution Bill before the Franchise Bill should come into actual operation. His proposal was that the Franchise Bill should be suspended till January 1, 1887. Mr. Gladstone explained that he was in sympathy with the honourable member, and that he was willing to go with him as far as he could towards the attainment of the object he had in view. He hoped that some security could be given that a redistribution bill should be passed before the new enfranchisement came into operation. But his view was that that object could not be attained in the form in which it was now proposed. When the proper time came he would be perfectly ready to support the proposal of the member for Wolverhampton. The amendment was withdrawn. (16.) There was a motion regarding the suspension of the franchise to convicted persons, which was negatived, and another proposing to give the franchise to men serving in the sea or land forces, which was withdrawn. (17.) Mr. Thomas Collins proposed that in the case of constituencies return-

ing two members to Parliament each elector should be
entitled to give a single vote for one candidate, and no
more, but the amendment was withdrawn after a discussion. (18.) Mr. H. H. Fowler then moved a clause to the
effect that the act shall commence and take effect from
January 1, 1885. Mr. Gladstone said that the bill as it
originally stood had a clause enacting that the act would
take effect from the date of its passing, but this was withdrawn. A proposal was then made that it should not
come into operation until the Redistribution Bill was
passed, but the House refused to adopt it. A motion was
then made by Mr. Grey that the bill do not come into
force until January 1, 1887, and that was withdrawn
agreeably to the sense of the House. The only remaining
method, therefore, consistently with what has been hitherto done, was the adoption of a plan which would enable
the present house to deal with redistribution, but which
should not absolutely make the operation of the new
constituencies contingent upon the passing of a measure
of redistribution. The clause would therefore be heartily
accepted by the government. After a debate the House
divided, and the clause carried by a majority of 256 to
130. (19.) Mr. Houldsworth moved for an extension of
the seven-mile limit in cities and boroughs, but Mr.
Gladstone opposed it on the ground of its being an extension of the principle of dual voting, and it was rejected by a majority of 99. (20.) Lord Algernon Percy
then moved that the franchise should be extended to
every man, not otherwise qualified, who should pay the
income-tax; but this was negatived by a majority of 78.
There were a number of less important amendments proposed, and which were either negatived or withdrawn.
The bill was then *reported.*

On June 23 the bill was considered by the House. A number of motions were made, but no substantial altera- tion was made on the bill. Mr. Anderson's clause re- garding the absence of members was negatived as irrele- vant. The clause giving a qualification to those who paid income-tax was rejected by a majority of 84. Mr. Kennard's motion to remove the disqualification upon
the constabulary was withdrawn. A variety of un- important amendments were made, and the discussion of details was continued on June 24, when the bill was or- bered to be read a third time on Thursday.

On June 26 Mr. Gladstone moved the third reading of the Franchise Bill, and referred to many ominous declar- ations that had been made, or indications given, as to the future fate of the bill, both in the House and outside of the House, sometimes by persons of great importance; and stated that he had refrained advisedly, and so had his colleagues, he believed, without exception, from noticing them. The opinion of the government with regard to quarrels and collisions, if they were to arise, was that the proper rules applicable to the case were contained in those few and well-known words of Shakspere:—

> " Beware
> Of entrance to a quarrel; but being in,
> Bear't, that th' opposed beware of thee."

He would have wished to preserve silence to the end, but some declarations made in the House had been so explicit that he did not feel authorized so to preserve it. One of those declarations was from an honourable mem- ber who said that he would not affect to deny that great danger overhung the bill, and he evidently spoke on the basis of something more than a mere private opinion, as indeed he was entitled to do. Another right honourable gentleman said, within the last few days, that no practical man believed that the bill had the ghost of a chance. These were indications which it was not possible wholly to pass by. The right honourable gentleman urged that no one complete bill had ever been presented to Parliament on the subject of reform. The whole government plan had never been so presented. And what would have been the position of the government if redistribution had been combined with the franchise? Here we are at June 26 with only one bill. He announced that the government were prepared to deal with redistribution during the next session, and he thought when an assurance of that kind was given it amounted to a covenant between the government and the House. He said that he should regard a quarrel as a calamity grievous to the country, bringing into question the Parliamentary institutions under which we have lived so long, a conflict the results of which, if there were in the country men of revolutionary opinions, might have been acceptable to such men, but which it was the solemn duty of the government to use every reasonable means to avoid. For that reason, in every question that came up the government sought to avoid a conflict between the Houses of the legislature. It has been said that this is a bill to secure the permanent existence of a Liberal government. That is not a rational argument. He concluded, "I think we have given sufficient evidence of our desire to avoid a quarrel. I am bound to say that I hold the question of this evidence to be a matter of the greatest importance, because even the remote probability of a conflict between the two Houses upon such a question as this, I take to be the most serious prospect that has been opened during my recollection since the crisis of the corn-laws was opened to the view of Parliament. I will not undertake to put a limit to the mischiefs and the difficulties which might result. Most grave I am confident—too painfully confident—they will be. But what the ultimate issue of it will be, I have not a doubt. That the duty of preventing it by every reasonable means was the most sacred duty incumbent upon us on this occasion next to the great business of enfranchising a vast mass of the population I do not doubt; and the second duty as well as the first of our obligations, which we have carefully and strenuously endeavoured to fulfil."

Sir Stafford Northcote: "I was anxious to follow the right honourable gentleman after the speech—the extra-ordinary speech he has just made. That speech was not a speech on the merits or demerits of the Franchise Bill, which we are now asked to read a third time. It was a speech upon the question whether the House of Lords is any longer to form a part of the legislature of this country. It was a speech upon the question whether the House of Lords is to be at liberty to examine and vote upon, and to take any part of the legislation which affects the constitution of this country; or whether the House of Lords is bound at the will of a majority of the House of Commons, or something even worse than that, at the will of an imperious minister, to listen to threats, and, affected by those threats, to refuse to do the duty which lies upon them. I submit that it is not for us to discuss how or what course the House of Lords may think it right to take upon any measure which comes up from the House of Commons, and has to be examined by that assembly; but when the right honourable gentleman comes forward and in a most theatrical manner makes a declaration, the meaning of which it is impossible to misunderstand, he is raising an issue which the country must take care to notice—perhaps in a manner different from that which he expects. We have had great reason to question the wisdom and the propriety of the course which the government have adopted in the matter of this Franchise Bill. We have had still greater reason to distrust a measure which has been brought forward, as this has been, as an obviously and confessedly incomplete part of a most important measure. I have from time to time had occasion to ask why we should be expected to pass a bill for the extension of the franchise without dealing with the question of redistribution, and the answer which I have received, the arguments which have been raised, and the indications which have been given, have convinced me that a much larger question is at issue than the mere question whether it is convenient to take these measures together or separately. It has convinced me that we have never been informed, not only of the minute details of the plan of the government, but of the real meaning and object of the great constitutional changes we have been invited to undertake. We have never been told what is the point at which the government is driving."

Mr. Goschen observed that he had felt it his duty to oppose the bill at every stage, not because it was inopportune or incomplete, but because of its opening the franchise to two millions of voters. But he had not noticed any political forces inside or outside the House which associated themselves with that opposition. The leader of the opposition, the Conservatives of the House, have not opposed the vital principle of the bill. Even the Conservative leaders out of the House have taken a

MR. GLADSTONE'S FIRST BILL OF 1884.

MR. GOSCHEN'S SPEECH.

**MR. GLAD-
STONE'S
FIRST BILL
OF 1884.** similar course. This has led him (Mr. Goschen) to the conclusion that the country now looks upon the principle of the extension of the household franchise as being accepted, and would insist upon any government that came into office submitting proposals embodying that which is the vital principle of this bill.

**Mr. A. J.
Balfour.** Mr. A. J. Balfour thought the prime minister would have deferred to a future occasion those vain threats to the House of Lords. If a conflict was to take place at all it would be one between the two Houses, and not one between the House of Lords and the country. The bill originated at the conference at Leeds. The said conference gave its order to the cabinet; the cabinet gave its orders to the House of Commons, and now the House of Commons wanted to give its orders to the House of Lords.

**Mr. Newde-
gate.** Mr. Newdegate said that if the House of Lords passed the measure, he as a humble but sincere constitutional member of the House was of opinion they would create a necessity for some body like the senate of the United States, which should be able to stand between the country and the dictation of a single chamber, or the arbitrary will of a too powerful minister.

**Sir W. B.
Barttelot.** Sir W. B. Barttelot held that the prime minister had endeavoured to dictate to the House of Lords. He thought it would be to the interest of the country that they should go to the country to see whether the people were so anxious for reform as they were represented to be.

Sir H. James. The attorney-general (Sir Henry James) remarked that since the noble lord who led the opposition in the other House had thought it right in a campaign which he had undertaken on behalf of his party to address persons outside the House of Lords, and to give reasons why the House of Lords should throw out the bill, it was quite right for some one in a responsible position to warn them of the consequences that might follow. The recent elections had been referred to; but it must be remembered that all the candidates had expressed themselves in favour of the bill.

Mr. Lewis said he would defy the attorney-general to produce any words of a responsible leader of the Conservative party in the House of Lords, in which he said he would pledge the House of Lords to pursue a certain course with regard to the bill.

Mr. Healy, Mr. Warton, and Mr. Frederick Milner then addressed the House, after which the question was put that the bill should be read a third time. It was then read a third time, *nemine contradicente*, and was passed. A dispute afterwards arose, and on June 27 a motion was made for the deletion of the words "*nemine contradicente*," but this was negatived by a majority of 43.

The Franchise Bill was then introduced into the House of Lords, and set down for the second reading on July 7.

The Earl of Kimberley, on moving that the bill be read a second time, said that from the moment that a system of household franchise was established in boroughs it was apparent that the same system must be established throughout the country. It was not because the agricultural classes were more dangerous or less capable than the urban classes that they were excluded from the franchise. They are shrewd men who understand their own interests, and well acquainted with land. To give, therefore, a vote to the agricultural labourers is a Conservative proposal. The bill before the House is a moderate measure, and sedulously avoids interfering with the old franchises of the country. The noble lord then described the various franchises in existence in the three kingdoms

MR. GLAD-
STONE'S
FIRST BILL
OF 1884. and the changes proposed, in the same way as done by
Mr. Gladstone in his speech on the second reading in the
House of Commons. He then said that their lordships
would see that the bill, if passed, would establish an
identity of franchise throughout the United Kingdom. It
was also an aim of the bill to get rid of illusory qualifications, such as rent-charges and joint-ownership, which
give rise to faggot-votes, and which were clearly an invasion of the true principle of voting. The general result
would be to add about two millions to the roll. With
reference to Ireland, it seemed at first a difficult problem
to approach; but when the government came to be of
opinion that there was no danger more serious than that
of leaving to Ireland a real and substantial grievance, it
Lord Kim-
berley's
speech. was resolved that Ireland should be dealt with on the
same terms as the rest of the United Kingdom. But,
unhappily, the second reading is to be met by a resolution the first portion of which says—"That this
House, while prepared to concur in a well-considered and
complete scheme for the extension of the franchise," &c.
The noble lord thought the bill a well-considered measure, for the House of Commons had been considering it
from February to the end of June, and had no less than
twenty-three sittings over it. It is also a complete bill,
and could not be more complete unless it went the length
of manhood suffrage. But what is complained of is, that
it is not accompanied by a measure of redistribution. The
government conceive that they would fail to carry the
two measures if they were to associate them together.
They hold themselves, however, pledged to deal with the
question of redistribution next session, and to make it
perfectly clear that the Franchise Bill would not come
into operation until the Redistribution Bill had been

fully considered; they consented to an amendment that
the Franchise Bill should not come into effect till January 1, 1885, which of course means that the voters cannot
be on the register till January 1, 1886. But what he
understood the noble lords to fear was that the Redistribution Bill might be of such a nature that there would
be no chance of its passing. The prime minister has
given the outlines of what is intended. It is to be a very
considerable measure of redistribution. It is not intended
to establish equal electoral districts. It would be necessary that the principle of proportion should be applied to
a greater extent than it now is, but it is not likely that
the government should adopt any strict system of proportion between population and representation. There are
other questions: that of the number of members for Ireland, the question as to enlarging the membership of the
House, minority representation, and what is called proportional representation; all of these will require consideration. But the noble lord did not think that the
allegation of the measure not being well considered or
complete, or the objection of the bill not being accompanied by redistribution or its not being acceptable to
Parliament, were the sole motives for the proposed resolution. It had been said that there was a desire to force
a dissolution of Parliament. That might be a good party
move; but would it be for the interest of the country? A
House that is not representative, that cannot be suddenly
changed, that in its composition remains the same from
year to year and from Parliament to Parliament, ought
to be careful, ought to consider whether it is more safe
to place itself permanently in antagonism to the other
House, to one great party in the state, and to associate
itself with one section of the country. Let the House

MR. GLAD-
STONE'S
FIRST BILL
OF 1884.

remember what took place in 1867. It was asked by a Conservative minister to take a "leap in the dark," and it did so. It is now asked to pass a bill that is desirable in itself, and the noble and learned lord says, "Do not take the leap." The noble lord (Lord Kimberley) said that the bitterest enemies of the aristocracy were longing and praying for the House to reject the bill. "Will you not disappoint their expectations? You have the opportunity, if you pass the bill, of seeing one of the greatest constitutional changes which have been made for many years take place in singular calmness. I am the last man to exaggerate danger or to appeal to popular and violent passions, but I think there is no man in this House who

Lord Kim-
berley's
speech.

will not agree with me, that if this bill is rejected there must be a bitter and exacting controversy in which must be involved the question of the action of this House That being so, I ask the House to pause. You are now at the parting of the ways. Pause before you take the way that is not that of peace. I know from the unusual and ominous assembly of noble lords opposite what we may have to expect. I well know the eloquence and power with which you will be addressed by the noble and learned earl. But notwithstanding that, I shall venture not to part with the hope that you will not be led away by his subtle and practised advocacy to take a step which all must admit to be most grave, and which many believe to be most perilous. I move the second reading of the bill."

Lord Cairns'
amendment.

Earl Cairns then moved the following resolution:— "That this House, while prepared to concur in a well-considered and complete scheme for the extension of the franchise, does not think it right to assent to the second reading of a bill having for its object a fundamental change in the constitution of the electoral body of the United Kingdom, but which is not accompanied by provisions for so apportioning the right to return members as to ensure a true and fair representation of the people, or by any security in the proposals of the government that the present bill shall not come into operation except as part of an entire scheme." His lordship said that he did not intend to raise any question about the franchise itself, nor did he understand the House of Commons to have done so. The question he did intend to raise was whether it was consistent with what had been the practice of the country, and safe with regard to the constitution, to have a large extension of the franchise unaccompanied by a measure for the redistribution of political power? The noble earl (Lord Kimberley) had said that there never had been a case in which a complete reform bill had been presented to or passed by Parliament. He (Earl Cairns) must take isssue with the noble earl on that point. The reform bills for the three countries were each complete in themselves, inasmuch as each contained complete provisions both as regarded the extension of the franchise and the redistribution of seats. Look at what effect the bill will produce. In certain given constituencies the electorate would be raised nearly fourfold, and thus for all practical purposes the representation of public opinion would be annihilated. The government has said that the redistribution of seats must be a large one, much nearer the redistribution of 1832 than that of 1867. Now it was necessary to keep in view the problem to be solved when a scheme of redistribution falls to be dealt with. It is said that England and Wales are not over represented, that Scotland is under represented. Some say that Ireland is not over represented, some that it is. Then how

are the members to be got for the great county constituencies in England, and likewise for the northern part of
the country? Then there is the main question with regard to the south and the north of Ireland; and how are
the additional members for Scotland to be provided? Are
they to be got from England or Ireland, or by an increase
of the total number of the House? Then there is the
question of proportional representation. All these prob-
lems have to be solved. The next question is whether
the question of redistribution and the question of enfranchisement ought to go together or can be safely separated.
The argument of the government is that they could not
be passed in the same session, and next, that it must
first be known what is the numerical extent of the elec-
Lord Cairns torate under the new franchise in the different parts of
the country. The prime minister likewise said that the
one question raised national considerations, and that the
others only raised selfish and local ones. He (Lord Cairns)
did not object to keeping the two measures distinct as
regards discussion, and even as regards bills, provided
that arrangements were made whereby the one measure
would not come into force without the other. Authorities
have settled the question in that way. The noble earl,
the secretary of state for the colonies (Lord Derby), so
settled it in his speech in 1866. So did the secretary of
state for war (Marquis of Hartington) in 1878. It has
been said, Why should not a clause be introduced which
would prevent the act coming into operation until the
Redistribution Bill has been passed? The government,
however, declined this course. If they are prepared to
meet the difficulty by a special provision they have only
to say so. Then why is it that the question has been
forgotten, year after year, until 1884? The noble earl

(Lord Kimberley) says that the Houso can accept the assurance of the government that, if nothing happens to prevent it, they are determined to bring in and pass a measure of redistribution. But suppose it does not satisfy those who are not the supporters of the government, what will happen? The government say: "You must either take it or leave it. If you do not take it you leave the elections to the new electorate without any redistribution at all." It is calling upon Parliament to legislate under duress. From many other causes a Redistribution Bill may not pass. If an election took place in these circumstances you would get a convention Parliament elected by those who are the mere temporary depositaries of power. They would be the masters of the situation, and you would have a fundamental change in the constitution simply by an accident. "It is this danger—I call it a grave and serious danger—that I ask your lordships to guard against. It is idle to say that we oppose ourselves to any wish of the country in this matter. We appeal to the country. It is a calumny to say that we set ourselves against the country or against a measure of reform. We desire that that which has been done on all former occasions in the reform of the constitution should be done now, and that a peril and danger of that character should, if possible, be avoided. My lords, I have endeavoured briefly, and I hope fairly, to place before your lordships the bearing of this question. I have preferred to confine myself to argument, and I have not referred to any of those considerations by which this question has been surrounded out of doors. Your lordships have received, with regard to the decision to which you ought to come on this motion, a considerable quantity of good advice and some menace. The advice

MR. GLAD-STONE'S FIRST BILL OF 1884.

Lord Cairns.

2 A

has come from various sources, but the menace has come mainly from one quarter, and that quarter, I venture to think, one from which menace to this House was neither fitting nor constitutional. My lords, it would be inconsistent with the dignity of this House to respond to the menace. I feel persuaded that in the course which your lordships will take you will be of opinion that any menace such as we have heard of can only recoil on the heads of those, however eminent they may be, by whom the menace was uttered; and as to your lordships, I feel persuaded that in your decision upon the matter you will not be deterred by threats from supporting this amendment if you approve of it, and that, on the other hand, you will not be provoked, as some might be, by threats, to support the amendment unless it has your entire approval. I believe that the amendment which I now propose has the approval of the great majority of this House, and I believe it will have the approval of the country. In that belief I place the amendment in your lordships' hands."

The Duke of Argyll rose to support the bill. He said that his noble friend (Lord Kimberley) had referred to the peculiar constitution of the House of Lords, and the enormous privileges the members enjoyed in having a voice in the legislation of the country; but this was balanced by an immense disadvantage in being shut out of the other House of Parliament. He was glad to see so many country peers present, as he thought they were quite as competent to judge of public affairs as those who habitually attend the sittings of the House. But how is the House to exercise the great privilege which belongs to it by hereditary right? The votes of the House are not decisive of the fate of the governments. Let the

House—especially the cross bench, mind—apply itself to the proposed bill He remembered the time when the Liberal party were deeply engaged in seeing how many votes would be added by a £6 rental franchise, or a rating franchise, and so on, till Mr. Disraeli said: "Let us go down to something like principle—let us found our new franchise upon household suffrage." The lesson to be drawn from that is, that all anxiety in regard to numbers was a mistake. Why, in a very few years after the great measure of 1867 there came in the strongest Tory govern- ment which the country had seen for generations. The assimilation of the county franchise to the burgh fran- chise is a necessity; and no alarming consequences will follow even if the Franchise Bill is dissociated from the bill for redistribution. The effect will be to strengthen the county constituencies, and their voice will be heard upon the distribution of seats. His grace concluded with an appeal to the House to pass the measure.

The Duke of Richmond and Gordon surported the amendment. He said that after the enfranchisement of 1867 it was certain that a similar extension of the fran- chise to the rural population would follow. He objected, however, to swamping the existing constituencies by im- porting into them the lowest class of voters in the country. He held that the government should provide for a redis- tribution of voters to take place at the same time as the extension of the franchise. His grace agreed with the opinion expressed on former occasions by Lord Derby and the Marquis of Hartington. He had also the highest respect for the opinion of Mr. Goschen. What security had the House that the government will be able to in- troduce a redistribution bill, or that it will be a satisfac- tory one? He was not opposed to an extension of the franchise, but he declined to fix the franchise until he knew how it was to be distributed.

The Earl of Jersey supported the bill, but was of opinion that it was very necessary that an extension of the franchise should be accompanied by a redistribution bill. It would, however, be quite possible for their lordships to pass an amendment, which would delay the operation of the Franchise Bill until after the passing of a measure of redistribution, and both bills might then come into operation at one and the same moment. He fully admitted the right of that House to reject the measure; but the question was, Would it be wise to refuse to go into committee on a bill which their lordships did not disapprove on its main principle?

The Earl of Fife said that if there had been a redistribution bill tacked on to the Franchise Bill neither of them would have passed this year at all; and, indeed, if one was to believe all the sinister reports one heard, one would have to conclude that the impossibility of passing two bills united was the real cause for wishing them to be introduced together. The Redistribution Bill could easily be introduced and passed next session if the opposition choose. No opposition had been offered to the Franchise Bill. The only object of attack was the want of a redistribution bill. The two bills were essentially different. The one dealt with large questions of electoral principles applicable to all parts of the country alike, while the other depended on details, local and personal, and naturally raising a host of totally different objections which had best be separately dealt with. They all recognized the constitutional theory, that the House of Lords had the right to delay legislation when the voice of the other House was uncertain, or that of the country doubt-

ful But it was flying in the face of all evidence to maintain such now to be the case. Practically governments,
like individuals, must bow to the necessities of time and
space, and when the head of a responsible government
distinctly stated that he could not see his way to treat in
one session the two parts of a reform bill, it seemed to
him that to oppose that procedure was to say that neither
part should be dealt with at all.

Lord Balfour thought that the recommendation of
Lord Jersey to pass the second reading, and introduce
an amendment in committee to postpone the operation
of the bill until a redistribution bill was passed, would
not do. Their lordships would not only be charged with
delaying the bill, but doing it in a dishonest way. There
were elements of much greater agitation in this course
than in the course proposed by the amendment. The
noble and learned lord (Cairns) did not oppose the principle of reform. He accepted it, and all he said was that
it must be accompanied by redistribution. Nor did he
see how it could be said that they were defying the will
of the people, because the people had never been asked
whether they would sanction an extension of the franchise without redistribution. If a redistribution bill was
not passed, and an election took place, the result would
be the utter destruction of the balance of power between
the urban and rural interests of the country. From a
speech of the president of the board of trade (Mr. Chamberlain) it appeared that he was not in favour of the
representation of minorities, and with this he could not
agree. It was of great importance that they should see
the whole scheme of the government; and though he
denied that there would be a spontaneous agitation
against their lordships' House—not for delaying the will

of the people—but simply for asking that an opportunity
should be given for the will of the people to be declared
on a matter of vital importance to them, he should
cheerfully vote for the amendment of the noble and
learned earl, and maintained that if there was to be a
quarrel it had not been of their seeking. If there was
to be one, however, they would not forget the concluding
part of the quotation made by the prime minister, and
bear themselves bravely in that quarrel.

Viscount Powerscourt referred to a statement made to
the effect that it would be dangerous to reduce the Irish
franchise. He feared that if this were not done it would
increase the hostility which existed among that people
against the continuation of the Union. He supported
the second reading of the bill.

Viscount Torrington observed, that in order to guard
themselves from being compelled to accept a bad redistribution bill from the present Parliament, or a much
worse one from the next, they must retain their control
over the franchise, which, in his judgment, could only be
done by throwing out this imperfect measure.

Earl Stanhope approved of the extension of the franchise to the agricultural labourer. He thought him
quite equal in many respects to the artisan, and quite as
well qualified for the exercise of the franchise. This extension was the logical result of the Act of 1867; but the
question had not been put before the constituencies at
the last general election. However, everything depended
on the distribution of the votes. He strongly believed
that the government would have found the introduction
of a redistribution bill at the same time as the Franchise
Bill a much easier procedure than what they had now
undertaken.

Earl Cowper observed that there must be some cause for
fear of the present constituencies being swamped if the
classes to be enfranchised all voted together. But it was
a matter of experience that they did not, because of the
influence exercised upon them by those socially above
them. If, however, those who were called the "upper
classes" did not succeed in retaining their hold and in
leading and influencing those below them, there was no
hope or chance of their being able to hold their own by
any scheme of redistribution or by any minority clause.
The question of reform was a foregone conclusion. The
question now was what effect their conduct with regard
to the measure would have upon the present and future
condition of the House. He thought that what had
given the House a blow was the number of times they
had thrown out measures or passed such amendments
as destroyed them, and then after a display of opposition for a short time had eaten their own words. He
hoped they would be saved this time from being placed
in the dilemma of either having once more to give way
or of their taking a stand on an untenable position.
The mode of regarding their position in the estimation
of the public was in resisting some ill-advised, pernicious,
but popular measures passed by the other House in a
moment of party passion. But that opportunity had not
come. The bill was admitted on all sides to be good.
The question raised was a very complicated one, and one
which the people would not understand. It would be
supposed they were hostile to the measure. But if the
government should be mad enough to manipulate the
subject of redistribution for party purposes, the opportunity which their lordships wanted would have come.
But supposing the worst to happen, and an election to take

MR. GLAD-
STONE'S
FIRST BILL
OF 1884.

Earl Cow-
per.

place without redistribution, would it be a great calamity to the party to which the noble lords opposite belonged? Would the increase of county voters make all the county constituencies Liberal? It had not been proved that the government would have any advantage. There was only a desire to force a dissolution, and that was a most dangerous game.

The Marquis of Waterford observed that the effect of the bill in Ireland would be the enfranchisement of the disloyal and the swamping of the loyal classes. The government preferred to enfranchise all capable citizens, but the proof of capability which seemed to be satisfactory consisted in the occupation of a mud cabin with only one room. They did not consider that education had anything to do with capability, because 40 per cent of the new electors could not read nor write.

Lord Fitzgerald said that when the honour, interests, and stability of England were at stake they were safe in their lordships' hands; but when it came to be a party question they could only come to one conclusion. The noble marquis opposite held the issue in his hands. A dissolution might come about, but it would not matter who became prime minister. If it were the noble marquis he would be obliged to come in with a more extended bill than the one before them.

The Earl of Dunraven held that the proper course would be to read the bill a second time and to ensure that the bill should not be operative until a redistribution bill had been passed, either by an amendment in committee or by an instruction to the committee, or by refusing to go into committee until the Redistribution Bill had been before the House and read a second time. The bill is a good bill in its main provisions, which are household suffrage, the assimilation of the county to the borough franchise, and the application of the bill to Ireland. He was of opinion that it ought to be accompanied with a bill for redistribution. He was of opinion also that numbers should be represented, and that property should be considered as well as mere numbers. He approved entirely of many parts in the bill. He approved of the admission of the large number of county voters; but he claimed for them that they should have a right to make their voice heard in Parliament, and that they should not be entirely swamped by the votes in the boroughs.

The Duke of Marlborough thought the policy of the noble marquis opposite was one which was fraught with all the peril of a manœuvre in the face of an enemy, without any of the corresponding advantages that might ensue from victory. He did not believe that the House was in possession of the ultimate views of the noble marquis, for it was impossible that so experienced a tactician in parliamentary warfare should court so manifest a defeat. The faults and failings in the foreign policy of the government would be lost sight of in the question which would be practically alone before the country by the action of their lordships' chamber. He thought the Conservative meeting to condemn the bill a mistake, and the amendment unfortunate. He also questioned very much how far it was wise for that House to prescribe to the other the limits of its constitution and suffrage. It seemed to him that there was a general expression of opinion in favour of the bill. There was no necessity for Clerkenwell explosions to prove it. It was, in his opinion, a most conservative measure.

Earl Cadogan supported the amendment, and advocated

MR. GLADSTONE'S FIRST BILL OF 1884.

Duke of Marlborough.

Earl of Cadogan.

MR. GLAD-
STONE'S
FIRST BILL
OF 1884,

an appeal to the constituencies. In this question the House would yield to the constitutionally-expressed opinion of the country.

Earl of
Morley.

The Earl of Morley was struck with the unanimity with which the principle of the bill had been accepted, and yet the country would judge by results. They would see that their lordships had refused to discuss the bill itself; they would see that their lordships had rejected it. In every meeting, from Land's End to John o' Groats, it would be said that the lords took an opportunity of throwing out a bill with which they had no real sympathy.

Earl of
Carnarvon.

The Earl of Carnarvon was of opinion that while the Act of 1832 made many improvements and removed many abuses, it made changes which were unnecessarily destructive and sweeping, and fraught with unexhausted consequences of peril to the constitution. It swept away those small boroughs that gave admission of the grandest names to Parliament of which any country could boast. It swept away the representation of interests and gave it to numbers. It destroyed the representation of colonial interests and also the representation of labour. The Act of 1867 was objectionable in so far as the redistribution that took place was incommensurate with the franchise, and its tendency was somewhat to convert members into delegates. He had no fault to find with the extension of the franchise proposed in the present bill, but there were faults in it. The mode of dealing with Ireland, the want of the representation of minorities, the omission of a female suffrage, were all objectionable. But there was the omission also of all provision for the redistribution of electoral power. This is unfair to Parliament, unfair to the old voters, unfair to the new ones.

The Earl of Derby could understand the difficulty that
many felt with reference to the bills of 1832 and 1867;
but when this bill provides a mere extension of the franchise so as to assimilate the county to the urban franchise,
he would scarcely have thought it worth while to provoke
a violent collision between the House and the majority
of the nation in order that there should be adopted one
method and order of procedure rather than another. The
House has the right to do what is proposed by the amendment, but is it wise? The public do not read long
debates. All they will know about it is that the House
of Lords has thrown out the bill which was to give them
votes, and all your reasons and qualifications will go for
nothing. Then suppose you succeed. Suppose there is
a dissolution, what then? The cry for reform will not
be the reform of the House of Commons, but reform of
the House of Lords. He did not dispute the rights of
the House of Lords. Their theoretical powers were very
large; but is it for their interest to strain them? It is
said that it would be a misfortune to have an election
without redistribution. I grant it; but there are eighteen
months to enable Parliament to deal with redistribution.
It would be inconvenient for everyone to have no redistribution bill, but no conceivable gain to the Liberal
party. He then said, If you acknowledge the inconvenience of the one bill coming into operation without the
other, why not make a statutory provision against it?
The opposition do not ask that that should be done. He
was not prepared to say whether it was possible, but the
reasonable thing to do was to read the bill a second time
and endeavour to insert the provision you want in committee. But he contended that you cannot keep the new
voters indefinitely out of the exercise of their rights. He

MR. GLAD-
STONE'S
FIRST BILL
OF 1884.
also referred to the comments made upon his speech of
1866, and said that he did not deny that he should like
very well to see the whole subject dealt with in one bill;
but the question was not what was desirable, but what
was possible. The House of Commons was not now what
it was in 1866—obstruction as an organized. system was
not then known—no party existed who habitually endeavoured to defeat all legislation.

Lord Bra-
bourne.
Lord Brabourne approved of the extension of the franchise, but held that there should have been redistribution
as well. He thought the government should have taken
up the most difficult part of the subject first, and dealt
with redistribution before the franchise. He maintained
that if the bill were passed, it was the direct interest of
the Liberal party to postpone redistribution. He felt
himself compelled to vote for the amendment.

Earl of
Roseberry.
The Earl of Roseberry remarked that there was no
difference of opinion whatever as to the merits of the
bill. The whole question was whether redistribution
should accompany it. For the carrying through of a
redistribution bill afterwards the House have the pledge
of the government; and should that pledge not be observed he would join with the noble lords opposite in
any vote of censure they might bring forward for such
breach of faith. He could conceive, however, no greater
insult to a body of men like her majesty's government
than to suggest the idea that they have come here with
false professions. But the question would not rest altogether with government, nor even with Parliament.
There are many unrepresented and many inadequately
represented constituencies that would take good care
that the question of redistribution was not allowed to
slumber. Besides, he could not but see that the whole

question was one that did not concern the House directly
at all. Suppose the House of Lords to pass a bill to
reform themselves, and, passing it by acclamation with
only two or three dissentients, sent it down to the House
of Commons, and it was met by a lengthy resolution and
was turned out on the second reading. What would
the feelings of the Lords be in regard to the bill to reform
themselves? There is no difference between the cases.
His lordship concluded with a powerful appeal to the
House to accept the bill.

The Duke of Portland remarked that there was not a
single noble lord who was opposed to the extension of
the franchise. Redistribution was promised them, but
what security was there, if their lordships passed this
bill, that a redistribution bill would follow, or that it
would be a fair and honest bill? He denied that the
Conservative peers were opposed to the will of the
people. They were merely seeking to give the people a
means of expressing their will as to the course proposed.

The Earl of Dalhousie held that if the House was to
be logical, if their lordships did approve of the extension
of the franchise to the counties, then the proper and
natural thing for them to do would be to pass the second
reading of the bill, and so amend it in committee as to
ensure that it would not come into operation until a
measure of redistribution was passed. It would be desirable to have both bills taken up at once, but that was
impossible. The franchise had taken four months to pass
the Commons, and did any sane man believe that if
redistribution had been tacked on to it, the bill would
have had any chance of reaching that House in the present session? Again, their lordships would do well to

MR. GLAD-
STONE'S
FIRST BILL
OF 1884.

remember that that particular bill was one which referred exclusively to the constitution of the House of Commons, and affecting the representation rights of the people by whom the other House was elected. Did their lordships think they were choosing their battle-ground wisely in opposing the second reading of such a bill as that? It was making the ancient House of Peers the stalking-horse of the Conservative party. It was difficult for the House of Lords to recover lost ground after 1832. If they lost ground now they would never regain it. The Radical party were delighted at the prospect of the House of Lords throwing out the bill. A struggle on this question once begun could only have one end in these days, and that not a favourable one for their lordships.

Earl of Ravensworth.

The Earl of Ravensworth was old enough to remember that the two Houses of Parliament had collided before on several occasions, and no great damage had ensued. He only wished that all collisions were as harmless. He would support the amendment.

Marquis of Huntly.

The Marquis of Huntly contended that very little risk of harm was involved in the possibility of an election taking place next year before a measure of redistribution was passed. Most of the arguments that had come from the opposite side of the House dealt with the question of representation, and the manner in which the voting powers were to be distributed, but had nothing to do with the question of the equalization of the county and borough franchise.

The Earl of Galloway supported the amendment.

Earl of Camperdown.

The Earl of Camperdown said there really was no difference between the two sides of the House with reference to the principle of the bill, and that being so the

noble and learned lord who moved the amendment was Mr. Glad-stone's first Bill of 1884.
facing a great responsibility. He was declining to accept
the measure, not because he disliked it on its own merits,
but because he refused the guarantees which the government had given on the subject of redistribution, which
guarantees the other House had considered satisfactory.
He thought there should be some sort of compromise.
He never remembered a situation which appeared to him
so difficult to retreat from, and for which there appeared
to him so little of excuse.

The Earl of Wemyss said that less than the one-third Earl of Wemyss.
of the whole number of the House of Commons on the
occasion of the last election referred to the question of
electoral reform. Still, as the question stood, it was
inevitable that the bill should pass. He would, therefore,
vote for the second reading, provided a guarantee was
given for a redistribution of seats. Let them, either by
a clause in the bill or by an instruction to the committee,
ensure that the bill should not become an operative act
except in conjunction with a measure for the redistribution of seats. In the interests of true conservatism
he earnestly prayed that a majority of their lordships
might give a second reading to the bill.

The Archbishop of Canterbury could have wished that Archbishop of Canter-bury.
redistribution had been included in the bill, but he could
not think that having to wait for redistribution was a
sufficient reason for stopping the progress of the bill. To
stop it now, when it was evident that it might be amended
in committee and a clause inserted to secure redistribution, was tantamount to denying the principle of the
bill. He did not believe that the principle of the bill
was to be denied. He could not enter into the feeling of
danger. He trusted the good sense of the country; the

people to be enfranchised were very much like other people. The church trusted them.

The Lord-chancellor (Lord Selborne) characterized the demand for redistribution to accompany the extension of the franchise as a thing that could not be done. It was done in 1832, when the House of Commons had the command of its own time. But even then it took three sessions of two parliaments. It was not done in one session. Then in 1866 a Franchise Bill was brought into the House of Commons and afterwards a Redistribution Bill, but they were lost. In 1867 a bill was brought in, and it was passed in a state very different from what it was when it was introduced. But the redistribution was of a trifling and temporary character. A complete franchise and redistribution bill has never therefore been passed in a single session. Besides, it is natural that the extension of the franchise should precede redistribution. The true relation between the two subjects is this: enfranchisement when made will give you the proper basis for redistribution. The learned lord counselled the House to free itself from party bias. The hereditary constitution of the House, he said, could only be justified on the principle that it is independent of mere party influences, and likely on important occasions to exercise a dispassionate judgment in the interest of public security and of the stability of our constitutional system. If it allowed its independence to be subordinate to party discipline, to the commands of party leaders, to the party interests of the moment, then the authority and the power of the House are imperilled. He appealed to the House not to reject a measure the principle of which it professed to approve.

The Marquis of Salisbury stated that there was no

adverse feeling to the extension of the franchise upon the MR. GLAD-
STONE'S
FIRST BILL
OF 1884. ground of incapacity or unfitness on the part of those to be enfranchised. The question was—How is political power to be so distributed that all classes may receive their due position in the state, that all interests may be Lord Salis-
bury. respected, and that the balance of power between the rural and urban electors may be maintained? It was necessary also that minorities be represented. The ministry have engaged to bring in a redistribution bill, and the House did not question the honesty of their intentions; but the question was, Had they the power to fulfil the promise which they make? The House knows that they have not had much power over their proceedings for the last few years. But even if such a bill were passed would we be any better? What is wanted is not only a redistribution bill, but a redistribution bill that the House can handle. Something, if manifestly unjust, the House can modify. The noble marquis appealed to the people. He would not shrink from bowing to the opinion of the people whatever that opinion might be. The people had in no real sense been consulted, and he felt that the House as guardians of their interests were bound to call upon the government to appeal to the people, and by that appeal the House would abide.

Earl Granville remarked that, after all, it did appear Earl Gran-
ville. that there was something behind the amendment. It was a dissolution of Parliament that was wanted, and the noble earl had very great doubt whether it was a perfectly constitutional doctrine that the House should arrogate to itself the strongest prerogative of the crown.

The House divided. For the amendment, 205; against it, 146. Majority for the amendment, 59.

VOTED FOR THE SECOND READING.

MR. GLAD-STONE'S FIRST BILL OF 1884.

Canterbury, L., Archp.
Selborne, E. (L. Chancellor).
York, L., Archp.
Bedford, D.
Devonshire, D.
Grafton, D.
Marlborough, D.
Norfolk, D.
Saint Albans, D.
Somerset, D.
Westminster, D.
Ailesbury, M.
Normanby, M.
Northampton, M.
Camperdown, E.
Chesterfield, E.
Chichester, E.
Clarendon, E.
Cowper, E.
Derby, E.
Durham, E.
Fitzwilliams, E.
Fortescue, E.
Granville, E.
Innes, E. (D. Roxburgh).
Jersey, E.
Kimberley, E.
Leicester, E.
Minto, E.
Morley, E.
Northbrook, E.
Saint Germans, E.
Shaftesbury, E.
Spencer, E.
Suffolk and Berkshire, E.
Sydnev. E.

Yarborough, E.
Canterbury, V.
Gordon, V. (E. Aberdeen).
Hampden, V.
Leinster, V. (D. Leinster).
Powerscourt, V.
Bath and Wells, L., Bp.
Carlisle, L., Bp.
Chichester, L., Bp.
Durham, L., Bp.
Ely, L., Bp.
Exeter, L., Bp.
Manchester, L., Bp.
Oxford, L., Bp.
St. Asaph, L., Bp.
Winchester, L., Bp.
Abercromby, L.
Aberdare, L.
Acton, L.
Alcester, L.
Auckland, L.
Barrogill, L. (E. Caithness).
Belper, L.
Blackford, L.
Blantyre, L.
Boyle, L. (E. Cork and Orrery)
     [Teller].
Bramwell, L.
Brayl, L.
Breadalbane, L.
Calthorp, L.
Cawoys, L.
Carew, L.
Carlingford, L.
Carrington, L.
Carysfort, L.

Chesham, L.

Churchill, L.

Clements, L.

Clermont, L.

Clifford, L.

Coleridge, L.

Crewe, L.

Dacre, L.

De Clifford, L.

De Mauley, L.

Dorchester, L.

Dormer, L.

Dunning, L.

Elgin, L.

Emily, L.

Erskine, L.

Ettrick, L.

Fingall, L.

Fitzgerald, L.

Foley, L.

Granard, L.

Greville, L.

Haldon, L.

Hammond, L.

Hare, L.

Hatherton, L.

Hothfield, L.

Houghton, L.

Howth, L.

Kenmare, L.

Lawrence, L.

Leigh, L.

Loftus, L.

Lovat, L.

Lurgan, L.

Lyttelton, L.

Meldrum, L.

Methven, L

Moncrieff, L.

Monson, L. [Teller].

Monteagle, L.

Mount Temple, L.

Oxenfoord, L.

Ponsonby, L.

Ramsay, L.

Reay, L.

Ribblesdale, L.

Robartes, L.

Romilly, L.

Roseberry, L.

Sandhurst, L.

Sandys, L.

Saye and Sele, L.

Sefton, L.

Skene, L.

Somerton, L.

Strafford, L.

Strathedin, L.

Strathspey, L.

Sudeley, L.

Suffield, L.

Sundridge, L.

Tennyson, L.

Thurlow, L.

Truro, L.

Tweeddale, L.

Tweedmouth, L.

Vaux of Harrowden, L.

Vernon, L.

Waveney, L.

Wemyss, L.

Wenlock, L.

Wentworth, L.

Wolverton, L.

Wrottesley, L.

MR. GLAD-
STONE'S
FIRST BILL
OF 1884.

VOTED FOR THE AMENDMENT.

Beaufort, D.

Buckingham and Chandos, D.

Leeds, D.

Northumberland, D.

Portland, D.

Richmond, D.

Rutland, D.

Wellington, D.

Abercorn, M.

Abergavenny, M.

Ailsa, M.

Bristol, M.

Exeter, M.

Hertford, M.

Salisbury, M.

Winchester, M.

Abingdon, E.

Annesley, E.

Ashburnham, E.

Bandon, E.

Bathurst, E.

Beauchamp, E.

Belmore, E.

Bradford, E.

Brooke and Warwick, E.

Cadogan, E.

Cairns, E.

Caledon, E.

Carnarvon, E.

Clonmel, E.

Coventry, E.

De La Warr, E.

Denbigh, E.

Doncaster, E.

Eldon, E.

Ferrers, E.

Feversham, E.

Graham, E.

Haddington, E.

Harewood, E.

Harrington, E.

Harrowby, E.

Howe, E.

Kilmorey, E.

Lanesborough, E.

Lathom, E.

Leven and Melville E.

Lucan, E.

Lytton, E.

Macclesfield, E.

Malmesbury, E.

Manvers, E.

Mar and Kellie, E.

Miltown, E.

Morton, E.

Mount Edgcumbe, E.

Nelson, E.

Onslow, E.

Poulett, E.

Powis, E.

Radnor, E.

Ravensworth, E.

Redesdale, E.

Romney, E.

Rosse, E.

Rosslyn, E.

Sandwich, E.

Selkirk, E.

Soudes, E.

Stanhope, E.

Strange, E.

Strathmore and Kinghorn, E.

Tankerville, E.
Vane, E.
Verulam, E.
Waldegrave, E.
Wharncliffe, E.
Zetland, E.
Bolingbroke and St. John, V.
Clancarty, V.
Gough, V.
Hardinge, V.
Hawarden, V.
Hereford, V.
Hood, V.
Hutchinson, V.
Melville, V.
Sidmouth, V.
Strathallan, V.
Templetown, V.
Torrington, V.
Gloucester and Bristol, L., Bp.
Abinger, L.
Amherst, L.
Ardilaun, L.
Arundel of Wardour, L.
Ashford, L.
Aveland, L.
Bagot, L.
Balfour of Burleigh, L.
Bateman, L.
Bolton, L.
Borthwick, L.
Boston, L.
Botreaux, L.
Brabourne, L.
Brancepeth, L.
Brodrick, L.
Byron, L.
Castlemaine, L.
Castletown, L.

Chelmsford, L.
Churston, L.
Clanbrassill, L.
Clanwilliam, L.
Clinton, L.
Cloncurry, L.
Colchester, L.
Colville of Culross, L.
Crofton, L.
De Freyne, L.
Delamere, L.
De L'Isle and Dudley, L.
Denman, L.
De Ros, L.
De Saumarez, L.
Digby, L.
Dinevor, L.
Donnington, L.
Douglas, L.
Egerton, L.
Ellenborough, L.
Elphinstone, L.
Fisherwick, L.
Fitzhardinge, L.
Forbes, L.
Forester, L.
Foxford, L.
Gage, L.
Gerard, L.
Grantley, L.
Harlech, L.
Harris, L.
Hartismore, L.
Hastings, L.
Hawke, L.
Hay, L.
Headley, L.
Heytesbury, L.
Hopetoun, L.

MR. GLAD-
STONE'S
FIRST BILL
OF 1884.

Howard de Walden, L.
Hylton, L.
Inchiquin, L.
Keane, L.
Kenles, L.
Ker, L.
Kintore, L.
Lamington, L.
Langford, L.
Leconfield, L.
Lovel, L.
Lyveden, L.
Manners, L.
Massy, L.
Minster, L.
Moore, L.
Mostyn, L.
Mowbray, L.
Napier, L.
North, L.
Oranmore and Browne, L.
Ormathwaite, L.
Ormonde, L.
Pairhyn, L.
Poltimore, L.
Raglan, L.
Rayleigh, L.
Rodney, L.

Rossmore, L.
Rowton, L.
Sackville, L.
Salterford, L.
Saltoun, L.
Scarsdale, L.
Shute, L.
Silchester, L.
Somerhill, L.
Stanley of Alderley, L.
Stewart of Garles, L.
Templemore, L.
Tollemache, L.
Tredegar, L.
Trever, L.
Tyrone, L.
Ventry, L.
Walsingham, L.
Watson, L.
Westbury, L.
Wigan, L.
Willoughby de Broke, L.
Wimborne, L.
Windsor, L.
Worlingham, L.
Wyndford, L.
Zouche of Haryngworth, L.

The House of Lords had now really, though not formally, rejected the bill. The prime minister thereupon
summoned a meeting of the Liberal part to be held in
the large room of the Foreign Office, on July 10, at
half-past two o'clock. There were 256 present. He
addressed them at considerable length, and announced
that the cabinet had resolved to wind up the session and
hold an autumn session, when the bill would be again

introduced, and again sent up to the Lords. He charac- MR. GLAD-
terized the action of the Lords, in claiming an appeal to STONE'S
FIRST BILL
the people, as an unwarrantable innovation. Mr. Go- OF 1884.
schen addressed the meeting, and counselled moderation.

Mr. Bright was received with much cheering. He
said : " It appears to me, after the speech which Mr.
Gladstone has delivered to this meeting, and, no doubt,
to the whole country, that it is hardly necessary for any
of us to add anything to what has been said. I think
that speech, in every sense, most judicious. I believe
its effect throughout will be everything that we could
desire, and I have no objection to any single passage
in it. I hope that everybody who can be calm during
the next three months, like my right honourable friend
the member for Ripon, will be as calm as they can, and
will not unduly judge those who may show by their
expressions a little warmth on the great question which
is before the country. We have had crises on several
occasions. Mr. Gladstone recollects more of them, I
think, than I do, but I recollect very well the crises of
1831 and 1832. I recollect the crisis of 1846, when the
question of the corn-laws came to an issue, and I recollect
the crisis of 1866 and 1867; but looking back on these
periods, I do not think the advice of Mr. Goschen—and
I do not know whether it was given then, but I dare
say it was—I do not think it was generally followed.
The fact is, when these great questions came up it was
impossible throughout the country that at great meetings
—which Lord Salisbury despises, which he speaks of in
the most contemptuous manner—when these great questions come up before a nation, you must at least allow
the people to speak freely. I am a man of peace, and
should be sorry to see the slightest breach of the peace

MR. GLAD-
STONE'S
FIRST BILL
OF 1884.
in any part of the country; but let us not forget how
this state of things has been created, and who are responsible for it. We are not responsible. Lord Salisbury
and his friends tell us that people really do not care
about this measure. Certain newspapers dwell on the
fact that the people have been so quiet all during the session of Parliament. They have been, and most reasonably
so, because they had a government in which they had
confidence."

Motion by
the Earl of
Wemyss.
It was now obvious that the country was on the eve of
a tremendous agitation—thoughtful men on both sides
were anxious about the result. Before Parliament arose
an effort was made to put matters on a better footing, if
that were possible. The Earl of Wemyss acted as a sort
of intermediary, and on July 17 he moved a resolution
to the effect that the House of Lords was now prepared
to proceed with the consideration of the bill, on the understanding that an address be presented to Her Majesty
to summon Parliament to meet in the autumn to consider
a redistribution bill which the ministry had undertaken
to present to Parliament. It was an attempt to throw
oil on the troubled waters. It was rejected by a majority of 50. The courage of the Peers had not abated.

Appeal to
the people.
The session being ended and the government defeated
in the House of Lords, there was now to be an appeal to
the people. This was what the Conservatives called for
since the contest began, but *their* appeal to the people
was to the *constituencies,* by a dissolution of Parliament
in the usual way. The appeal of the Liberals was to the
people represented and unrepresented; and thus it was
the verdict of the whole people that was now to be
brought forth. The way in which this was to be done
was by demonstrations and processions and speeches and

resolutions. It now took place on a scale that never was
seen before. There had, perhaps, been single assemblies
of people larger in numerical strength—at least as large
—as any of the assemblies that now took place, but there
was not the number of them, there were not the numbers
engaged in them, there was not the number of resolutions
passed at them, as in the autumn of 1884. The country
from end to end, from side to side, looked for months as
if it were one continued holiday. The country had never
exhibited such unanimity, and there were no riots, no
breaches of the peace, no call even for the police. There
was a little show of temper at one or two places in connection with an attempt on the part of the Conservatives
to get up similar demonstrations. They, however, proved
a failure. Even Lord Salisbury got tired of attempting
to make a show of the "Conservative working-man," and
it became known before the end of September that the
appeal to the *people* by the Liberal party had been successful. It was felt that there must be a surrender by
the Lords.

The autumn session of 1884 commenced on October
23, and the Franchise Bill was formally reintroduced
into the House of Commons on November 6. Mr. Gladstone moved the second reading. He referred at some
length to the subject of menace that had been charged
against him. He denied that he had been guilty of
menace to the House of Lords. The language he used
was respectful and was simply a warning, which did not
proceed from insolence nor wantonness, but from a
sense of duty and a desire to preserve an ancient institution. The question of reform always possesses great historical and political interest, but there are not the difficulties involved nor the questions raised that beset the

*Mr. Glad-
stone's
second Bill
of 1884.*

*Demonstra-
tions.*

*Mr. Glad-
stone's
second Bill
of 1884.*

*Autumn
session.*

MR. GLAD-
STONE'S
SECOND BILL
OF 1884.
movement of 1831–2. There were questions of property in seats then raised that don't arise now. There was a question of retaining a non-representative element in the chamber. Happily there is no such principle now at is-Reform Bill
again intro-
duced. sue. The question of the franchise is one of extreme simplicity, if dealt with by itself. The right honourable gentleman then announced that the government would endeavour to pass the Franchise Bill, and afterwards to deal with redistribution. He explained at some length his views on the principles that should regulate the subject of the distribution of political power, and concluded with moving the second reading of the bill.

Mr. E. Stanhope rose to propose the following amend-Amendment
proposed. ment on behalf of Lord Randolph Churchill:—"That in the opinion of this House any measure purporting to provide for the better representation of the people in Parliament must be accompanied by provisions for a proper arrangement of electoral areas." The honourable Mr. Stanhope's
speech. member concurred with the prime minister in the desire he expressed that some settlement might be arrived at on this matter favourable to the wishes of the people, and he was sorry that the government had not made an effort on this occasion to have this accomplished. The great question of electoral reform should be put before the House as a scheme fairly adjusted to the wants of the country, that they might have an opportunity of considering it as a whole, and that it might come into effect as a whole. Because they had not been able to detect either in the speech of the prime minister or in the bill itself any guarantee of a substantial character for securing these all-important results, it was his duty to move the amendment standing in his name. Mr. Ecroyd seconded the motion.

Mr. Gorst could not agree with the previous speaker in thinking that there was no possibility of a compro- mise. He would not discuss the amendment. It was the same as that proposed by Lord John Manners, and since that time a great deal had happened. The Con- servative party had been defeated by a very large majority, and if parliamentary government was to be carried on, there must be some questions on which the minority must yield to the majority. Procedure was one of them. The result of the autumn agitation was that the people were not to dissent from the majority of the House of Commons. As to a guarantee, the government was pledged up to the hilt to go on with redistribution, and they could not resile from it without a gross breach of faith.

A lengthy debate ensued, and all the arguments for and against combining a Redistribution Bill with the Franchise Bill were reproduced, but to no purpose. There were indications of a desire on the part of the Conservatives to come to some arrangement, but the time for that had not yet arrived.

The House divided—

For the amendment, - - - - - -	232
Against, - - - - - - -	372
Majority for second reading, - - -	140

The House went into committee on November 10, when Colonel Stanley moved that the passing of the bill be made conditional upon the passing also of the Redistribution Bill. This was rejected by a majority of 85. The bill then passed through committee, and was reported to the House. The third reading was fixed for the 11th, and when the 11th arrived a debate of a rather depress-

ing character ensued, from which the spirit of compromise was yet absent, which ended in the Franchise Bill
being read a third time, and passed without a division.

The final ordeal through which the Franchise Bill had
to pass was now at hand. The autumn agitation was
now to bear fruit. The lords were satisfied that their
case was hopeless. Not only was there to be reform,
but there was to be a Franchise Bill, without a Redistribution Bill accompanying it. The government had won
in reality as well as in form. It was not a matter of
surprise, therefore, that negotiations were talked about
—that they were commenced—that they were carried
through. An arrangement had been arrived at, and at
a meeting of the Conservative party on November 18
Lord Salisbury made the announcement that the contest
was over. He referred with satisfaction to the concessions made by the government, which he regarded as
practically vindicating the course taken by the Lords.
He remarked that the Peers would now have some means
of assuring themselves that the promised Redistribution
Bill would be of a moderate and equitable character, that
its rapid advancement would be guaranteed, and that its
main provisions would be made known to them before
they passed the measure for the extension of the franchise.

The Franchise Bill having been sent up to the House
of Lords and read a first time, the second reading was
moved by Lord Kimberley on November 18, the evening
of the day on which the Conservative meeting took place.
The terms of arrangement between the two great parties
were announced to the House, and all further opposition
was withdrawn. The bill was read a second time without a division. The next procedure took place on Decem-

ber 1, when Mr. Gladstone moved for leave to bring in the Redistribution Bill. He stated that the counties at present have representation to the extent of one member for 70,800 persons; the boroughs one member for 41,200 persons; the average being one member for 54,200 persons. The first schedule of the bill has been framed on the principle that towns under 15,000 inhabitants shall pass into the counties. The second schedule contains towns up to 50,000 that will be restricted to one member. The effect of these two schedules will be to liberate not less than 160 seats. To that number falls to be added six seats that have to be revived. Now, by the act of 1832 there were only 143 seats made available in this way for redistribution, which will show the scope of the present measure. The right honourable gentleman then proceeded to state in what way redistribution would take place, which will be noticed further on in describing the bill. The result, however, he gave as follows: That England would have the six vacant seats; Wales and Ireland would remain as they were; and Scotland would have an increase of twelve. These twelve bring up the members of the House to 670. The general principle of the bill was one member to one seat. There was little or no discussion, and the bill was read a first time.

On December 4 the second reading of the Redistribution Bill took place, on which occasion Mr. Courtenay raised a discussion on the subject of proportional representation. His proposal was negatived, the bill was read a second time, and the committee stage fixed for February 19, 1885. On the same night the Franchise Bill passed through committee in the House of Lords without amendments, and was ordered to be reported. Upon December 5 the Franchise Bill was read a third time and

Marginal notes:

MR. GLADSTONE'S SECOND BILL OF 1884.

Redistribution Bill.

Second reading of Redistribution Bill.

Franchise Bill received royal assent.

passed, and on December 6 it received the royal assent.
The Redistribution Bill was afterwards submitted to
much discussion, and then passed into law.

The *extent* generally of the changes to be produced by
the two bills will be very considerable. The number of
new votes to be introduced into the constitution is com-
puted to amount to 2,000,000, which will have the effect
of raising the electorate of the United Kingdom to over
5,000,000. The changes to be produced by redistribution
will, however, be the most important part of the entire
scheme of reform. (1) There are 79 small boroughs in
England and 22 in Ireland to be disfranchised, and the
Haddington and Wigtown districts of burghs are likewise
to lose the franchise. (2) There are five counties of cities
or towns to be included in counties at large, namely,
Berwick-on-Tweed, Haverfordwest, Lichfield, Carrick-
fergus, and Drogheda. (3) There are to be disfranchised
the two boroughs of Macclesfield and Sandwick. (4) There
are 36 boroughs in England and 3 in Ireland that are to
lose one member each. (5) There are certain boroughs
to have their membership raised to the undernoted
figures:—

Birmingham,	7 members.
Bradford,	3 do.
Bristol,	4 do.
Kingston-upon-Hull,	3 do.
Leeds,	5 do.
Liverpool,	9 do
Manchester,	6 do.
Nottingham,	3 do.
Salford,	3 do.
Sheffield,	5 do.
Swansea (district),	2 do.
Wolverhampton,	3 do.

Aberdeen,	-	-	-	-	-	2 members.
Edinburgh,	-	-	-	-	-	4 do.
Glasgow, -	-	-	-	-	-	7 do.
Belfast, -	-	-	-	-	-	4 do.
Dublin, -	-	-	-	-	-	4 do.

Mr. Glad-
stone's
second Bill
of 1884.

(6) There are to be a number of new boroughs created. (7) A number of boroughs are to have their boundaries altered. (8) Many boroughs are to be divided, and a member given to each division. (9) Large counties are to be dealt with in a similar way. (10) The numerical strength of the House is to be raised. The gross number of members is to be 670, of which England is to have 465, Wales 30, Ireland 103, and Scotland 72. The changes made are as follows: England gets 6 more, being the disfranchised seats; Wales and Ireland no more; and Scotland is to be raised from 60 to 72.

Extent of Reform.

VI. REFORM—ITS RESULTS AND FURTHER OBJECTS.

The reform of the machinery of government, and specially of the representation of the people in the Commons House of Parliament, has been the business of the country at different times since the beginning of the century, and particularly during the last twelve months. Reform is an interesting process to the philosophical student. It means the country growing out of the old system into the new, out of a lower into a higher form of political life, out of a sphere of bondage into a state of self-government. These are the objects of reform as entertained by the British citizen. There is involved a two-fold process in the subject of reform—one of preparation and one of reconstruction. They ought to accompany one

Further Objects of Reform.

another. It is a simple matter to find room for reform in any constitution, for that must be so long as it stops short of perfection; but to reform it when the materials are not ready is disappointing. It means relapse. In this country we do not realize it so much as the French do. They have experienced it perhaps more than any modern nationality. With us progress has been, as some suppose, very slow, but there has been no retrogression. There has always been an aptitude for the exercise of the franchises conferred, and for the responsibilities they have involved. And yet there has been no special effort made to fit the people for the duties of citizenship. There has been no special training in connection with our municipal institutions to qualify the people for the exercise of the functions of political life. There has been no school or university teaching, nor books specially directed to that end. There have been, however, other agencies in operation, such as a free press, general education, the right of public meeting, the liberty of co-operation by means of trades-unions and political associations; these have contributed to the educating up of the working-man to the "capable" standard of citizenship; and to all those far-seeing and single-minded men who at different times have helped to the attainment and protection of those blessings, the thanks of the British workmen are especially due. They have prepared him for taking a part in the great business of political life.

What has been attained, however, is the association of the people for acquiring and maintaining a command over the House of Commons. That is the direct and immediate result of parliamentary reform. Before 1832 the people had little or no control over it. It really did not represent them. But the entrance of the middle-classes

into the constitution secured by that act made a great ɪ
difference, the entrance of the artisans by the acts of ɪ
1867–8 made another difference, the act of 1884 admitting o
the agricultural and mining classes has consummated
parliamentary reform for a time, and made the House of
Commons in reality the People's House. There are more
of the people still to be there, but they are not yet ready.
It is a question of time when women must be admitted—
not merely women householders. If there had been a
representation of the sex in Parliament in earlier times
there would not have been in existence such laws as exclude them from succession to landed property and from
some control over their children.

The further efforts at reform are not difficult to fore-
cast. The representative of a constituency must be a
delegate. He is not to be a master but a servant, and if
he is to be a servant he must be paid. This is a logical
outcome of national self-government.

The last stage in this strange eventful history is still
to be reached. It began with the despotism of the
monarch, then of the aristocracy, then of the three estates
of the realm. The process is now being reversed, and
can only terminate, perhaps at some distant day, in a republic, when the second chamber and the sovereign will
both be elective, just as the House of Commons is; when
the different estates in their different capacities will be
representative of the nation which elects them; when, in
short, the entire system of government will be directed to
one end—the progress, the security, and the happiness of
the people.

INDEX.

Address to King on 1831 Bill, 158; King's Circular, 159.

Agitation, 47, 49, 54, 81, 113.

Althorp, Lord, his motion, 82; his speech on first Bill of 1831, 92; speech on second Bill, 124; speech on third Bill, 140.

Anderson, Mr., speech on 1884 Bill, 281; second speech, 307; amendment, 355.

Argyll, Duke of, speech on 1884 Bill, 370.

Baines, Mr., his Bill, 200; second Bill, 200.

Balfour, Lord, speech on 1884 Bill, 373.

Balfour, Mr. A. J., speech on third reading of 1884 Bill, 362.

Baring, Mr., speech on Address to the King, 156.

Barons, their contest with King John, 14; with King Edward, 14; with other monarchs, 16; their usurpation, 17; they are humbled by King Henry VII., 18.

Barron, Mr., speech on 1884 Bill, 330.

Barttelot, Sir W. B., speech on 1884 Bill, 337; amendment, 351; speech on third reading, 362.

Baxter, Mr., speech on Lord Palmerston's Bill, 193; speech on 1884 Bill, 299.

Beach, Sir M. H., speech on 1884 Bill, 321.

Bentinck, Mr. C., amendment on 1884 Bill, 354.

Berkeley, Mr., his Ballot Bills, 175, 200.

Biddell, Mr., speech on 1884 Bill, 327.

BILLS, REFORM:

Mr. Pitt's Bill, 36; rejected, 39.

Mr. Flood's Bill, 40; withdrawn, 47.

Mr. Lambton's Bill, 61; rejected, 61.

First Bill of 1831 introduced, 83; for Scotland and Ireland, 108; Bills lost, 110.

Second Bill, 113; passed the Commons, 126; taken to the Lords, 127; thrown out, 136.

Third Bill, introduced into Commons, 139; passed, 142; taken to the Lords, 143; carried, 160.

Mr. Locke King's Bill of 1851, 169.

Lord John Russell's Bill of 1854, 170; abandoned, 174.

Mr. Locke King's Bill of 1858, 175.

Mr. Caird's Bill of 1858, 175.

Mr. Berkeley's Ballot Bill, 175.

Mr. Disraeli's Bill of 1859, 175; rejected, 187.

BILLS, REFORM—continued:

Lord Palmerston's Bill, 187; withdrawn, 199.

Mr. Baines' Bill, 200; second Bill, 200.

Mr. Berkeley's Bill, 200.

Mr. Gladstone's Bill of 1866, 201; Redistribution Bill, 222; Scotch and Irish Bills, 226; Bills lost, 231.

Mr. Disraeli's Bill, 242; Bill carried through, 261.

Mr. Gladstone's first Bill of 1884, 270; lost in the Lords, 385; re-introduced in Commons, 393; passed, 398; Redistribution Bill, 397; Bills passed, 398. (See under Reform.)

Blandford, Marquis of, his motion, 81; negatived, 82.

Blennerhasset, Mr., speech on 1884 Bill, 284.

Brabourne, Lord, speech on 1884 Bill, 380.

Braxfield, Lord, charge in Muir's trial, 52.

Bright, Mr., speech on Mr. Disraeli's Bill, 178; second speech, 182; speech on Lord Palmerston's Bill, 194; on 1866 Bill, 207; second speech, 216; on Mr. Disraeli's second Bill, 244; speech on 1884 Bill, 297; speech at Foreign Office, 391.

Broadhurst, Mr., speech on 1884 Bill, 325.

Brodrick, Mr., amendment on 1884 Bill, 350.

Brougham, Lord, speech on second Bill of 1831, 133; on third Bill, 151.

Burdett, Sir F., his motion of 1819, 55; his speech on Marquis of Blandford's measure, 1830, 82.

Burke, Mr., speech on Mr. Flood's Bill, 46; on Mr. Grey's motion, 49.

Burt, Mr., speech on 1884 Bill, 336.

Cadogan, Earl of, speech on 1884 Bill, 370.

Caird, Mr., his Bill, 175.

Cairns, Sir H., speech on 1866 Bill, 215; his amendment on 1884 Bill, 366.

Cameron, Dr., amendment on 1884 Bill, 350.

Campbell, Mr. J. A., speech on 1884 Bill, 306.

Camperdown, Earl of, speech on 1884 Bill, 382.

Canning, Mr., speech on Reform 1822, 66.

Canterbury, Archbishop of, speech on 1884 Bill, 383.

Cardwell, Mr., speech on Mr. Disraeli's Bill, 183.

Carnarvon, Earl of, speech on 1884 Bill, 398.
Chamberlain, Mr., speech on 1884 Bill, 309.
Churchill, Lord R., speech on 1884 Bill, 283.
Clarke, Mr. G., speech on 1884 Bill, 284.
Cobden, Mr., speech on Mr. Hume's Bill, 169.
Collings, Mr. J., speech on 1884 Bill, 301.
Collins, Mr. T., amendment on 1884 Bill, 356.
Combination Laws repealed, 79.
Commons, House of, 19; origin, 19; its functions at first, 19; its rise, 21; nation no control over it, 24; not representative in 1688, 25; discontent, 31; opposition to reform, 32; state of the representation, 33; corruption, 34.
Compromise on subject of 1884 Bill, 396.
Constitution of 1688, 25; working of same, 25; laws passed under it, 26; government tyrannical, 30; constitution of 1832, 163; of 1867, 263.
Country. See under *Nation.*
Cowper, Earl, speech on 1884 Bill, 375.
Crampton, Mr., speech on second Bill of 1831, 121.
Cranborne, Lord, speech on 1866 Bill, 218; also on voting papers, 257; on third reading of 1867 Bill, 258.
Croker, Mr., speech on second Bill of 1831, 119.
Cross, Sir R., speech on 1884 Bill, 318.
Cubitt, Mr., speech on 1884 Bill, 305.

Dalhousie, Earl of, speech on 1884 Bill, 381.
Dalrymple, Mr., speech on 1884 Bill, 334.
Dawnay, Colonel, speech on 1884 Bill, 298.
Dawnay, Mr. Guy, speech on 1884 Bill, 322.
Derby, Earl of, speech on 1884 Bill, 379.
Discontent after 1688, 31.
Disraeli, Mr., speech on 1859 Bill, 175; on Lord Palmerston's Bill, 192; on 1866 Bill, 219; electioneering speech, 231; his announcement of Reform, 234; resolutions, 235; explanations, 238; his Bill of 1867, 242; his speech, 242; his reply, 244, 252; his new proposal, 255; Bill carried, 260.
Dissolution of Parliament in 1831, 113.
Distress in the country, 54.
Drummond, Mr., speech, 167.
Du Cane, Mr., speech on Lord Palmerston's Bill, 197.
Dunkellin, Lord, amendment on 1866 Bill, 230.
Dunraven, Earl of, speech on 1884 Bill, 376.
Durham, Lord (Mr. Lambton), Bill of 1821, 61; rejected, 61; speech on third Bill 1831, 148.

Ebrington, Lord, speech on 1884 Bill, 308.
Ecroyd, Mr., amendment on 1884 Bill, 354.

Elcho, Lord, speech on 1866 Bill, 216.
Eldon, Lord, speech on third Bill of 1831, 149.
Election in 1831, 113.
Electorate. See under *Redistribution.*
Ellenborough, Lord, speech on third Bill of 1831, 143.
Estates, the Three, 12; the *status quo* in 1688, 21; the constitution of the Estates, 23; their tyranny, 30; no check on them, 31; discontent, 31.
Exeter, Bishop of, speech on third Bill of 1831, 146.

Fawcett, Mr., speech on 1866 Bill, 207.
Female Suffrage, 249, 355.
Feudal System, 13.
Fife, Earl of, speech on 1884 Bill, 372.
First Reform. See under *Reform.*
Fitzgerald, Earl of, speech on 1884 Bill, 376.
Flood, Mr., his Reform Bill, 40; his speech, 40.
Folkestone, Lord, speech on 1884 Bill, 335.
Forster, Mr., speech on 1884 Bill, 295; second speech, 314.
Fowler, Mr. H. H., speech on 1884 Bill, 282; second speech on Bill, 329; his amendment on 1884 Bill, 357.
Fox, Mr., speech on Flood's Bill, 46; speech on Mr. Grey's motion, 49.
Franchise before First Reform, 33, 34; after it, 164; prior to 1867 and after it, 263, 264; in 1884, 398.
Friends of the People, Society of, 47.

Gage, Lord, speech on third Bill of 1831, 144.
Gascoigne, General, his amendment destroyed first Bill of 1831, 110.
Gibson, Mr., speech on 1884 Bill, 281.
Gladstone, Mr., his speech on Mr. Disraeli's Bill, 186; speech on Mr. Baines' Bill, 200; his own Bill of 1866, 201; speech, 201; speech in Liverpool, 210; speech in the House, 213; his reply, 220; speech on Redistribution Bill, 222; second speech on Bill, 230; speech on Mr. Disraeli's second Bill, 243; his amendment, 247; speech on Bill, 254; first Bill of 1884, and speech, 270; second speech, 331; speech on amendments, 352; speech on third reading, 358; speech on re-introducing Bill, 393.
Gorst, Mr., speech on 1884 Bill, 395.
Goschen, Mr., speech on 1884 Bill, 286; second speech, 338; speech on third reading, 361.
Government, theory of, 9; arbitrary, 9; constitutional, 10; tyranny of the Three Estates, 30; discontent, 31.
Graham, Sir J., speech on Mr. Disraeli's Bill, 185.

Grant, Mr. C., speech on first Bill of 1831, 106.

Grant, Mr. R., speech on first Bill of 1831, 102.

Grantham, Mr., speech on 1884 Bill, 331.

Granville, Earl, speech on 1884 Bill, 385.

Grey, Mr. A., speech on 1884 Bill, 322; amendment, 356.

Grey, Earl, his motion as Mr. Grey on Reform, 48; moves second reading in House of Lords of Reform Bill of 1831, 127; speech, 127; his speech on third Bill, 143; reply, 153; recalled to power, 158.

Grey, Sir George, speech on Lord Palmerston's Bill, 193.

Grosvenor, Earl of, amendment on 1866 Bill, 209; speech, 214.

Haddington, Lord, speech on third Bill of 1831, 144.

Hamilton, Lord George, speech on 1884 Bill, 313.

Hamilton, Lord A., motion in 1821, 63.

Harrowby, Lord, speech on third Bill of 1831, 145.

Hartington, Lord, speech on 1884 Bill, 302.

Hay, Sir John, speech on Bill of 1884, 280.

Hope, Mr. B., speech on 1884 Bill, 323.

Horsman, Mr., speech on Mr. Disraeli's Bill, 181.

Houldsworth, Mr., amendment on 1884 Bill, 357.

House of Commons. See under Commons.

House of Lords. See under Lords.

Hume, Mr., speech on first Bill of 1831, 92; speech on Address to King, 156; motion in 1848, 165; Bill of 1852, 170.

Huntly, Marquis of, speech on 1884 Bill, 382.

Inglis, Sir R. H., speech on first Bill of 1831, 90.

Ireland, Bill for, introduced, 108, 191, 226; exclusion from the Franchise Bill of 1884, 350.

James, Sir H., speech on 1884 Bill, 341; speech on third reading, 362.

Jeffrey, Lord, speech on first Bill of 1831, 100.

Jersey, Earl of, speech on 1884 Bill, 372.

Kimberley, Lord, speech on 1884 Bill, 363.

King's Circular, 159.

Laing, Mr., speech on Bill of 1866, 205; motion on Mr. Disraeli's second Bill, 250; second motion, 256.

Lamb, Mr., speech on Sir F. Burdett's motion, 58.

Lambton, Mr. See under Durham.

Lansdowne, Lord, speech on third Bill of 1831, 147.

Leatham, Mr. E. A., speech on 1884 Bill, 300.

Lefevre, Mr. S., speech on 1884 Bill, 319.

Leighton, Mr., amendment on 1884 Bill, 350.

Lewis, Mr., speech on 1884 Bill, 363.

Limited Monarchy, 10.

Locke, Mr. J., speech on Lord Palmerston's Bill, 198.

Locke King, Mr., motion in 1851, 169; his Bill in 1852, 170; motion for Abolition of Property Qualification, 175; proposed Reform Bill, 175; Bill dropped, 175; Bill of 1858, 175; Bill in 1864, 199.

Lords, House of, 14; establishment of, 14.

Lowe, Mr., speech on Bill of 1866, 205; second speech, 217; speech on Mr. Disraeli's Resolutions, 240; speeches on Bill of 1867, 248, 259.

Lowther, Mr. James, speech on 1884 Bill, 301.

Lowther, Mr. J. W., speech on 1884 Bill, 308.

Lubbock, Sir J., speech on 1884 Bill, 290.

Lyndhurst, Lord, speech on second Bill of 1831, 135; on third Bill, 151.

Lytton, Sir E. B., speech on Lord Palmerston's Bill, 196.

Macaulay, Mr., speech on first Bill of 1831, 93; on second Bill, 115; on third Bill, 141; speech on Address to the King, 156; speech on Lord Palmerston's Bill, 198.

M'Laren, Mr., amendment on 1884 Bill, 352.

Magna Charta, 14; confirmations of, 15.

Manners, Lord J., amendment on 1884 Bill, 295.

Marlborough, Duke of, speech on 1884 Bill, 377.

Marriott, Mr., speech on 1884 Bill, 325.

Mellor, Mr., speech on 1884 Bill, 308.

Mill, Mr., speech on the Tory party, 229; on Female Suffrage, 249; on Minority Representation, 250.

Minority Representation, 250.

Monarchy, Arbitrary, 9; Limited, 10; Constitutional, 10.

Morley, Earl of, speech on 1884 Bill, 378.

Morley, Mr. J., speech on 1884 Bill, 328.

Muir's Trial, 52; Lord Braxfield's charge, 52; debate in House of Commons, 53.

Mulholland, Mr., speech on 1884 Bill, 300.

Nation, Position of, in 1688, 24; no control over Commons, 24.

Newdegate, Mr., speech on Lord Palmerston's Bill, 195; on 1884 Bill, 362.

Newport, Lord, speech on 1884 Bill, 336.

Northcote, Mr. H. S., speech on 1884 Bill, 298.

Northcote, Sir S., speech on Mr. Disraeli's Bill, 183; speeches on Bill of 1884, 294, 340; speech on third reading, 360.

O'Connell's motion on Reform, 81; rejected, 82; his speech on first Bill of 1831, 103. O'Donoghue, The, speech on 1884 Bill, 335. Osborne, Mr., speech on third reading of 1867 Bill, 259.

Paine, Thos., his writings, 47; trial and escape, 50.
Pakington, Sir J., speech on 1866 Bill, 228.
Palmerston, Lord, speech on first Bill of 1831, 93; speech on Mr. Disraeli's Bill, 184; speech on Bill of 1860, 187.
Parnell, Mr., speech on 1884 Bill, 288.
Peel, Sir Robert, speech on first Bill of 1831, 97; speech on its rejection, 111; on second Bill, 126; on third Bill, 139.
Peel, Sir R. (son), speech on 1884 Bill, 316.
Percy, Lord A., amendment on 1884 Bill, 357.
Pitt, Mr., motions for Reform, 35; resolutions, 35; rejected, 36; his last attempt, 36; his speech, 37; his defeat, 39; speech on Flood's Bill, 45; on Grey's motion, 48.
Plunkett, Mr., speech on 1884 Bill, 329.
Porchester, Lord, speech on third Bill of 1831, 141.
Portland, Duke of, speech on 1884 Bill, 381.
Power, Mr. O'Connor, speech on 1884 Bill, 339.
Powerscourt, Viscount, speech on 1884 Bill, 374.
Prerogative, Royal, 13–15.
Property Qualification abolished, 175.

Raikes, Mr., speech on 1884 Bill, 304.
Ravensworth, Earl of, speech on 1884 Bill, 382.
Redistribution by first Reform Act, 162; by second, 263; by third, 398.
Redman, Mr., speech on 1884 Bill, 327.

REFORM PERIODS, 21, 163, 263.
First Reform:
Constitution of 1688, 25; opposition to Reform, 32; state of representation, 33; corruption, 34.
Mr. Pitt's motion, 35; resolutions, 36; rejected, 36; his last attempt, 36; his speech, 37; defeat, 39.
Mr. Flood's Bill, 40; Mr. Wyndham's speech, 44; Mr. Pitt's, 45; Mr. Fox's, 46; Mr. Burke's, 46; Bill withdrawn, 47.
Mr. Grey's motion, 48; Mr. Pitt's speech, 48; Mr. Fox's reply, 49; Mr. Burke's speech, 49.
Postponement of Reform, 54.

First Reform—continued:
Sir F. Burdett's motion, 55; Mr. Lamb's speech, 58; Bill rejected, 59.
Lord John Russell's motion in 1819, 59; speech, 59; motion withdrawn, 61.
Mr. Lambton's Bill of 1821, 61; rejected, 61.
Lord J. Russell's resolution in 1821, 61; lost, 62.
Lord A. Hamilton's motion in 1821, 63; rejected, 64.
Lord J. Russell's motion in 1822, 64; his speech, 64; Mr. Canning's speech, 66; motion rejected, 78.
Lord J. Russell's motion in 1826, 79; speech, 79; Mr. Hobhouse's speech, 80; motion rejected, 81.
Marquis of Blandford's motion, 81; Sir F. Burdett's speech, 82; motion negatived, 82.
Lord Althorp's and Lord J. Russell's motions, 82; motions rejected, 82.
Mr. O'Connell's motion, 83; rejected, 83.
First Bill of 1831 introduced in the Commons, 83; Lord J. Russell's speech, 83; Sir R. H. Inglis' speech, 90; Lord Althorp's speech, 92; Mr. Hume's speech, 92; Mr. Macaulay, 93; Lord Palmerston, 97; Sir R. Peel, 97; Mr. Stanley, 100; Lord Jeffrey, 100; Mr. R. Grant, 102; Mr. O'Connell, 103; Lord J. Russell's reply, 103; Bill read first time, 104; second reading moved, 104; opposed by Sir R. Vyvyan, 104; Mr. Shiel's speech, 105; Mr. C. Grant, 106; Mr. Ward, 106; Mr. Stanley, 106; majority of one, 108; Scotch and Irish Bills introduced, 108; House in committee, 109; Gen. Gascoyne's amendment, 109; carried, 110; great confusion, 110; Lord Wharncliffe's notice of motion, 111; Sir R. Peel's speech, 111; Parliament dissolved, 113; new elections, 113.
Second Bill introduced, 113; Sir R. Peel's speech, 113; second reading carried, 113; in committee, 114; amendments, 114; third reading moved, 115; Mr. Macaulay's speech, 115; Mr. Croker, 119; Mr. Crampton, 121; Mr. Wynn, 122; Sir Charles Wetherell, 123; Lord Althorp, 124; Sir R. Peel, 126; Bill passed the Commons, 126; taken to the Lords, 127; read first time, 127; Earl Grey moves second reading, 127; his speech, 127; Lord Wharncliffe's speech, 132; Duke of Wellington's, 133; Lord Brougham, 133; Lord Lyndhurst, 135; Bill thrown out, 136; motion in Commons that Ministers do not resign, 137; great indignation in the country, 138.
Third Bill introduced into Commons, 139;

First Reform—continued:

Sir R. Peel's speech, 139; Lord Althorp, 140; Lord Porchester, 141; Mr. Macaulay, 141; second reading carried, 142; bill passed, 142; second reading in the Lords, 143; Earl Grey's speech, 143; Lord Ellenborough, 143; Lord Haddington, 144; Lord Gage, 144; Lord Shrewsbury, 144; Lord Harrowby, 145; Duke of Wellington, 146; Lord Wharncliffe, 146; Bishop of Exeter, 146; Lord Lansdowne, 147; Lord Durham, 148; Lord Eldon, 149; Lord Tenterden, 150; Lord Brougham, 151; Lord Lyndhurst, 151; Earl Grey's reply, 153; second reading carried by a small majority, 153; committee, 154; Earl Grey requires permission to create peers, 154; Ministers resign, 154; Address to the Crown, 155; Mr. Baring's speech, 156; Mr. Hume, 156; Mr. Macaulay, 156; Address carried, 158; Duke of Wellington failed to form a Ministry, 158; Earl Grey recalled, 158; King's Circular, 159; third Bill carried and received royal assent, 160; extent of Reform, 162; results, 163; defects, 163.

Second Reform:

Mr. Hume's motion of 1848, 165; Mr. Drummond's speech, 167; Mr. Cobden, 169; motion negatived, 169; Mr. Locke King's motion in 1851, 169; rejected, 170; Mr. Hume's Bill of 1852, 170; rejected, 170; Mr. Locke King's motion of 1852 rejected, 170; Lord J. Russell's Bill, 1854, 170; speech, 170; Bill abandoned, 174; property qualification abolished, 175; Mr. Locke King's Bill of 1858, 175; Mr. Caird's Bill, 175; Mr. Berkeley's Ballot Bill, 175; Mr. Disraeli's Bill of 1859, 175; his speech, 175; Lord J. Russell, 178; Mr. Roebuck, 178; Mr. Bright, 178; amendment by Lord J. Russell, 179; his speech, 180; Lord Stanley, 180; Mr. Horsman, 181; Mr. Bright, 182; Sir S. Northcote, 183; Mr. Cardwell, 183; Lord Palmerston, 184; Sir J. Graham, 185; Mr. Gladstone, 186; Mr. Roebuck, 187; Bill rejected, 187; Lord Palmerston's Bill, 187; Lord J. Russell's speech, 188; Irish and Scotch Bills, 191; Mr. Disraeli's speech, 192; Mr. Baxter, 193; Mr. Rolt, 193; Mr. Bright, 194; Sir G. Grey, 195; Mr. Newdegate, 195; Sir E. B. Lytton, 196; Lord J. Russell's reply, 196; Mr. Walter, 197; Mr. Du Cane, 197; Mr. J. Locke, 198; Mr. Macaulay, 198; Bill read a second time, 199; withdrawn, 199; Mr. Locke King's Bill, 199; Mr. Baines' motion, 200; rejected, 200; Mr. Berkeley's motion, 200; Mr. Baines' Bill, 200.

Second Reform—continued:

Mr. Gladstone's Bill of 1866, 201; speech, 201; Mr. Laing, 205; Mr Lowe, 205; Mr. Villiers, 206; Mr. Fawcett, 207; Mr. Bright, 207; Earl Grosvenor's motion, 209; agitation, 210; meeting in Liverpool, 210; Mr. Gladstone's speech there, 210; speech in the House, 213; Lord Grosvenor's speech, 214; Lord Stanley, 215; Sir H. Cairns, 215; Lord Elcho, 216; Mr. Bright, 216; Mr. Lowe, 217; Lord Cranborne, 218; Mr. Disraeli, 219; Mr. Gladstone's reply, 220; majority of 5 for government, 222; Redistribution Bill, 222; Mr. Gladstone's speech, 222; Scotch and Irish Bills, 226; fusion of the Bills, 228; debate, 228; Sir J. Pakington's speech, 228; Mr. Mill's speech, 229; Lord Dunkellin's amendment, 230; Mr. Gladstone's speech, 230; government defeated, 231; ministry resign, 231.

Mr. Disraeli's platform speech, 231; his announcement, 234; resolutions, 235; explanations, 238; Mr. Lowe, 240; Bill of 1867, 242; Mr. Disraeli's speech, 242; Mr. Gladstone's, 243; Mr. Roebuck, 244; Mr. Bright, 244; Mr. Disraeli's reply, 246; Bill read a second time, 247; debate, 247; Mr. Gladstone's amendments, 247; Mr. Lowe, 248; Mr. Mill, 249; Mr. Laing, 251; Mr. Disraeli's reply, 252; Mr. Gladstone, 254; Mr. Disraeli's new proposal, 255; Mr. Laing's second amendment, 256; voting papers, 257; Mr. Torrens' motion, 257; Lord Cranborne, 259; Mr. Lowe, 259; Mr. Osborne, 259; Bill carried in Commons, 260; debate in the Lords, 260; received royal assent, 261; extent of the reform, 262.

Third Reform:

Effect of second reform, 264; Mr. Trevelyan's motions, 267, 268, 269.

Mr. Gladstone's first Bill of 1884, 270; Sir J. Hay's speech, 280; Mr. Salt, 281; Mr. Anderson, 281; Mr. Gibson, 281; Mr. Fowler, 282; Lord R. Churchill, 283; Mr. Blennerhasset, 284; Mr. E. Clarke, 284; Mr. Walter, 284; Mr. W. H. Smith, 285; Mr. Goschen, 286; Mr. Parnell, 288; Mr. Trevelyan, 289; Sir J. Lubbock, 290; Sir S. Northcote, 294; Mr. Forster, 295; read first time, 295; Lord J. Manners' amendment, 295; Mr. Bright's speech, 297; Col. Dawnay, 298; Mr. H. S. Northcote, 298; Mr. Baxter, 299; Mr. C. Ross, 299; Mr. E. A. Leathem, 300; Mr. Mulholland, 300; Mr. J. Collings, 301; Mr. James Lowther, 301; Lord Hartington, 302; Mr. Raikes, 304; Mr. G. Russell, 305; Mr. Cubitt, 305; Mr. Spencer, 306; Mr. J. A. Campbell,

Third Reform—continued:
306; Mr. Anderson, 307; Col.Walrond, 307; Mr. Mellor, 308; Mr. Ritchie. 308; Lord Ebrington, 308; Mr. J. W. Lowther, 308; Mr. Chamberlain, 309; Lord G. Hamilton, 313; Mr. Forster, 314; Sir R. Peel, 316; Mr. Craig-Sellar, 316; Mr. C. Russell, 317; Sir R. A. Cross, 318; Mr. S. Lefevre, 319; Sir M. H. Beach, 321; Mr. A. Grey, 322; Mr. G. Dawnay, 322; Mr. Woodall, 323; Mr. B. Hope, 323; Mr. Stansfeld, 324; Mr. Marriott, 325; Mr. Broadhurst, 325; Mr. Biddell, 327; Mr. Redmond, 327; Mr. Morley, 328; Mr. Plunket, 329; Mr. H. H. Fowler, 329; Mr. Stuart Wortley, 330; Mr. Barron, 330; Mr. Grantham, 331; Mr. Gladstone, 331; Mr. Dalrymple, 334; Mr. Williamson, 335; Lord Folkestone, 335; The O'Donoghue, 335; Lord Newport, 336; Mr. Burt, 336; Sir W. B. Barttelot, 337; Mr.Goschen, 338; Mr. O'Connor Power, 339; Sir S. Northcote, 340; Sir H. James, 341; carried in the Commons, 342; votes of the members, 342; Mr. Brodrick's amendment, 350; Col. Stanley's amendment, 350; Mr. Leighton's amendment,350; Dr.Cameron's amendment, 350; Sir W. B. Barttelot's amendment, 351; Sir E.Watkin's amendment, 351; Mr. M'Laren's amendment, 352; Mr. Gladstone's speech, 352; Mr. Cavendish Bentinck's amendment,354; Mr. Warton's amendment, 354; Mr. Ecroyd's amendment, 354; Mr.Anderson's amendment,355; Mr.Woodall's amendment, 355; Mr. A. Grey's amendment, 356; Mr. H. H. Fowler's amendment, 357; Mr. Houldsworth's amendment, 357; Lord A. Percy's amendment, 357; Bill reported, 357; third reading, 358; Mr. Gladstone's speech, 358; Sir S. Northcote, 360; Mr. Goschen, 361; Mr. A.J.Balfour, 362; Mr. Newdegate, 362; Sir W. B. Barttelot, 362; Sir H. James, 362; Mr. Lewis, 363; Bill passed, 363; in the Lords, 363; read first time, 363; second reading moved, 363; Lord Kimberley's speech, 363; Lord Cairns' amendment, 366; speech, 366; Duke of Argyll, 370; Duke of Richmond, 371; Earl of Jersey, 372; Earl of Fife, 372; Lord Balfour, 373; Viscount Powerscourt, 374; Viscount Torrington, 374; Earl Stanhope, 374; Earl Cowper, 375; Marquis of Waterford, 376; Lord Fitzgerald, 376; Earl of Dunraven, 376; Duke of Marlborough, 377; Earl of Cadogan, 377; Earl Morley, 378; Earl of Carnarvon, 378; Earl Derby, 379; Lord Brabourne, 380; Earl of Roseberry, 380; Duke of Portland, 381; Earl

Third Reform—continued:
of Dalhousie, 381; Earl of Ravensworth, 282; Marquis of Huntly, 382; Earl of Camperdown, 382; Earl of Wemyss, 383; Archbishop of Canterbury, 383; Lord Selborne, 384; Lord Salisbury, 385; Earl Granville, 385; amendment carried, 385; votes of members, 386.
Meeting of Liberals in Foreign Office, 390; Mr. Bright's speech, 391; Earl Wemyss attempts to mediate, 392; appeal to the people, 392; demonstrations, 393.
Autumn session, 393; Bill again introduced, 393; Mr. Gladstone's speech, 393; Mr. E. Stanhope's amendment, 394; Mr. Gorst's speech, 395; read second time, 395; passed through committee, 395; compromise, 396; read second time in House of Lords, 396; Redistribution Bill introduced in the Commons, 397; read second time, 397; Franchise Bill passed the Lords and received royal assent, 397; Redistribution Bill passed, 398; extent of reform of 1884, 398; results, 399; further objects, 401.
Representation, state of, in 1688, 33; corruption, 34; after 1688, 164; in 1867, 263; in 1884, 398.
Richmond, Duke of, speech on 1884 Bill, 371.
Riots, 49.
Ritchie, Mr., speech on 1884 Bill, 308.
Roebuck, Mr., speech on Mr. Disraeli's first Bill, 178; second speech, 187; speech on his second Bill, 244.
Roseberry, Earl of, speech on 1884 Bill, 380.
Ross, Mr. C., speech on 1884 Bill, 299.
Russell, Mr. C., speech on 1884 Bill, 317.
Russell, Mr. G., speech on 1884 Bill, 305.
Russell, Lord John, motion in 1819, 59; speech, 59; motion withdrawn, 61; Resolutions in 1821, 61; lost, 62; motion in 1822, 64; lost, 78; motion in 1826, 79; speech, 79; motion in 1830, 82; rejected, 83; introduces first Bill of 1831, 83; speech, 83; reply, 103; Bill of 1854, 170; speech, 170; Bill abandoned, 174; speech on Mr. Disraeli's Bill, 178; his amendment, 179; speech, 180; speech on Lord Palmerston's Bill, 188; reply, 196.

Salisbury, Lord, speech on 1884 Bill, 385.
Salt, Mr., speech on 1884 Bill, 281.
Scotland, in 1793, 50.
Second Reform. See under *Reform*.
Selborne, Lord, speech on 1884 Bill, 384.
Sellar, Mr. Craig, speech on 1884 Bill, 316.
Shiel, Mr., speech on first Bill of 1831, 105.
Shrewsbury, Lord, speech on third Bill of 1831, 144.

Smith, Mr. W. H., speech on 1884 Bill, 285.
Spencer, Mr., speech on 1884 Bill, 306.
Stanhope, Earl, speech on 1884 Bill, 374; amendment, 394.
Stanley, Col., amendment on 1884 Bill, 350.
Stanley, Lord, speech on Mr. Disraeli's Bill, 180; on Bill of 1866, 215.
Stanley, Mr., speech on first Bill of 1831, 100; second speech, 110.
Stansfeld, Mr., speech on 1884 Bill, 324.

Tenterden, Lord, speech on third Bill of 1831, 150.
Theory of Government, 9.
Third Reform. See under *Reform*.
Three-corner Constituencies, 350.
Torrens, Mr., motion as to Voting Papers, 257.
Torrington, Viscount, speech on 1884 Bill, 374.
Trevelyan, Mr., motions on Reform, 267, 268, 269; speech on 1884 Bill, 289.
Trial of Muir, at Edinburgh, 57; trials in England, 53.

Villiers, Mr., speech on 1866 Bill, 206.
Votes of the Members of the House of Commons on 1884 Bill, 342; votes of the Lords, 386.
Voting Papers, 257.

Vyvyan, Sir R., speech on first Bill of 1831, 104.

Walrond, Col., speech on 1884 Bill, 307.
Walter, Mr., speech on Lord Palmerston's Bill, 197; speech on 1884 Bill, 284.
Ward, Mr., speech on first Bill of 1831, 106.
Warton, Mr., amendment on 1884 Bill, 354.
Waterford, Marquis, speech on 1884 Bill, 376.
Watkins, Sir E., amendment on 1884 Bill, 351.
Wellington, Duke of, speech on second Bill of 1831, 133; on third Bill, 146; failed to form ministry, 158.
Wemyss, Earl, speech on 1884 Bill, 383; attempt at mediation, 392.
Wetherell, Sir Charles, speech on second Bill of 1831, 123.
Wharncliffe, Lord, notice of motion, 111; his speech on second Bill 1831, 132; on third Bill, 146.
Williamson, Mr., speech on 1884 Bill, 335.
Women, Enfranchisement of, 249, 355.
Woodall, Mr., speech on 1884 Bill, 323; amendment on 1884 Bill, 355.
Wortley, Mr. S., speech on 1884 Bill, 330.
Wyndham, Mr., speech on Flood's Bill, 44.
Wynn, Mr., speech on second Bill, 1831, 122.

THE END.

GLASGOW: W. G. BLACKIE AND CO., PRINTERS, VILLAFIELD.